*Oracle Press*™

Mastering JavaFX® 8 Controls

Hendrik Ebbers

New York   Chicago   San Francisco
Athens   London   Madrid   Mexico City
Milan   New Delhi   Singapore   Sydney   Toronto

Cataloging-in-Publication Data is on file with the Library of Congress

McGraw-Hill Education books are available at special quantity discounts to use as premiums and sales promotions, or for use in corporate training programs. To contact a representative, please visit the Contact Us pages at www.mhprofessional.com.

Mastering JavaFX® 8 Controls

1234567890   DOC DOC   10987654

ISBN   978-0-07-183377-6
MHID   0-07-183377-3

Sponsoring Editor
Brandi Shailer

Editorial Supervisor
Janet Walden

Project Manager
Hardik Popli,
Cenveo® Publisher Services

Acquisitions Coordinator
Amanda Russell

Technical Editor
Simon Ritter

Copy Editor
Kim Wimpsett

Proofreader
Lisa McCoy

Indexer
Karin Arrigoni

Production Supervisor
Jean Bodeaux

Composition
Cenveo Publisher Services

Illustration
Cenveo Publisher Services

Art Director, Cover
Jeff Weeks

For Silke—*Because you helped me every day writing this book. I wrote this book in my free time, so there were weeks where I completely disappeared from normal home life. You managed everything alone, and in addition you backed me when I became frustrated about this project. Without you, I couldn't have managed this.*

For the JavaFX community—*Because without the awesome community, I would have never been in the position to write this book.*

For my father—*Because you taught me that you can create everything you imagine if you have enough courage to take hold of it.*

For all of my friends and family—*Because you heard me talking about this book too many times but still listened to me.*

About the Author

Hendrik Ebbers is senior Java architect at Materna GmbH in Dortmund, Germany. His main focus besides research and development is primarily in the areas of JavaFX, middleware, and DevOps. Additionally, Hendrik is founder and leader of the Java User Group Dortmund and gives talks and presentations in user groups and international conferences. He blogs about UI-related topics at www.guigarage .com (or on Twitter @hendrikEbbers) and contributes to some open source projects such as DataFX, BoxFX, AquaFX, and Vagrant-Binding.

About the Technical Editor

Simon Ritter works as a Java technology evangelist for Oracle Corporation and Sun Microsystems before that. He has been developing Java code since JDK 1.0 and has been involved in JavaFX since its launch as a scripting language.

Contents

Introduction

JavaFX from a Developer's Point of View

My background is in a lot of Swing development and web application creation. For web applications, I mostly used plain HTML or JSF to create the views, and I did some little applications with most of the other technologies (Adobe Flex, Flash, Android, Wicket, GWT, and so on) to learn more about these UI toolkits over the years.

For me, JavaFX is a perfect combination of most of the best practices that have come out of these technologies. For a Swing developer, most of the basic JavaFX APIs are easy to learn because the main concepts seem to be similar when looking at the framework. Under the hood, most of the technologies are different, but you can structure an application in a better way by using FXML and CSS, for example. Compared to HTML applications, JavaFX development is much easier for me because theoretically, you can do whatever you want and don't need to think about cross-browser behavior and all that stuff. You can create the complete view by using What You See Is What You Get (WYSIWYG) editors like Scene Builder and use your favorite Java IDE for development.

JavaFX offers a small learning curve, so you'll be able to create your first applications quickly. In addition, because of the good documentation and structure of the APIs, you probably won't make as many mistakes as you might have when learning Swing or HTML, for example. But, there are some places where you need to know the underlying technology well, and some parts are hard when you experiment the first time with them. When creating my first custom JavaFX control, I needed a lot of help to understand all the concepts and APIs involved. That was before JavaFX 8, though, and most of the documentation that is available today didn't exist. For me, as a Java developer, JavaFX is the best choice to develop applications that don't need to be captured in a browser.

With the release of Java 8, JavaFX is the default UI toolkit for Java. In this book, you will learn how to master JavaFX, especially the control API, to create applications based on these technologies. You can get all the scripts and programs featured in this book online (see the section "Retrieving the Examples" for details).

With this book, you will perform the following tasks:

- Create a structure for JavaFX applications
- Understand the general APIs of JavaFX
- Define layouts for all the views of an application
- Use the JavaFX bindings and property APIs to bind controls and a custom data model
- Understand the basic APIs and technologies of the scene graph
- Explore all the basic control types that are part of JavaFX
- Use FXML to separate the view layer
- Style specific controls or a complete application by using CSS
- Create custom controls the right way

This book contains 10 chapters and one appendix.

Chapter 1: The History of Java UI Toolkits   This chapter gives a short overview of Java UI toolkits and how UI toolkits and their features have evolved over the past few years.

Chapter 2: JavaFX Basics   In this chapter, you will find short descriptions of the JavaFX core APIs and useful tools.

Chapter 3: The Scene Graph   This chapter covers the core concepts of the scene graph and the associated APIs.

Chapter 4: Laying Out and Transforming Nodes in the Scene Graph   This chapter starts with an overview of the transformation types that can be used in JavaFX. The second part describes the layout algorithms of JavaFX and how to define custom layouts.

Chapter 5: JavaFX Basic Controls   After describing the core concepts of the `Control` class, this chapter gives an overview of all the basic control types that are part of JavaFX and shows how to use the controls and their features.

Chapter 6: Additional JavaFX Controls   This chapter discusses more complex controls such as the `TableView` and `DatePicker`. The chapter ends with an interview with Jonathan Giles.

Chapter 7: Additional JavaFX Nodes   In addition to the already described controls, JavaFX contains some useful node types such as charts and the WebView. This chapter covers these special node types.

Chapter 8: Integrating JavaFX, Swing, and SWT   This chapter covers some best-practice workflows for integrating JavaFX in Swing or SWT. This can be useful when migrating a Swing or SWT application to JavaFX.

Chapter 9: Styling a Control   This chapter describes the CSS support of JavaFX. After a short general introduction of CSS, this chapter covers different use cases for styling controls and applications in JavaFX. In addition, the chapter concludes with an interview with Claudine Zillmann.

Chapter 10: Custom Controls   This chapter shows how you can create custom JavaFX controls. In a hands-on example, you'll use all the APIs and techniques discussed in the earlier chapters. The chapter ends with an interview with Gerrit Grunwald.

Appendix: JavaFX Resources and Where to Go from Here   The appendix gives you a general overview of other useful resources for JavaFX.

Intended Audience

This book is suitable for the following readers:

- Developers who need to write JavaFX applications
- Developers who want to know more about the differences between Swing and JavaFX
- Developers who want to create a desktop application and are searching for the right technologies

Retrieving the Examples

You can download all the samples shown in this book from the Oracle Press web site at www.OraclePressBooks.com. The files are contained in a ZIP file. Once you've downloaded the ZIP file, you need to extract its contents. In addition, all the samples are provided at GitHub: https://github.com/guigarage/mastering-javafx-controls.

I created a general web page about the book that you can find at www.guigarage.com/javafx-book/.

I hope you enjoy this book and JavaFX!

Acknowledgments

When writing this book, I stumbled over some topics where I couldn't offer enough expert knowledge to provide the solutions and descriptions in the right way. Thanks to the JavaFX community, a lot of experts helped me out, and I want to thank each of them:

Jonathan Giles: I had a lot of questions about specific APIs, and you always had the perfect answer.

Simon Ritter: You did a great review of the whole book and often moved the topics in the right direction.

Claudine Zillmann: You are my CSS guru.

Gerrit Grunwald: You were the perfect person to discuss the general structure of the topics.

Thank you also to Johan Vos for many productive discussions, Tom Schindl for showing me how to combine JavaFX and SWT, Arnd Kleinbeck and Simon Skoczylas for reviewing some of my chapters, and Alexander Casall, Mark Heckler, Dierk König, and Carl Dea for your contribution of several cool tips and tricks.

In addition, I want to thank Amanda Russell and Brandi Shailer at McGraw-Hill Professional. You both managed the whole development process of this book, reviewed my chapters, and always offered useful tips and tricks.

CHAPTER
1

The History of
Java UI Toolkits

Almost 20 years have passed since Java was first released in 1995; the eighth major version was released in 2014. During these two decades, the IT world has rapidly evolved. The size, speed, and requirements of computer hardware have changed dramatically, as have the user interfaces of software. In 1995, computers were mainly used in offices, making a decorative user interface (UI) unimportant for most applications. Most dialogs consisted only of labels, text fields, and buttons. More complex graphical user interface (GUI) elements such as tables or tab panes were not supported by most of the UI toolkits. But as computing has evolved from a specialized niche to part of everyday life for millions of people worldwide, the importance of a polished, practical, and purposeful UI has become paramount. It is now normal to have a computer or tablet-based device at home to manage music, photos, or other private documents, and most people using applications today do not have technical backgrounds, which is why applications have to be intuitive and easy to use. A good layout and modern UI controls and effects can help generate a better user experience. By using up-to-date technologies and frameworks, developers can create outstanding web, desktop, and mobile applications, and that's why UI toolkits, including the Java UI toolkits available with the Java Development Kit (JDK), have evolved over the last 20 years.

This chapter will give you an overview of the important Java-based UI toolkits and some rising trends. Today, most applications have their own style, and the views are laid out in a pixel-perfect way. You'll find out how that came to be.

Java SE UI Toolkits

Several generations of UI toolkits have been introduced in the JDK over the years to allow developers to create state-of-the-art applications with Java. JavaFX is the newest framework to provide the ability to create and design desktop applications with Java. Before I discuss the controls of JavaFX in depth, it is important to take a short look at the history of Java-based UI toolkits that are part of Java Standard Edition (Java SE). By doing so, you will get an overview of the fundamental differences and similarities between several generations of UI toolkits, specifically in relation to the JavaFX controls.

AWT

The first version of the Java Abstract Window Toolkit (AWT) was introduced in 1996; AWT is an abstraction of the underlying native user interfaces. Since Java runs on various platforms, AWT supports only the least common denominator of these platforms, so it has only a small number of supported components. Standard controls such as buttons and text fields are available, but more complex components such as tables are not part of the toolkit. By using AWT, developers create GUI components in Java code. Simultaneously, a native graphical component is created as a counterpart by the operating system, and a peer class is used as the link between these two instances. (These kinds of components are called *heavyweight* components.) Developers can define the attributes of a component, such as the visible text of a button, by using the Java class. However, the Java application has no influence on the graphical representation of the components because the operating system (OS) is responsible for rendering the controls.

AWT was improved with Java 1.1; it included new features such as event listeners and new components such as the scroll pane. However, the great advantage of AWT is also its worst weakness: By using the toolkit, each Java-based application takes on the native look and feel of the operating system automatically. On Windows, the typical Windows buttons and combo boxes will be shown if you create an app by using the framework, for example. On Mac OS, all components are rendered by using the Aqua look (Apple's default UI definition). It's almost impossible to create new components or modify the look of a control to deliver an application with a unique appearance.

Java Foundation Classes and the Emergence of Swing

In parallel with Java 1.1, Netscape developed the Internet Foundation Classes (IFC) library that represents a completely platform-independent UI toolkit for Java. Unlike AWT, IFC does not create a wrapper around native components; it provides controls that are completely managed and rendered by pure Java. This technology was originally designed to display applets in the Netscape browser, and the main objective of IFC was to create browser-independent applications that have the same appearance on any OS. In 1997, Sun Microsystems and Netscape announced the intention to merge IFC into Java.

The Java Foundation Classes (JFC) framework is the result of integrating IFC into Java. The classes in the framework include AWT, Java2D, Swing, and some additional APIs. JFC has been part of Java SE since 1998, which means Swing has been part of Java SE since version 1.2 (Java 2) and has become the main UI toolkit of Java.

Swing

Unlike the base development of IFC, which was written from scratch as a new API, Swing's control classes are based on AWT; however, the internal architecture of the framework is completely different from AWT. This approach was chosen for compatibility purposes. Swing offers a set of so-called *lightweight* components that are completely managed and rendered by Java. Because of this, you can achieve the same graphical representation of components across operation systems. From a technical point of view, the graphical output of Swing is based on Java2D, an API for rendering two-dimensional objects that is also part of JFC. Although the features of Java2D and Swing are not "state of the art" anymore, these were modern APIs with many incredible options when JFC was released. Even today, you can create astonishingly good results by using Swing.

All UI controls in Swing are based on the JComponent class, which extends the AWT Component class. This ensures that the main concepts for using Swing components are already known by AWT developers, and AWT layout managers, for example, can be used to lay out Swing-based applications without any learning curve. Figure 1-1 shows a general overview of the class hierarchy of AWT and Swing components.

By using the Java2D API, you can change the appearance of Swing-based components at any time or even create new components from scratch. Swing uses a Model-View-Controller (MVC) approach internally, in which the graphical representation of components is separated from the model in a special UI class. The base skin of a Swing button is defined by the ButtonUI class, for example. Since the operating system doesn't draw the components in Swing, the controls will have the same look across OSs. To achieve this, Swing includes the LookAndFeel API. By using LookAndFeel (LAF), you can define your own style for the complete Swing component set. In fact, Swing comprises a set of cross-platform LAFs and system-dependent LAFs. If you want to develop an application that always looks like the underlying operating system, you set the OS-specific look and feel for Swing. A Java version for Mac OS includes the Aqua LAF, for example. This will render all components so that they look like native Mac OS controls. If your application is running on a Windows system, it can use the Windows LAF that is part of Java on every Windows-based PC. New versions of these LAFs have native support for creating controls that you can't

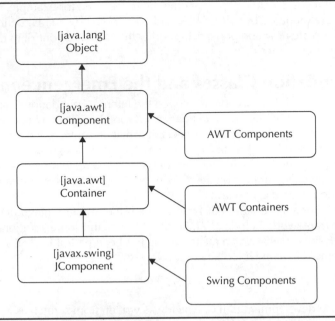

FIGURE 1-1.   *Class hierarchy for AWT and Swing*

distinguish from native ones. The framework offers some helper methods as well. By using them, you can configure Swing to always use the provided system look and feel depending on which platform the application is running.

Another advantage Swing has over AWT is the rich set of components it includes. For example, in Swing, you can find tables, lists, and tree-based controls to represent the application data in the way that best fits your application view. These controls can handle lists of data by using renderers to support large amounts of data and show or process them in the interface without any problems. Above all, these new and flexible components are the reason why Swing is used to develop business applications. With Swing's ability to manage and render controls that support LAFs and its internal use of Java2D, along with the many open source libraries and frameworks that can be used to extend functionality, Swing deposed AWT and remained for several years the standard UI toolkit for creating graphical desktop applications in Java.

From today's point of view, Swing also has some weaknesses. One weakness is that many graphical effects that are standard in today's modern applications cannot be implemented by using Swing (or they need a lot of hacks and workarounds). Examples include reflections and blur effects. Animations are also missing from Swing's API, and a Swing-based dialog needs a lot of boilerplate code. Although creating special skins for controls or creating new components from scratch is possible in Swing, it is difficult to do. It requires a lot of training, and there are many pitfalls you can trip over before being ready to develop usable components for Swing. These are crucial reasons why Swing needed to be replaced by a new UI toolkit. Hence, JavaFX emerged and has been the recommended UI toolkit since Java 8.

Before diving into the history and features of JavaFX, I'll briefly cover a few other UI toolkits and place them in the historical context of the default Java SE toolkits.

Additional UI Toolkits

In addition to the default toolkits that are part of Java SE, some other UI-based frameworks have been developed over the years. SWT and Apache Flex are two examples of toolkits developed during the reign of Swing. SWT is based on Java, but Apache Flex has nothing to do with Java and even offers some concepts that JavaFX has picked up.

SWT

Parallel to the release of Java 2 in 1998, IBM decided to implement its next generation of development tools in Java. The first generation of IBM's development environment, VisualAge for Java, was based on Smalltalk and used the common widget (CW) framework to create the surface. This API was a thin layer on top of the native components of the operating system and therefore resembled AWT. For the developers at IBM, it was important that the new development environment, which today is known as Eclipse, would be based on a native look and feel. Since Swing could not provide these requirements by supporting platform-specific LAFs, the developers decided to create a separate UI toolkit with the same features as CW. The result was the Standard Widget Toolkit (SWT).

Like AWT, SWT provides wrappers on top of native controls. The native controls are provided via the Java Native Interface (JNI), but SWT includes an API to write your own GUI components. Additionally, SWT provides a larger set of default controls than AWT does. All components that are not supported by an underlying OS are emulated in Java. Tables, for example, are supported by the Microsoft Windows platform, and SWT can depend on native components by using JNI. On an OS that doesn't support tables, SWT will use a fallback and manage and render a table control completely in Java. With this functionality, developers can create an application with a native appearance and add controls or change the skin of controls to define a unique look for the app. Compared to Swing, SWT requires fewer system resources because most of the controls are managed by the OS and not by Java. Today, SWT is still the default UI toolkit of Eclipse and is also used in many projects that are based on the Eclipse rich client platform (RCP).

Apache Flex

In recent years, other languages have breathed new life into the field of UI toolkits. Apache Flex is an example of a toolkit developed in the last few years, and it was clearly designed for creating rich clients. It is based on Adobe Flex, which was passed to the Apache Foundation in 2012. Internally, Flex is based on Flash for rendering and offers its own programming language called ActionScript.

Flex offers some interesting techniques and concepts that have been sought after in Java UI toolkits. For example, with its MXML library, Flex provides an XML-based file format to define user interfaces and their layout. In these files, the structure of a view with all embedded controls and their attributes can be defined. Version 4 of Flex introduced Spark as a new architecture to skin and create controls in Flex. In Spark, all controls are split in two files: a skin file that is written in MXML and that defines the look of the component and an ActionScript class that defines the model and the controller. In addition, Flex provides support for effects and transformations.

The Way to JavaFX

As you can see, there are plenty of UI toolkits on the market, both based on Java and other languages. But no toolkit is perfect. Sometimes a cool feature is incompatible to the main architecture of a toolkit and can't be added. Additionally, sometimes different UI toolkits have different philosophies. Some rely on native controls, while others have extended support for skinning. Another feature that has become more important over the years is the way the metadata of controls, such as the background or border and the layout of views, is described. Most modern toolkits remove this information from the source and add file types such as MXML in Flex or the XML layout in Android to define this information. Old Java-based UI toolkits like Swing can't handle these needed features.

From F3 to JavaFX 8

The JavaFX story started with the F3 API developed by Chris Oliver at SeeBeyond. The company required a modern UI toolkit to create new desktop applications that looked superior to the competition, so Oliver started developing the F3 framework, and it was acquired by Sun Microsystems as part of the SeeBeyond acquisition during the API's development. Oliver continued on at Sun to lead the development of F3, which was renamed and introduced as JavaFX at JavaOne in 2007. The first version of JavaFX was published one year later. However, version 1 of JavaFX (JavaFX Script) has very little to do with the current version; it was a script-based language for the Java platform that could interoperate with Java code.

After Oracle's acquisition of Sun Microsystems, version 2 was announced that would be based completely on the Java API, which would allow any Java developer to use it with any IDE. By doing this, the barrier of entry to using JavaFX was reduced, and the competition for a great UI toolkit was leveled. JavaFX Script was also discontinued with this release. JavaFX supports a lot of effects, transformations, and animations, all of which will be covered in the following chapters.

What Kinds of Applications Can Be Built with JavaFX?

So, what kinds of applications can you build with JavaFX? As an initial answer, I would say every kind of application. For sure, some types of applications are a better match to a JavaFX-based technology stack than others, such as business applications that use databases or servers as the back end. All the needed components are part of the JDK and the JavaFX library, so you can create an application mostly the same way as you would have with Swing.

But JavaFX can do so much more. I have seen some 2D games that were created by using JavaFX with the great performance and features of the JavaFX scene graph API or the JavaFX canvas API. Additionally, JavaFX offers 3D support to create 3D landscapes. By adding embedded support to Java, JavaFX allows you to create the UI and user interaction for smart embedded devices. Using JavaFX in this way is as easy as developing a desktop application. You can even develop a media center because the API to play media files is part of JavaFX. As you can see, there is a lot of potential when using JavaFX as the UI toolkit to develop applications.

In reality, most of the applications that will be developed with JavaFX will be business applications, so this book will concentrate on the APIs and knowledge that you need to know to develop these kinds of applications. But even when developing data-centric applications, you can use the creative power of JavaFX. By using the JavaFX effects, animations, or multitouch input, you can create an application with an outstanding user experience.

JavaFX Compared to HTML5 and Web-Based Technologies

Today, a lot of applications that are created are web applications or rich Internet applications (RIAs), also called plain HTML apps, that run in a browser such as Firefox or Chrome. Most of these applications are written in HTML5, CSS, and JavaScript. Other technologies can also be used to create RIAs: Technologies such as Adobe Flash/Flex and Silverlight can be used to create applications that are running inside a browser with a browser plug-in.

These rich Internet applications could also be created with JavaFX. (Although you can integrate a JavaFX application as an applet in a web page, this workflow isn't best practice anymore, as it will create some problems; therefore, it won't be discussed in this book.) I discussed the non-HTML technologies earlier in the chapter, so now it's time to take a deeper look at plain HTML RIAs and how they compare to applications created with JavaFX.

First, it's hard to compare HTML with JavaFX because of some big differences: HTML runs inside a browser, and JavaFX applications are desktop applications running directly in the OS. Additionally, HTML is only a markup language, and you can't define application logic with HTML. A developer needs to use a combination of HTML, JavaScript, and CSS to create an interactive application.

Here is the default structure of an HTML-based RIA: By using HTML, you define all components that appear on a web page and structure them. If you need application logic, you can use JavaScript to add the logic to your application. Additionally, in most applications, CSS is used to define special skins for the app and all components that are part of the application. This is a technology stack that is unusual for a desktop application; however, JavaFX provides a comparable set of technologies. Specifically, the layout of all views can be done by using FXML, which is an XML-based markup language for defining JavaFX views. For the skinning of an application, JavaFX supports CSS; it doesn't use the same attributes that are used in HTML web applications, but the CSS syntax is the same. Instead of JavaScript, you can use Java to define the logic and interaction of a JavaFX application.

JavaFX offers all the benefits that a developer might know from HTML application development. For example, the structure of the views isn't created in code; the markup language FXML is used to define the layout of all application dialogs. As a result, the layout of an application can be done by a designer who doesn't need to understand Java code. Additionally, CSS is used to define custom skins of controls. By using CSS, it is easy to change the font of all buttons that are used in a JavaFX application, for example. There is another big benefit in JavaFX too: The APIs are ready for extensions. In HTML, you can't use other tags than the defined ones, and CSS provides some default attributes and a set of additional ones that are browser-specific. With FXML, you can easily integrate any custom control, and you can define new CSS attributes with a Java API. As a result, you can easily add components to an application that are not part of the default framework.

HTML applications do have some advantages over JavaFX ones, however. HTML is always running in a browser, and a normal user doesn't need to install anything to run web applications. By contrast, JavaFX applications mostly run on the desktop, and if they are not packaged as native applications, the user will need the Java runtime on the OS. And if a JavaFX application is running in a browser, the user will need the applet plug-in. JavaFX 8 fixes this issue by offering a tool that can package JavaFX applications as native ones and add the needed Java runtime to the package automatically. As a result, no additional software is needed on a client computer. Still, HTML applications are easier to administer because most users have a browser, but often cross-browser development is a necessity.

You could say that there is no final rule which of these two technologies should be used for application development. Both have benefits and are stronger in some areas. But JavaFX has learned a lot from HTML and has taken some of the best parts of it to offer a great infrastructure and ecosystem for application developers.

Java-Based Web Frameworks

In addition to creating plain HTML web applications, developers can use Java to develop web applications with frameworks such as JSF, Wicket, Play, or GWT. All these frameworks will create applications with views that are rendered as HTML views in a browser. Normally, the Java code is running on a server, and HTML views are created that will be sent to the client. In all these frameworks, Java can be used to define the application logic, and sometimes even the views can be created in Java. In the end, all the frameworks will create HTML and JavaScript. Because of this, it is often more complicated to create pixel-perfect applications with these frameworks. Comparing all these frameworks to JavaFX is beyond the scope of this book.

Summary

UI-related technology has become more important in the past few years because developers are creating more impressive UIs than ever before. JavaFX is the newest in a series of UI toolkits, and it supports all modern UI methods and patterns. Without a doubt, JavaFX will become the most important UI toolkit for Java applications in the next few years and will be used on various platforms. Therefore, it is important for every Java application developer to know and understand the core concepts of JavaFX. One of the most important parts of the framework is the controller API, a core focus of this book.

CHAPTER
2

JavaFX Basics

avaFX is a toolkit specifically used for creating graphical user interfaces, and therefore it includes much more than just a collection of controls. This chapter briefly introduces the various components, APIs, and tools of JavaFX. You'll need this basic knowledge in later chapters because the control APIs either interface to the other JavaFX APIs or use them internally. Developers who want to create a JavaFX-based application need to know the basics covered in this chapter. However, since you don't need to know all features in depth to be able to customize the JavaFX controls, this chapter will serve only as an overview of them. To acquire deeper knowledge on any of these topics, consult *Quick Start Guide to JavaFX* (McGraw-Hill, 2014), *JavaFX 8: Introduction by Example* (Apress, 2014), or *Pro JavaFX 8* (Apress, 2014).

NOTE
In the Appendix of this book you will find some more starting points for these topics.

Your First JavaFX Application

Almost every book starts with a "HelloWorld" example when teaching a new programming language or framework. Even though this is not a book for learning JavaFX from the ground up, let's follow that trend and start with a basic `HelloWorld` application, shown here:

```java
package com.guigarage.masteringcontrols;

import javafx.application.Application;
import javafx.scene.Scene;
import javafx.scene.control.Button;
import javafx.scene.layout.StackPane;
import javafx.stage.Stage;

public class HelloWorld extends Application {

    @Override
    public void start(Stage primaryStage) throws Exception {
        Button button = new Button("Hello World");

        StackPane myPane = new StackPane();
        myPane.getChildren().add(button);

        Scene myScene = new Scene(myPane);

        primaryStage.setScene(myScene);
        primaryStage.setWidth(800);
        primaryStage.setHeight(600);
        primaryStage.show();
    }

    public static void main(String[] args) {
        launch(args);
    }
}
```

When you start the program, a dialog will appear onscreen. Figure 2-1 shows how this dialog looks on Mac OS X. This example is one of the easiest graphical applications that can be created; however, even in its simplicity, this application uses a number of JavaFX APIs. When looking at the import statements of the Java file, for example, you can see that classes from the following three JavaFX packages are loaded for this simple program:

- `javafx.application`
- `javafx.stage`
- `javafx.scene`

In the following sections, I will discuss the classes and APIs used in this program so you can gain a better understanding of how JavaFX is working.

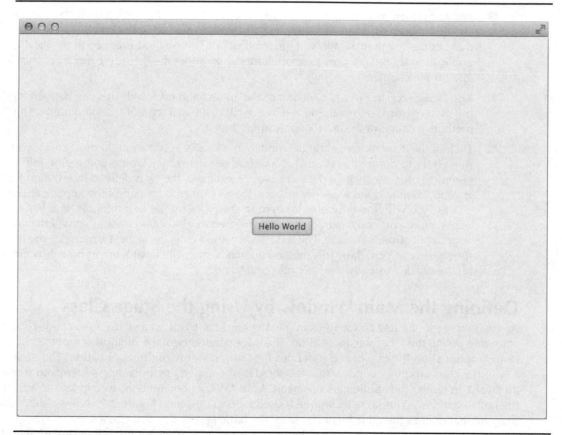

FIGURE 2-1. *Your first JavaFX application: HelloWorld*

NOTE
*As mentioned in Chapter 1, JavaFX has been bundled with the JDK
and JRE since Java SE 8. Therefore, to compile and run a JavaFX
application, no additional software is needed. You can develop the
HelloWorld class shown previously with any Java IDE or even with a
simple text editor.*

JavaFX Application Life Cycle

As you can see in the `HelloWorld` example program, each JavaFX application needs to extend the
`javafx.application.Application` class, which defines the life cycle of an application. This is
covered by the following methods that are called automatically by the JavaFX Framework:

- `Application.init()` can be used to define and prepare everything before the
  application starts. This method is called in a special thread, the JavaFX launcher thread.

- `Application.start(Stage stage)` is called to start the application. This method
  should be used to define the complete application and its view by adding a scene
  that defines the main window of the application. This method is called in the JavaFX
  application thread. I'll provide more information about the threading model of JavaFX
  later in the chapter.

- `Application.stop()` is called once the application is closed. This can happen for
  different reasons; one example is if a user clicks the exit icon of the main frame. This
  method is called in the JavaFX application thread.

- Each of these methods can be overridden in a JavaFX application. In most cases, you
  need only to define the `start(...)` method because that's where you define the
  complete user interface. In the `HelloWorld` example, the UI is defined by a button that
  is wrapped in a `StackPane` control, and the `main` method is part of the `Application`
  `class`. You will find this behavior in most JavaFX examples and tutorials. In a large
  application, you could extract the `main` method to any other classes that will manage
  your application, of course. The `main(...)` method calls the static `launch(...)` method of
  the `Application` class. This method internally starts the JavaFX environment by creating
  all the needed threads, the life cycle, and so on.

Defining the Main Window by Using the Stage Class

As you can see in the `HelloWorld` example, the `Application.start(Stage stage)` method
is used to define the UI of the application. The stage parameter of the method is provided by the
JavaFX application life cycle, and it defines the main window of the application. The `Stage` is
a wrapper class around a window that is offered by the underlying operating system and is used
by JavaFX to render the application onscreen. As in AWT, a peer entity is used in Java to access
the native window. (The same technique is used for pop-ups, too.) Figure 2-2 shows a short UML
diagram that defines the class hierarchy of all the basic JavaFX `Window` classes.

As you can see, a stage is a special window. It provides some additional information and
methods to define and skin the main window of the JavaFX application. Table 2-1 describes all
the properties that are part of a stage.

All mentioned properties are implemented by using the JavaFX property API, which is used a
lot in JavaFX and will be used in most of the examples in this book. Don't worry if you haven't

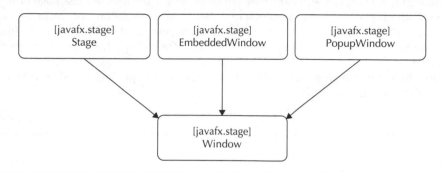

FIGURE 2-2.   *JavaFX Window class hierarchy*

Property	Type	Description
fullScreen	ReadOnlyBooleanProperty	If true, the application is shown as an undecorated full-screen window.
fullScreenExitKey	ObjectProperty<KeyCombination>	This specifies a key combination that allows the user to exit full-screen mode.
fullScreenExitHint	ObjectProperty<String>	This defines informational text that will be shown when the application enters full-screen mode.
iconified	ReadOnlyBooleanProperty	This defines whether the stage is iconified.
maxHeight	DoubleProperty	This defines the maximum height of the stage.
maximized	ReadOnlyBooleanProperty	This defines whether the stage is maximized.
maxWidth	DoubleProperty	This defines the maximum width of the stage.
minHeight	DoubleProperty	This defines the minimum height of the stage.
minWidth	DoubleProperty	This defines the minimum width of the stage.
resizable	BooleanProperty	If this property is set to false, a user can't resize the stage.
title	StringProperty	This defines the title of the stage. If the stage is decorated with a title bar, the string will be shown in it.

TABLE 2-1.   *Properties of the Stage Class*

heard about the property API until now. All properties of the Stage class have normal getter and setter methods like you know from other JavaBean implementations; however, by using the property API internally, the implementation of these getter and setter methods is different from the one you know from plain old Java objects (POJOs). The API will be shown in more depth later in this chapter.

In addition to the properties of the Stage class, its parent class, Window, defines a set of properties, as described in Table 2-2.

Property	Type	Description
eventDispatcher	ObjectProperty<EventDispatcher>	Specifies the event dispatcher for this node. The default EventDispatcher will receive all input events and send these events to event handlers and filters.
focused	ReadOnlyBooleanProperty	Defines whether the window can get the input focus.
height	ReadOnlyDoubleProperty	Defines the height of the stage.
onCloseRequest	ObjectProperty<EventHandler<WindowEvent>>	Specifies a handler that is called when an external request to close the window is received. This can happen when a user tries to close the window.
onHidden	ObjectProperty<EventHandler<WindowEvent>>	Defines a handler that is called when the window has been hidden.
onHiding	ObjectProperty<EventHandler<WindowEvent>>	Defines an event handler that is called just before the window will be hidden.
onShowing	ObjectProperty<EventHandler<WindowEvent>>	Defines an event handler that is called just before the window will be shown.
onShown	ObjectProperty<EventHandler<WindowEvent>>	Defines a handler that is called just after the window is shown.
opacity	DoubleProperty	Defines the opacity of the stage as a value between 0.0 and 1.0.

TABLE 2-2. *Properties of the Window Class*

Property	Type	Description
scene	ReadOnlyObjectProperty<Scene>	Specifies the scene of this stage.
showing	ReadOnlyBooleanProperty	Defines whether the stage is shown onscreen.
width	ReadOnlyDoubleProperty	Specifies the current width of this stage.
x	ReadOnlyDoubleProperty	Specifies the x-location of the stage on the screen.
y	ReadOnlyDoubleProperty	Specifies the y-location of the stage on the screen.

TABLE 2-2. *Properties of the Window Class* (continued)

In addition to the properties, the Stage class and the Window class contain some useful methods to interact with instances from Java code. Tables 2-3 and 2-4 contain an overview of these methods.

Method	Description
void close()	Closes the stage.
observableList<Image> getIcons()	Returns a list of icons that will be used to decorate the window. The visualization depends on the OS.
modality getModality()	Returns the modality for this stage.
window getOwner()	Returns the owner window for this stage if it's not a top-level window.
stageStyle getStyle()	Retrieves the style attribute for this stage.
void initModality(Modality modality)	Specifies the modality for this stage. This must be called before the stage will be shown. Otherwise, an Exception will be thrown.
void initOwner(Window owner)	Specifies the owner window for this stage. This must be called before the stage will be shown. Otherwise, an Exception will be thrown.
void initStyle(StageStyle style)	Specifies the style for this stage. This must be called before the stage will be shown. Otherwise, an Exception will be thrown.
void showAndWait()	Shows this stage and waits until it will be closed. This method must be called on the JavaFX application thread.
void toBack()	Sets the window to the background.
void toFront()	Brings the window to the foreground.

TABLE 2-3. *Methods of the Stage Class*

Method	Description
void centerOnScreen()	Sets the x and y properties on this window so that it is centered on the screen
void fireEvent(Event event)	Fires a specified event
void hide()	Attempts to hide the window
void requestFocus()	Requests that the window gets the focus
void sizeToScene()	Sets the width and height properties of this window to match the size of its defined scene

TABLE 2-4. *Methods of the Window Class*

NOTE
The shown methods and properties contain some classes and functionality that weren't described until now. The defined classes like EventHandler are part of the JavaFX framework and will be described later in the book in more detail.

As shown in Table 2-5, the style of a stage can be defined. By using a style, you can simply change the decoration and behavior of a stage instance. Table 2-5 provides an overview of all supported types.

By setting some of these properties in the start (...) method of an application, you can specify the look of the main window. Here is an example of a decorated frame:

```
@Override
public void start(Stage primaryStage) throws Exception {
    ...
    primaryStage.setScene(myScene);
    primaryStage.initStyle(StageStyle.UTILITY);
    primaryStage.setTitle("Utility App");
    primaryStage.getIcons().add(new Image("http://www.guigarage.com/
                                    demo_icon_16.png"));
    primaryStage.getIcons().add(new Image("http://www.guigarage.com/
                                    demo_icon_32.png"));
    primaryStage.getIcons().add(new Image("http://www.guigarage.com/
                                    demo_icon_64.png"));
    primaryStage.getIcons().add(new Image("http://www.guigarage.com/
                                    demo_icon_128.png"));
    primaryStage.setWidth(300);
    primaryStage.setHeight(200);
    primaryStage.show();
}
```

Type Variant	Description	
`StageStyle` `.DECORATED`	Default type of a stage. This is a typical application frame.	⊖ ○ ○ DECORATED
`StageStyle` `.UNDECORATED`	The undecorated style has no title bar but has a shadow.	
`StageStyle` `.TRANSPARENT`	The transparent style just has the color that is defined as background color.	

`StageStyle`
`.UNIFIED`
	The unified style has a title bar as decorated but with no border. This makes it possible to create dialogs with typical toolbars. This is a conditional feature. To check whether it is supported, you can use the following call:
	
	`javafx.application.Platform`
	`    .isSupported(javafx`
	`    .application`
	`    .ConditionalFeature.UNIFIED_`
	`    WINDOW);`
	
	If the feature is not supported by the platform, this style downgrades to `StageStyle.DECORATED`.
		⊖ ○ ○ UNIFIED

`StageStyle` `.UTILITY`	The utility style has a smaller title bar and can't be maximized. It is ideal for utility dialogs.	⊖ ○ ○ UTILITY

TABLE 2-5. *Stage Styles*

FIGURE 2-3.   *Application on different operating systems*

Figure 2-3 shows the application running on Mac OS and Windows 7. Now that the application is created and the window is specified, controls can be added to the surface.

The Scene Graph

Another API used in the HelloWorld application is the scene graph. In JavaFX, each window contains a so-called scene graph, which is an acyclic-directed graph that can be accessed by the Scene class in JavaFX. A scene graph manages all the items that will be rendered on the screen. None of these items can have more than one parent, and each element that is part of the scene graph is called a *node*. Examples for nodes include a rectangle, a button, or a panel that holds other nodes. Because the scene graph manages all of these nodes in an internal model, it knows which nodes should be displayed at what location onscreen and which components and areas need to be repainted. Each scene graph has a root node that, by default, is a group that holds all the other nodes in any hierarchy. The StackPane control is the root node of the HelloWorld application, and it holds only one node: the Hello World button.

```
Button button = new Button("Hello World");

StackPane myPane = new StackPane();
myPane.getChildren().add(button);

Scene myScene = new Scene(myPane);
```

The actual layout of the buttons is taken from StackPane. Unlike Swing, in which a JPanel class is the default container and different layout managers such as BorderLayout and FlowLayout are used for positioning elements, JavaFX provides different panes that are responsible for grouping and laying out the child nodes.

By using the JavaFX scene graph, developers can use significantly more features than in Swing. The scene graph supports transformations such as scaling or rotation, and you can add and display 3D objects in it. Since the scene graph is the global administrative body of all controls in JavaFX, its structure and API will be described in more detail in Chapter 3. (The application life cycle and the stage API will not be covered further.)

Now that I've discussed three of the JavaFX APIs that were used in the HelloWorld application (application, stage, and scene graph), I'll present the entire structure of JavaFX and its various APIs.

Technical Design of the JavaFX Toolkit

As you already know from many other frameworks, the JavaFX toolkit is composed of different APIs. JavaFX can be roughly divided internally into three layers:

- Native layer
- Private layer
- Public layer

For a better overview, Figure 2-4 shows a graph in which the different layers and their components are shown schematically.

JavaFX developers should only ever work with the public APIs. As with all other components of the JDK, it is not recommended to use private APIs to program, even with JavaFX. These classes may change at any time, and any Java update can create an incompatibility for your application. For this reason, the components of the native and private layers are presented here only briefly.

The Native Layer

The native part of JavaFX is not written in Java. Instead, these components are native libraries that grant access to the native OS layer. A big part of the native libraries of JavaFX are the Prism implementations. Prism is a technology-independent layer to render the JavaFX views. Because high-performance graphics are one of the most important issues for UI toolkits like JavaFX, there are several operating system or hardware-oriented implementations of Prism. On Windows, this works normally with a Direct3D version, while on other systems, an OpenGL-based implementation of Prism is used. In addition to these implementations, the native layer still contains implementations of the media and web engines. With these implementations, it is possible in a JavaFX application to show media content, such as movies and music, or embed web pages directly in an application. By using native interfaces, JavaFX has achieved very good performance in these areas. As mentioned, the native parts are not developed in Java. This is also the reason why JavaFX can't simply be delivered as a one-JAR framework: The native components are specific to operating systems and need to be delivered as compiled libraries. Although most parts of JavaFX are open source, a few fonts and the VP6 codec are not, which creates license issues.

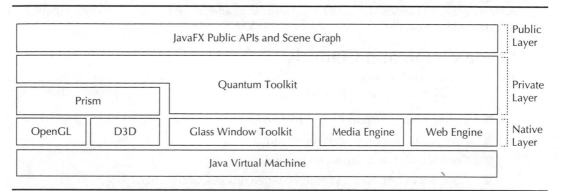

FIGURE 2-4. *JavaFX library stack*

NOTE
JavaFX has some optional APIs and features. The media support is an example of an optional feature. You can check for the availability of these optional features in code by using the `Platform .isSupported(...)` *method. All optional features are defined by the enumeration* `javafx.application.ConditionalFeature`.

Private API Layer

The private APIs contain internal classes that are part of the JRE. These classes are defined in special packages (`com.sun.*`). The definition of the Prism API is, for example, part of the private APIs. All these APIs are closed under the `com.sun` package, and a developer should never use them because these APIs can change in each new Java version.

Public API Layer

The most important part for each developer is the public part of the architecture stack. This part contains all the JavaFX classes that can and should be used when developing an application. Because of this, the next section will introduce all the main public APIs of JavaFX.

JavaFX Public APIs

JavaFX has a lot of different classes packed into its public framework. All of these classes are allocated in different APIs. By taking a look at the package structure of JavaFX (see Table 2-6), you can learn about the core APIs.

The following sections contain overviews of all the different APIs. Most of them will be covered again later in the book when their interoperability with specific controls is shown. Here, I'll primarily show some special features of the APIs because developers should know the basic purpose and usage of them to understand all the examples in this book.

Application and Life Cycle

The application API was discussed earlier in reference to the `HelloWorld` application.

Stage API

All the important classes that are part of `javafx.stage.*` were discussed when explaining the `HelloWorld` application.

Scene Graph and Controls

The scene graph API is one of the biggest parts of JavaFX. It contains the definition of the scene graph and all kinds of nodes. To simplify, you can group all the nodes in four categories, as shown here:

- Simple nodes, such as lines or rectangles
- Groups and panes, such as the `FlowPane`
- Controls, such as buttons and text fields
- Complex nodes, such as rendered video, images, and web pages

The main focus of this book is on the APIs that are part of the `javafx.scene` package and its subpackages.

Package	Description
javafx.application	This contains general application classes and utilities (as described for the HelloWorld application).
javafx.stage	The stage API contains all classes to create and manage windows such as frames or pop-ups.
javafx.scene	This is the biggest part of JavaFX that contains the scene graph and all nodes. Layout panes and controls are part of this package too.
javafx.event	The event API specifies how general events are defined in JavaFX. An example for an event is a mouse click that is fired as a JavaFX event to defined listeners.
javafx.beans	This package includes the property API. This API adds new syntax to JavaFX beans by defining bindable properties.
javafx.collections	A set of collections is part of JavaFX. This special collection offers listener support so that changes of the collection content can be observed.
javafx.concurrent	JavaFX offers some helper classes for asynchronous handling.
javafx.animation	This package defines an animation API to create smooth animations.
javafx.fxml	With FXML, JavaFX offers an XML-based language to separate the definition of the user interface from the application logic of your code.
javafx.css	Nodes can be styled by using CSS. This package provides a set of helper classes if you want to access the CSS support in JavaFX.
javafx.print	The JavaFX printing API is the content of this package.
javafx.embed	This package contains APIs for interoperability with Swing and SWT.
javafx.geometry	This includes some general geometrical classes such as rectangles or direction enums.
javafx.util	This is a bundle of general helper classes.

TABLE 2-6. *JavaFX Public Packages*

Event Handling

JavaFX offers event handling for different types of input. For this reason, there are different event types in JavaFX, such as MouseEvent, KeyEvent, and TouchEvent. Event handlers can be easily registered for the different input events. The following code snippet shows how to register an event handler to a button that will fire with every touch on the screen:

```
button.setOnTouchPressed(new EventHandler<TouchEvent>() {

    @Override public void handle(TouchEvent event) {
        touchx = event.getTouchPoint().getSceneX();
        touchy = event.getTouchPoint().getSceneY();
    }
});
```

The event handlers define how a user can interact with a JavaFX application. Mostly, the event handlers are registered to single controls like a `Button` instance. When covering different controls later in this book, I'll explain the specific event types that are supported by these controls in addition to the input events. An example of this kind of action event is the one that occurs when the pop-up list of a combo box will be shown or hidden.

Property API

JavaFX includes the `Property` interface, which extends property handling and binding with some great features and a simple but powerful API. Most of the JavaFX beans use the property API to grant access to their fields. Normally, next to the getter and setter methods, there is a new method to access the property. Here is an example for a `DoubleProperty` instance:

```
private DoubleProperty cellWidth;

public final DoubleProperty cellWidthProperty() {
    if (cellWidth == null) {
        cellWidth = new SimpleDoubleProperty(64);
    }
    return cellWidth;
}

public void setCellWidth(double value) {
    cellWidthProperty().set(value);
}

public double getCellWidth() {
    return cellWidth == null ? 64.0 : cellWidth.get();
}
```

As you can see, there is no `double cellWidth` field in the code. Instead, the attribute is wrapped in a property instance. The getter and setter methods work directly with the property instance and set or request the current value from the property. JavaFX offers a set of basic property classes for primitive data types like `String` or `double`. All these basic implementations are part of the package `javafx.beans.property.*` Next to all these `Simple**Property` classes, there are some special implementations, such as read-only implementations, that can be used if you want to close your field to external changes. In this case, only removing the setter method is not enough because you can still access the property instance. It's recommend you use `ReadOnly**Property` classes, like `ReadOnlyDoubleProperty` in this case.

By using this design for properties in JavaFX, you will get a lot of benefits in your code. First, JavaFX properties offer support for `javafx.beans.value.ChangeListener`. So, you can add listeners to every property, as shown here:

```
SimpleStringProperty textProp = new SimpleStringProperty();
textProp.addListener(new ChangeListener<String>() {

    @Override
    public void changed(ObservableValue<? extends String> observableValue,
                        String oldValue, String newValue) {
        System.out.println("Value changed: " + oldValue + " -> " + newValue);
    }
});
```

Second, JavaFX properties have support for binding. For this, the `Property` interface offers the following methods:

- `void bind(javafx.beans.value.ObservableValue other);`
- `void unbind();`
- `boolean isBound();`
- `void bindBidirectional(javafx.beans.property.Property other);`
- `void unbindBidirectional(javafx.beans.property.Property other);`

By using these methods, you can create bindings between JavaFX properties easily. For instance, you can use a binding to express a direct relationship between variables. Changes made to an object will be automatically reflected to any bound object. In the following example, the value of a slider will be bound to another one. Now whatever slider is changed, the other one will adopt its value.

```
Slider mySlider1 = …;
Slider mySlider2 = …;
mySlider1.valueProperty().bindBidirectional(mySlider2.valueProperty());
```

JavaFX provides two types of binding: bidirectional and unidirectional. The slider example uses a bidirectional binding. With this binding, you can change any of the two sliders, and the other one will change. With the use of the `bind(…)` method, you can create a unidirectional binding. Here, only one property is bound to the other one: Changing the first slider will affect the second one, but if you change the second slider, this will have no effect on the first one.

With the shown methods, you can easily bind two or more properties with the same value type, but sometimes you need a more complex binding. Suppose you need to bind a slider value to the visible property of a label. The label should appear once the slider value reaches a maximum. The JavaFX property API offers some conversion methods for these needs. Most property types provide specific methods that create a new binding. Here is a sample that uses some of these methods:

```
Slider mySlider1 = new Slider();
Label myLabel = LabelBuilder.create().text("ALERT!").visible(false).build();
myLabel.visibleProperty().bind(mySlider1.valueProperty().multiply(2).greaterThan(100));
```

In line 3, the `valueProperty` is converted to a new double binding that is always double the size of the wrapped property. Now by calling the `greaterThan(…)` method, you create a Boolean binding that is wrapped around the double binding. This binding's value is `true` while the wrapped value is > 100. So if the value of the slider is greater than 50 (50 * 2 > 100), the label will be visible. In addition to these functions, there is the utility class `javafx.beans.binding.Bindings` that provides a lot of additional functions and support.

Collections

JavaFX offers some new collection types by extending the `List`, `Map`, and `Set` interfaces. All of these can be found in the `javafx.collections` package. All the new collections are observable and offer support for change listeners. By using the `ObservableList`, for example, you can easily register a `ListChangeListener` to receive events for each change that is made to the content of the list. Here is a code snippet that shows how you can use this API:

```
ObservableList list = FXCollections.observableArrayList();
list.addListener(new ListChangeListener() {
@Override
public void onChanged(ListChangeListener.Change change) {
    System.out.println("OnChange event:");
    while (change.next()) {
            if(change.wasAdded()) {System.out.println("Elements added. Range:"
                + change.getFrom() + "-" + change.getTo())};
            if(change.wasRemoved()) {System.out.println("Elements removed.
                Range:" + change.getFrom() + "-" + change.getTo())};
            if(change.wasReplaced()) {System.out.println("Elements replaced.
                Range:" + change.getFrom() + "-" + change.getTo())};
            if(change.wasPermutated()) {System.out.println("Elements
                permutated. Range:" + change.getFrom() + "-"
                + change.getTo())};
        }
    }
});
```

As you can see in the code of the `ListChangeListener`, you can analyze the change that was done on the list content and check what ranges have changed and what kind of change it was. Additionally, there is a utility class called `FXCollections`. If you know the `java.util.Collections` class, you will be familiar with this new utility class. By using the class, you can simply create new instances of the JavaFX collection types or execute special operations such as shuffling the content of a list. In the previous code snippet, the `FXCollections` class is used to create the `ObservableList` instance.

Concurrent API

As previously stated, JavaFX is a single-threaded system. All rendering and interaction happen on the JavaFX application thread. Much of the time, you need more than one thread in your application. If you want to access a database, for example, you shouldn't do this on the application thread. The action can block the thread for a long time, and the result will be a frozen application because the thread can't be used for rendering and user interaction. To help the developer in these cases, JavaFX contains some helper classes to create asynchronous activities. The `javafx.concurrent` package contains the `Worker` interface that provides APIs that are useful for creating background workers that will communicate with the UI. The two classes `Task` and `Service` implement the `Worker` interface.

In addition to these classes, the `Platform.runLater(…)` method is useful. With the help of this method, a runnable can be executed on the JavaFX application thread. (Swing developers may know the equivalent method `SwingUtilities.invokeLater(…)`.)

Animations

As a modern UI toolkit, JavaFX offers a great API to create animations. JavaFX supports two different types of methods to create animation: transitions and timeline animations. A transition is the easiest way to create an animation. By using a specific transition class, you only need to define the values that should be reached by the animation and the duration. Additionally, you can define more properties that will influence the behavior of the transition. Here is a short example of a transition that fades a rectangle out and in when it's running:

```
FadeTransition ft = new FadeTransition(Duration.millis(360), rectangle);
ft.setFromValue(1.0);
ft.setToValue(0.1);
ft.setCycleCount(Timeline.INDEFINITE);
ft.setAutoReverse(true);
ft.play();
```

Timeline animations are more complex than transitions. These animations provide the ability to change properties along the progression of time. Unlike transitions, you can add keyframes to timeline animations and define values at certain times.

FXML

To separate the view definition and the application logic, you can use FXML to define the view. FXML is an XML-based language that defines the structure of a user interface. By using FXML, designers can define the complete user interface of an application without mastering any Java code. The FXML files can be loaded at runtime and don't need to be compiled. A basic view structure that is defined in an FXML file looks like the following code:

```
<?xml version="1.0" encoding="UTF-8"?>
<?import java.lang.*?>
<?import java.util.*?>
<?import javafx.scene.control.*?>
<?import javafx.scene.image.*?>
<?import javafx.scene.layout.*?>
<?import javafx.scene.paint.*?>
<AnchorPane id="AnchorPane" prefHeight="720.0" prefWidth="1280.0"
xmlns:fx="http://javafx.com/fxml/1" xmlns="http://javafx.com/javafx/2.2">
  <children>
    <ImageView fitHeight="720.0" fitWidth="1280.0" AnchorPane.
        bottomAnchor="0.0" AnchorPane.leftAnchor="0.0"
        AnchorPane.rightAnchor="0.0" AnchorPane.topAnchor="0.0">
      <image>
        <Image url="@wallpaper/wp3.png" />
      </image>
    </ImageView>
  </children>
</AnchorPane>
```

FXML is the preferred way to define the views of applications in JavaFX. FXML supports all the default JavaFX controls, and you can use FXML to lay out reusable components such as a login form. FXML supports custom controls, too. Because of this, it will be used in later chapters of this book.

CSS Support

All JavaFX controls can be skinned by CSS. Each control has a set of properties, such as foreground color or font size, that are related to its appearance onscreen, and these properties can be defined by CSS. A perfect example that shows what you can do with CSS in JavaFX is the AquaFX library that provides skins to all the default JavaFX controls to make them look like native Mac OS controls. You can find the open source library and documentation at http://aquafx-project.com.

By using CSS, you can define a new look for a control type or a single instance. The following code snippet shows some CSS code that skins a single button:

```
.custom-button {
    -fx-padding: 10;
    -fx-background-color: #FFAA99;
    -fx-font: 24px "Serif";
}
```

When working with controls or creating custom ones, you will normally work a lot with CSS and its internal JavaFX APIs. JavaFX's support for CSS will be covered later in this book.

Printing

With version 8, APIs for printing support were added to JavaFX. By using these APIs, you can easily print nodes or a complete scene graph from a JavaFX application. This book will not cover printing in detail. To take a short look at the API and its methods, the following code snippet contains a method that can be used to print a JavaFX node:

```
public void print(final Node node) {
    Printer printer = Printer.getDefaultPrinter();
    PageLayout pageLayout = printer.createPageLayout(Paper.A4,
        PageOrientation.PORTRAIT, Printer.MarginType.DEFAULT);
    double scaleX = pageLayout.getPrintableWidth() / node.getBoundsInParent().
        getWidth();
    double scaleY = pageLayout.getPrintableHeight() / node.
        getBoundsInParent().getHeight();
    node.getTransforms().add(new Scale(scaleX, scaleY));


    PrinterJob job = PrinterJob.createPrinterJob();
    if (job != null) {
        boolean success = job.printPage(node);
        if (success) {
            job.endJob();
        }
    }
}
```

Interoperability with Swing

JavaFX offers support to include JavaFX in Swing, and vice versa. As a result, the migration from Swing to JavaFX can be much easier for a Swing-based application. The complete APIs that are provided by JavaFX in this context will be shown later in the book.

Tools

In addition to the general support in the most popular IDEs, there are already some visual tools to help developers create applications with JavaFX. The three most prominent tools are covered here.

All three tools should be known to JavaFX application developers and are also used in some of the examples in this book.

Scene Builder

By using Scene Builder, developers can quickly create attractive graphical interfaces. Developers can easily add graphical components via drag and drop to the working view and lay out all controls of a dialog by using a WYSIWYG editor. In addition, new styles and style sheets can be configured and stored. The created views will be stored as FXML files. These FXML files can be embedded in any JavaFX application and used to represent the view of the application. Scene Builder is much more than a simple layout tool for dialogs. Thanks to its direct support of CSS transformations, effects, and other JavaFX technologies, you can create complex graphical views using Scene Builder. Figure 2-5 shows Scene Builder.

Scenic View

Three of the JavaFX chief developers (Jasper Potts, Jonathan Giles, and Richard Bair) run a blog where they introduce interesting JavaFX features and news; see http://fxexperience.com. Additionally, they offer the Scenic View tool for download on this blog (http://fxexperience.com/scenic-view/). With the

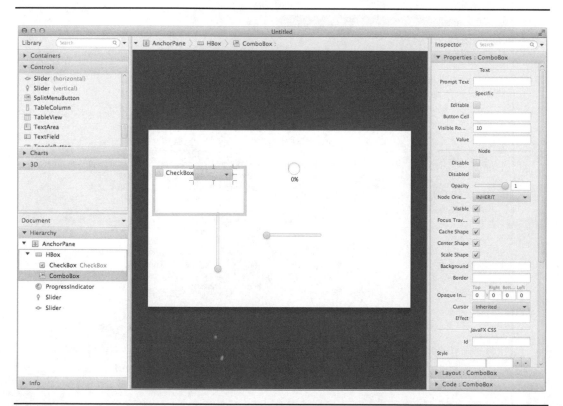

FIGURE 2-5. *Scene Builder workspace*

help of this tool, it is possible to analyze the scene graph. You can look at the layout and the transformation of individual nodes or even directly edit their properties. You should use the Scenic View application primarily to find bugs and check a view for pixel perfection. Figure 2-6 shows Scenic View.

FX Experience Tools

In addition to the tool Scenic View, the FX Experience blog offers another tool named FX Experience Tools. You can download the code and the application at GitHub. You will find more information about the tool here: http://fxexperience.com/2012/03/announcing-fx-experience-tools/.

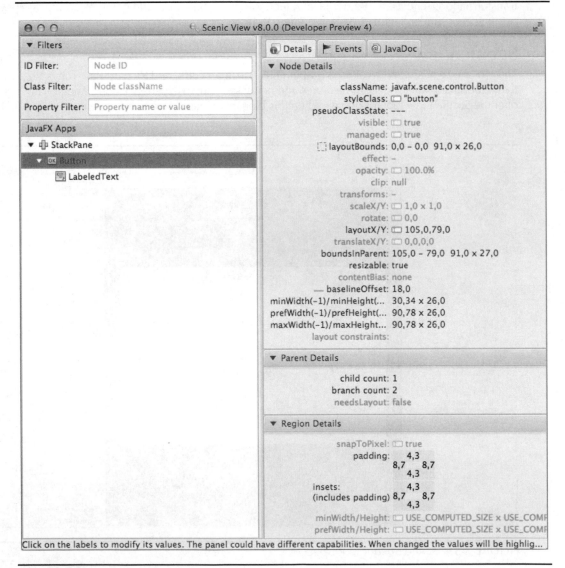

FIGURE 2-6.   *Scenic View*

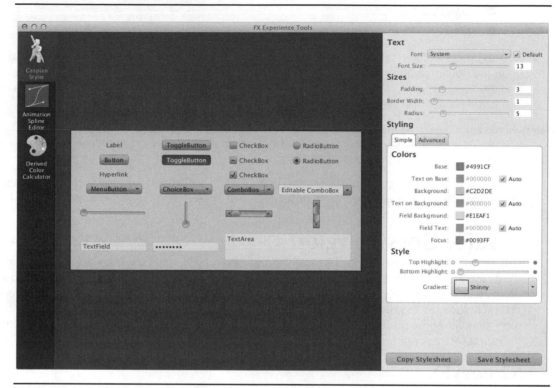

FIGURE 2-7. *FX Experience Tools*

You can use the tool to customize the skin of an application. Although you may not create completely self-created skins, you can easily configure the basic colors of a graphical interface and create a blue skin, for example. Figure 2-7 shows FX Experience Tools.

Deployment/Native Builds

Java provides different ways to deploy a JavaFX application. An application can be packed in a JAR that can be started by a double-click, for example. This way is well known to most developers and is not anything special. Since Java 8, the javafxpackager tool allows you to create self-contained, native applications. By using this tool, you can create an app that is more user friendly than a simple JAR. These applications include all application resources, the Java and JavaFX runtimes, and a launcher. By using them, the user will have the same experience as when installing or launching a native application. By using the javafxpackager tool, an application can be distributed as one of the following formats:

- ZIP file
- EXE or MSI for Windows

- DMG for Mac OS
- RPM or DEB for Linux

To create a native self-contained application by using the javafxpackager tool, you should read the documentation of the tool, available at the command line. Most important for this goal are the -deploy and -native flags. Here is a short example for a shell command that will create a native installer of a demo application:

```
javafxpackager -deploy -native -outdir packages -outfile DemoApp
    -srcdir dist -srcfiles DemoApp.jar -appclass de.guigarage.demo.Main
    -name "Demo" -title "Demo Application"
```

All of JavaFX's functionality can be used in ANT, too. JavaFX contains a JAR with some specific ANT tasks. The <fx:deploy> task needs to be used in an ANT script to create a self-contained app.

JavaFX Goes Polyglott

Thanks to JSR-223, Scripting for the Java Platform, several scripting languages are available on the JVM. You can simply use JavaFX classes in these scripting languages, and there are frameworks that integrate JavaFX with these script languages in a more natural way. It is not part of this book to teach you how to program in these script languages, but because some of them are currently very popular, some projects may depend on them. The following is a brief overview of the three most important script languages.

GroovyFX

With GroovyFX, you can use JavaFX in Groovy in a much simpler and more natural way. By using the Groovy Builder patterns, you can eliminate boilerplate code and create code that is easier to write and read, and then simply use JavaFX in Groovy without this framework. GroovyFX is open source and can be downloaded here: http://groovyfx.org. You can see the convenience of the code by creating a `HelloWorld` application. To create a JavaFX application, you need only to pass a closure to the `GroovyFX.start(…)` method. Inside the closure, you can define the complete UI. The following code shows a simple `HelloWorld` Groovy application that uses GroovyFX. Figure 2-8 shows the running application.

```
import static groovyx.javafx.GroovyFX.start
start {
    stage(title: 'GroovyFX Hello World', visible: true) {
        scene(fill: BLACK, width: 500, height: 250) {
            hbox(padding: 60) {
                text(text: 'Groovy', font: '80pt sanserif') {
                    fill linearGradient(endX: 0, stops: [PALEGREEN, SEAGREEN])
                }
                text(text: 'FX', font: '80pt sanserif') {
                    fill linearGradient(endX: 0, stops: [CYAN, DODGERBLUE])
                    effect dropShadow(color: DODGERBLUE, radius: 25, spread: 0.25)
                }
            }
        }
    }
}
```

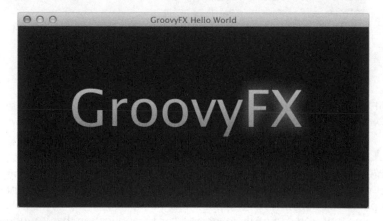

FIGURE 2-8. *GroovyFX application*

ScalaFX

Next to Groovy, Scala is the most successful programming language that can run on top of the JVM. You can find a good introduction to Scala at the Typesafe website (http://typesafe.com/platform/tools/scala), which was founded by the creators of Scala in 2011 and which provides support for Scala. If you want to write a Scala-based JavaFX application, you should take a look at ScalaFX, which is a domain-specific language (DSL) written within Scala that sits on top of JavaFX. Thanks to this, you can use a simple pattern to define the scene graph of your application. Here is a short example of a Scala application that defines a JavaFX view by using ScalaFX:

```scala
package hello
import scalafx.application.JFXApp
import scalafx.application.JFXApp.PrimaryStage
import scalafx.geometry.Insets
import scalafx.scene.Scene
import scalafx.scene.control.Label
import scalafx.scene.layout.BorderPane
import scalafx.scene.text.Font
object ScalaFXHelloWorld extends JFXApp {
  stage = new PrimaryStage {
    scene = new Scene {
      title = "ScalaFX"
      root = new BorderPane {
        padding = Insets(20)
        center = new Label("Hello World!!!") {
```

```
            font = new Font("Verdana", 24)
            style = "-fx-font-weight:bold"
          }
        }
      }
    }
  }
}
```

ScalaFX is open source software. You can find the download and some documentation on the ScalaFX website: https://code.google.com/p/scalafx/.

JavaFX and Nashorn

The Nashorn engine is a new part of Java SE 8 and provides a lightweight, high-performance JavaScript runtime on the JVM. It enables Java developers to embed JavaScript in Java applications or develop free-standing JavaScript applications that can be on top of the JVM by using the jjs command-line tool. You can easily interpret a JavaFX application that is written in JavaScript with Nashorn by only adding the -fx flag. For example, the following command starts Nashorn to run the javaFX.js file:

```
jjs -fx JavaFXscript.js
```

Nashorn provides some additional features to make developing JavaFX applications with JavaScript even easier. Most of the JavaFX classes are wrapped in scripts. By loading them, the imports of JavaFX are easily managed. Here are some examples:

Script	Managed Imports
fx:base.js	javafx.stage.Stage
	javafx.scene.Scene
	javafx.scene.Group
	javafx.beans.*
	javafx.collections.*
	javafx.events.*
	javafx.util-*
fx:fxml.js	javafx.fxml.*

Additionally, the primary stage of a JavaFX application is available in Nashorn as the global property $STAGE. By using this property, you can directly define your application view without using the Application class. Here is a JavaScript example that will run in Nashorn and that creates a simple JavaFX application:

```
load("fx:base.js");
load("fx:controls.js");
load("fx:graphics.js");
$STAGE.title = "Hello World!";
var button = new Button();
button.text = "Say 'Hello World'";
```

```
button.onAction = function() print("Hello World!");
var root = new StackPane();
root.children.add(button);
$STAGE.scene = new Scene(root, 300, 250);
$STAGE.show();
```

Summary

In this chapter, I covered the basics of JavaFX, including its APIs, tools, and JVM support. You quickly saw that even in the case of a simple HelloWorld example, JavaFX calls on a number of different APIs. All these APIs will be elaborated on in the following chapters.

CHAPTER 3

The Scene Graph

This chapter will provide a general overview of the scene graph and its functionality. The chapter will introduce the important public classes and their core functionalities, and it will show you how to create a scene graph and define a UI in it by using visual nodes such as buttons. In addition, you will learn how these elements can be laid out onscreen. Additionally, you'll learn about interacting with the scene graph and different ways to define the layout of the scene graph.

Using and Integrating the Scene Graph in a JavaFX Application

In a JavaFX application, each stage has its own scene graph instance. Within this scene graph, you define a hierarchy of components, called *nodes*. All nodes that are part of a scene graph will be organized in a tree structure. For a more detailed look, let's review the scene graph in the following JavaFX application:

```java
package com.guigarage.masteringcontrols;

import javafx.application.Application;
import javafx.geometry.Pos;
import javafx.scene.Scene;
import javafx.scene.control.Button;
import javafx.scene.layout.HBox;
import javafx.scene.layout.VBox;
import javafx.stage.Stage;

public class SceneGraphApp extends Application {

    @Override
    public void start(Stage primaryStage) throws Exception {
        HBox hBox = new HBox();
        hBox.setAlignment(Pos.CENTER);
        hBox.getChildren().add(new Button("Button 1"));
        hBox.getChildren().add(new Button("Button 2"));
        hBox.getChildren().add(new Button("Button 3"));

        VBox vBox = new VBox();
        vBox.getChildren().add(new Button("Button 4"));
        vBox.getChildren().add(new Button("Button 5"));

        hBox.getChildren().add(vBox);

        Scene mySceneGraph = new Scene(hBox);
        primaryStage.setScene(mySceneGraph);
        primaryStage.show();
    }

    public static void main(String[] args) {
        launch(args);
    }
}
```

FIGURE 3-1. *An application with a simple scene graph*

This example shows a scene graph with several components displayed in the stage of an application, as shown in Figure 3-1. As you can see in the source code, you add different nodes within a defined hierarchy to the scene graph; all components added to the scene graph need to extend the class javafx.scene.Node. When using these nodes, you create a tree structure of components; for instance, nodes can hold other nodes that are *children*, as needed. A node that has children is a *parent* node. The javafx.scene.Parent class inherits from the Node class and allows you to manage the child nodes. The VBox and HBox classes used in the example inherit from the Parent class, and the hierarchy of the application is created by using these two classes and the Button control. As with the HBox and VBox classes, every control is a node. You may notice that, like the Component class in Swing, the inheritance hierarchy of the Node class is a bit more complicated. This will be described in more detail later in this chapter (see the "Node Types" section).

The HBox and VBox classes manage the layout of child nodes by considering the preferred bounds of the child nodes. To display a component, you just need to add it to a visible scene graph. Each scene must have a root node, which is the main node of the scene graph and which contains all other nodes. Therefore, you need a Parent type. As you saw in the previous chapter's example, you can add a scene graph to a stage. By showing the stage on the screen when launching the application, the scene graph and all its visible nodes will be rendered on the surface. Figure 3-2 outlines a simplified structure of a JavaFX application.

The Scene Class

So far, you've seen that the Scene class that defines the scene graph holds the root node and its children. The Scene class also provides a number of features and an inheritance hierarchy. Before looking at those topics, let's first review the rest of the basic properties and functions of the Scene class. Table 3-1 provides an overview of the most important properties of the Scene class.

NOTE
You can access most properties either by using the JavaFX property API or (the POJO way) by using getter and setter methods. Table 3-1 and all following tables in this book will cover the JavaFX properties. Sometimes, only the properties that are specific to the current topic or that are used in common use cases will be shown in these tables. For additional information, refer to the JavaDoc or the JavaFX source code.

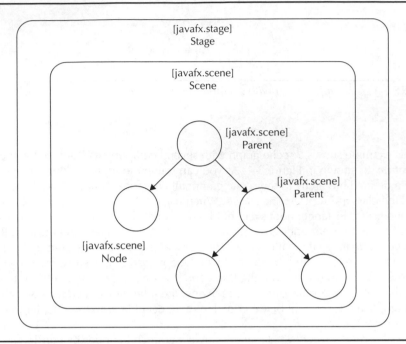

FIGURE 3-2. *Structure of a JavaFX application*

Property	Type	Description
Camera	`ObjectProperty<Camera>`	Defines the camera of the scene graph. Each scene has a camera, which maps the scene coordinates to the window of the application. In most cases (and the default), a parallel camera is used, which renders an application from a default perspective. So the application will look like a 2D application by default. By setting a `PerspectiveCamera`, the application can be rendered from another angle.

TABLE 3-1. *Properties of the Scene Class*

Property	Type	Description
Cursor	ObjectProperty<Cursor>	Defines the mouse cursor within the scene graph. Once the mouse enters the area of the scene graph, the cursor will change to the one specified by this property. The Cursor class provides a huge set of predefined cursors, such as a wait cursor. Additionally, developers can define custom cursors.
eventDispatcher	ObjectProperty<EventDispatcher>	Specifies the event dispatcher that handles the user events. In most cases, the default dispatcher should be used, and developers don't need to change it.
fill	ObjectProperty<Paint>	Specifies the background representation of the scene. For example, a color can be passed because javafx.scene.paint.Color inherits from javafx.scene.paint.Paint.
focusOwner	ReadOnlyObjectProperty<Node>	Specifies the currently focused component within the scene graph.
height	ReadOnlyDoubleProperty	Specifies the height of the scene.
nodeOrientation	ObjectProperty<NodeOrientation>	Defines the alignment of the nodes in the scene graph.
on...	ObjectProperty<EventHandler <? extends Event>>	Defines event handling properties. Event handling in the scene graph is implemented by using event handlers defined by the javafx.event.EventHandler class. The scene graph has different properties for supporting each input type. All of these event handler properties begin with *on**; examples are onMouseClicked and onTouchPressed.

TABLE 3-1. *Properties of the Scene Class* (continued)

Property	Type	Description
root	ObjectProperty<Parent>	Defines the main nodes in the scene graph. All nodes in the scene graph are arranged in the hierarchy under this node.
width	ReadOnlyDoubleProperty	Defines the width of the scene graph.
window	ReadOnlyObjectProperty<Window>	Defines the window in which the scene graph is displayed. In the examples in this book, the window is always the main stage of the application.
x	ReadOnlyDoubleProperty	Defines the x-position of the scene graph within the current window.
y	ReadOnlyDoubleProperty	Defines the y-position of the scene graph within the current window.

TABLE 3-1.   *Properties of the Scene Class* (continued)

The following code extends the sample application and uses properties such as the cursor and fill properties of the Scene class. The code shows two different ways to set a property: by calling the appropriate setter method, which is setFill() in this case, and by retrieving the property object using the appropriate method. The method mySceneGraph.nodeOrientationProperty() is used in this case, and it returns the property instance of type ObjectProperty<NodeOrienta tion>. The value of the property can be set by calling setValue(...). When looking at the source code of the Scene class, you can see that the setter method does the same thing. These properties provide better styling and give the application its first functionalities.

```
package com.guigarage.masteringcontrols;
import javafx.application.Application;
import javafx.geometry.NodeOrientation;
import javafx.geometry.Pos;
import javafx.scene.Camera;
import javafx.scene.Cursor;
import javafx.scene.PerspectiveCamera;
import javafx.scene.Scene;
import javafx.scene.control.Button;
import javafx.scene.layout.HBox;
import javafx.scene.layout.VBox;
import javafx.scene.paint.Color;
import javafx.stage.Stage;
```

```
public class SceneGraphApp extends Application {
    @Override
    public void start(Stage primaryStage) throws Exception {
        HBox hBox = new HBox();
        hBox.setBackground(null);
        hBox.setAlignment(Pos.CENTER);
        hBox.getChildren().add(new Button("Button 1"));
        hBox.getChildren().add(new Button("Button 2"));
        hBox.getChildren().add(new Button("Button 3"));
        VBox vBox = new VBox();
        vBox.setBackground(null);
        vBox.setAlignment(Pos.CENTER);
        vBox.getChildren().add(new Button("Button 4"));
        vBox.getChildren().add(new Button("Button 5"));

        Scene mySceneGraph = new Scene(hBox, 800, 600);

        mySceneGraph.setOnMouseClicked(e -> mySceneGraph.setRoot(vBox));
        mySceneGraph.setOnKeyTyped(e -> mySceneGraph.setRoot(hBox));
        mySceneGraph.setCursor(Cursor.HAND);
        mySceneGraph.nodeOrientationProperty().setValue(NodeOrientation.RIGHT_TO_LEFT);
        mySceneGraph.setFill(Color.BLACK);
        primaryStage.setScene(mySceneGraph);
        primaryStage.show();
    }
    public static void main(String[] args) {
        launch(args);
    }
}
```

This code uses various properties of the Scene class. A different background color and a mouse cursor are set for the scene graph, and the nodes' orientation is changed. To see the background color of the scene graph, the background of the HBox and VBox is set to null since these nodes have their own background color by default and their layout is always maximized in the scene graph. Button 1 is now on the right side of the window instead of the left side, and so on.

In addition, the hierarchy of the nodes in the sample application has changed. The VBox is no longer part of the hierarchy and is therefore not displayed. However, two of the EventHandler properties have been set. The event handlers that are defined here will always execute when a key or a mouse button is pressed in the scene graph; when that happens, the root node of the scene graph will change. You can see this behavior in action by clicking the black background of the demo application. Now Button 4 and Button 5 should appear. By pressing any key on the keyboard, the HBox with the corresponding button will appear again.

NOTE
Lambda expressions are used to define the EventHandler properties in the source code of the demo application. Lambdas are a new language feature introduced in version 8 of Java, so some developers may not have used them yet. JavaFX is well designed for the use of lambda expressions, which are simply source code. For this reason, I use them in this book as often as possible. In theory, all examples shown in the book can be refactored to a version that doesn't use lambda expressions. However, refactoring the previous example makes the two lines of code increase to 12 lines (as shown in the following listing) by using internal classes.

```
mySceneGraph.setOnMouseClicked(new EventHandler<MouseEvent>() {
        @Override
        public void handle(MouseEvent event) {
            mySceneGraph.setRoot(vBox)
        }
});
        mySceneGraph.setOnKeyTyped(new EventHandler<KeyEvent>() {
        @Override
        public void handle(KeyEvent event) {
            mySceneGraph.setRoot(hBox);
        }
});
```

Additionally, this structure creates code that is more complicated to read.

In addition to the properties described earlier, there are some useful methods defined in the Scene class, as described in Table 3-2.

Method	Description
`public <T extends Event> void addEventFilter(EventType<T> eventType, EventHandler<? super T> eventFilter)`	This method adds an event filter to the scene graph. The event handler that is set as an event filter will be handled before an event is passed to the normal life cycle of the event dispatcher. As a result, global event handlers can be created that have a higher priority than event handlers on child nodes.
`public Node lookup(String selector)`	This method can be used to search for a specific node in the scene graph. The selector string is defined as a CSS selector. An example of this method follows this table.
`public final <T extends Event> void removeEventFilter(EventType<T> eventType, EventHandler<? super T> eventFilter)`	By using this method, you can remove an event filter.
`public WritableImage snapshot(WritableImage image)`	This method creates a snapshot of the scene graph and renders it into the given image.
`public void snapshot(Callback< SnapshotResult, Void> callback, WritableImage image)`	This method creates a snapshot of the scene graph and renders it into the given image. Additionally, a callback is supported to react once the snapshot handling is finished.

TABLE 3-2. *Methods of the Scene Class*

The following example uses the event filter and snapshot features:

```java
package com.guigarage.masteringcontrols;

import javafx.application.Application;
import javafx.embed.swing.SwingFXUtils;
import javafx.geometry.Pos;
import javafx.scene.Scene;
import javafx.scene.control.Button;
import javafx.scene.image.WritableImage;
import javafx.scene.input.MouseEvent;
import javafx.scene.layout.HBox;
import javafx.scene.paint.Color;
import javafx.stage.Stage;
import javax.imageio.ImageIO;
import java.io.File;
public class SceneGraphApp extends Application {
    @Override
    public void start(Stage primaryStage) throws Exception {
        HBox hBox = new HBox();
        hBox.setBackground(null);
        hBox.setAlignment(Pos.CENTER);
        hBox.getChildren().add(new Button("Button 1"));
        Scene mySceneGraph = new Scene(hBox, 800, 600);
        mySceneGraph.addEventFilter(MouseEvent.MOUSE_CLICKED, e ->
                mySceneGraph.setFill(Color.GREEN));
        mySceneGraph.setOnKeyTyped(e -> saveSnapshotOnDisc(mySceneGraph));
        primaryStage.setScene(mySceneGraph);
        primaryStage.show();
    }
    public void saveSnapshotOnDisc(Scene sceneGraph) {
        WritableImage i = new WritableImage((int) sceneGraph.getWidth(), (int)
            sceneGraph.getHeight());
        sceneGraph.snapshot(i);
        try {
            ImageIO.write(SwingFXUtils.fromFXImage(i, null), "png", new
                        File("image.png"));
        } catch (Exception s) {
        }
    }
    public static void main(String[] args) {
        launch(args);
    }
}
```

This code adds an event filter for all mouse click events to the scene graph. As mentioned in the previous table, the defined event handler will be called before the events can be passed to the normal life cycle of the event dispatcher. The event handler will be called even if a button was clicked in the scene graph, for example. All click events will be handled directly and passed only to child components. In the application, you can simply click any point in the application window. Even if you click an empty area of the scene graph or the button, the background of the scene graph will change its color.

The second method of the scene graph that is used here is the `snapshot(...)` method to create a screenshot of the current scene graph. In the example, this method is called inside the `saveSnapshotOnDisc(...)` method. The snapshot is created and saved as a PNG file on the hard drive. By pressing any key, the `KeyEventHandler` creates the snapshot.

Event Handling

JavaFX knows several types of input events on which an application can react to user input. Event handlers for these event types can be used in the scene graph to create an interaction between the user and the application. All supported input events are defined in JavaFX as a derivation of the class `javafx.scene.input.InputEvent`. JavaFX can deal with considerably more input types than Swing. Additionally, all modern input types such as gestures and touch input are supported. By using these features, developers can define a better user experience than with any other Java UI framework. Figure 3-3 contains an overview of the supported event types and their inheritance.

In addition to the classic mouse and key events that already exist in AWT or Swing, touch and gesture events have been added to JavaFX, so you can use JavaFX on a multitouch environment such as a tablet and have your application respond to finger input by the user. For example, a pinch, shown in Figure 3-4, will be passed directly as a zoom event to the JavaFX scene graph.

NOTE
All modern MacBooks embed a multitouchpad that can interpret gestures. Most of them are supported in the Mac OS, and if a JavaFX program is running on such a system, the gesture events will be passed to the program. If you don't have a tablet but own a MacBook, you can easily test the gesture events by using the touchpad of your device.

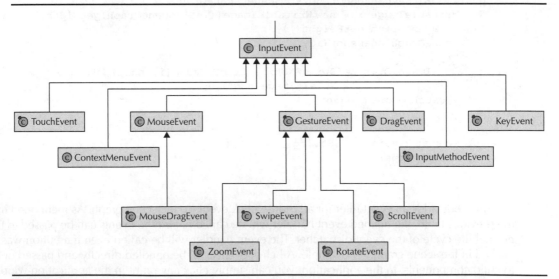

FIGURE 3-3. *Class hierarchy of JavaFX events*

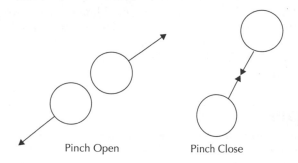

Pinch Open   Pinch Close

FIGURE 3-4. *Pinch events*

Many examples in this book will use input events to create some interaction, so there is no special example that contains all the different event types. The following code snippet shows how an `EventHandler` can be set to react after a special button is clicked:

...

```
Button myButton = new Button("Button 1");
myButton.setOnMouseClicked(e -> System.out.println("Mousebutton " +
    e.getButton() + " was clicked " + e.getClickCount() + " times. (" +
    e.getX() + "/" + e.getY() + ")"));
```

...

Each event that occurs on the scene graph will be handled by the event dispatcher of the scene graph. An event dispatch sends all received events to the registered event handlers and filters. Whenever an event occurs, four steps will take place:

1. Target selection
2. Route construction
3. Event capturing
4. Event bubbling

First, the target of the event will be determined. This step depends on the event type. If a mouse click occurs, the event target will be the topmost node at the position of the mouse cursor that has not set the `mouseTransparent` property to true. The target of a key event is the currently focused node. Touch and gesture events have some special rules for how the target node will be selected too. After the target node is defined, a route through the scene graph will be defined. This route contains all nodes between the root node of the scene graph and the target node. This route is called the *event dispatch chain*. In the event-capturing phase, the event will be passed through the chain. This dispatch starts with the scene graph instance and goes down the complete route to the target node. If any of these nodes has registered an event filter for the given event type, the event handler that is defined as the filter will be called. Each event has a consumed flag. Whenever any event handler consumes an event by setting this flag, the processing of the event will stop. If no registered filter consumes the event, the target node will be reached. At this moment, the last phase will start. In the event-bubbling phase, the event will return along the dispatch chain from the target to the root node of the scene graph. Here, each event handler that is registered for the given event type will be called. As long as no handler consumes the event, it will return to the next node up the chain until the root node is reached, and the event dispatching will stop.

Node Types

As mentioned earlier, any component that can be added to a scene graph has to extend the Node class. The inheritance of the Node class is a little more complicated than you might know from other cases such as Swing, for example. Figure 3-5 shows a diagram with the most important parts of the class hierarchy.

The diagram may be overwhelming at first, but all the classes in the diagram can split into three different main types: primitive nodes, LayoutPanes, and complex nodes such as controls.

Primitive Nodes

Among the primitive nodes are different shape types such as circles, rectangles, and lines. There are, thanks to the 3D support of JavaFX, still primitive three-dimensional shapes like a box. All

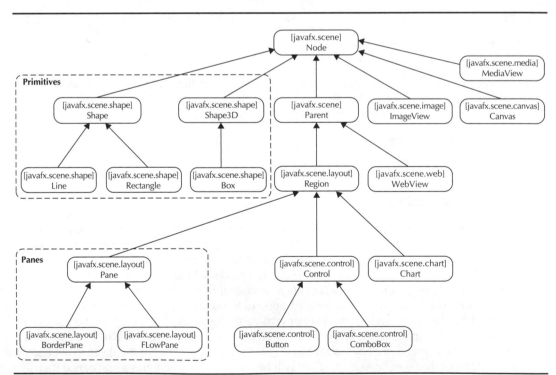

FIGURE 3-5. *Node class hierarchy*

these nodes can be easily added to a scene graph. In the following example code, a rectangle is added to the scene graph:

```java
package com.guigarage.masteringcontrols;
import javafx.application.Application;
import javafx.geometry.Pos;
import javafx.scene.Scene;
import javafx.scene.control.Button;
import javafx.scene.layout.HBox;
import javafx.scene.paint.Color;
import javafx.scene.shape.Rectangle;
import javafx.stage.Stage;

public class SceneGraphApp extends Application {
    @Override
    public void start(Stage primaryStage) throws Exception {
        HBox hBox = new HBox();
        hBox.setAlignment(Pos.CENTER);
        hBox.getChildren().add(new Rectangle(50, 50, Color.YELLOW));
        Scene mySceneGraph = new Scene(hBox, 800, 600);
        primaryStage.setScene(mySceneGraph);
        primaryStage.show();
    }
    public static void main(String[] args) {
        launch(args);
    }
}
```

As you can see, the shapes in the code are treated exactly as other nodes, in other words, like controls. The use of these elements is not different from other examples such as buttons in the scene graph. All the other elements that extend the Node class can be added in this way in the scene graph.

Using the scene graph even with primitives such as lines is one of the advantages of JavaFX over other UI toolkits like Swing. All visual elements are real nodes in the scene graph, and internally more complex components like buttons are composed by using a set of primitive shapes.

As you can see in Figure 3-6, a RadioButton control is internally composed from different nodes. To display the text information on the radio button, a LabeledText object is used. This is

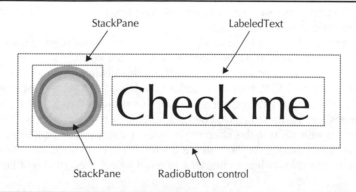

FIGURE 3-6. *Composition of a RadioButton*

a derivative of the `javafx.scene.shape.Text` class and mainly used in the skin of controls. The selection circle of the radio button is created by two nested StackPanes. These StackPanes are styled by CSS to get the specific look shown here. The individual nodes will be styled and laid out by the radio button skin. This special functionality will be explained in Chapters 9 and 10. In Swing, an inner canvas is used in which pixel graphics are painted to define the visual representation of a component. You won't find this technology in JavaFX nodes.

NOTE
JavaFX contains a special node type called `Canvas`. *This node provides paint functionality like you may know from Swing and Java2D, but the* `Canvas` *class is never used internally in JavaFX nodes. Here, CSS and other node types such as shapes are always used. The* `Canvas` *class will be described in Chapter 7.*

LayoutPanes

The LayoutPanes category of nodes contains all panes. These classes are responsible for the layouts and therefore the positioning of child components. I'll briefly describe the class hierarchy of the panes: Each node that needs to encapsulate a set of child nodes needs to extend the `javafx.scene.Parent` class. This class provides only the ability to wrap any type of node. As a next step, the `javafx.scene.layout.Region` class defines the `Region` type that is a resizable `Parent` class that can be styled using CSS. The `Parent` and `Region` classes can both contain a set of children. The children of a parent are defined as an `ObservableList<Node>`. Neither the `Parent` nor `Region` class provide public methods to change its children. The `javafx.scene.layout.Pane` class adds this feature. While the `Parent` class defines the `getChildrenUnmodifiable()` method that returns a read-only list of all children, the `Pane` class defines a `getChildren()` method that returns a modifiable list of children. Therefore, all default layout containers in JavaFX, such as `HBox` or `VBox`, extend the `Pane` class, and developers can add child nodes to them by calling `pane.getChildren().add(myButton)`, for example. All controls such as `Button` controls inherit from the `Region` class because they need to hold and lay out some primitive shapes that are needed to visualize the button. But developers can never easily add new nodes to a button. By using the descried class hierarchy, it will be more difficult for developers to use some of the node types in a wrong way.

All the nodes that implement different layouts to align its children extend the `Pane` class. Instances of these classes should be used when all the controls inside a scene graph need to be laid out. In the previous examples, you already saw two pane types: `HBox` and `VBox`. Table 3-3 describes the various layout panes.

Some panes, such as the `HBox` or `FlowPane`, can be easily used in code. Others, such as the `AnchorPane`, are flexible, and therefore they need more configuration in code to create a special layout. As a best practice, you should create these layouts in Scene Builder. When using Scene Builder, you create an FXML file that describes the layout. (FXML will be discussed in the "FXML" section, and an example with a complex layout that is created in Scene Builder will be shown.) To achieve the desired layout structure, you can nest different containers within a JavaFX application. The first demo application in this chapter wrapped a `VBox` inside an `HBox` to create a special screen layout, for example. As you will see later, it is easy to create your own LayoutPanes, too, but doing so requires knowledge about the internal layout mechanism of JavaFX.

Class	Description
AnchorPane	By using this pane, developers can define anchors to the top, bottom, left side, or center of the layout for each child node.
BorderPane	This pane arranges its child components in top, bottom, right, left, and center regions.
FlowPane	All child nodes will be placed in a horizontal or vertical sequence that wraps at the edge of the pane.
GridPane	This pane uses a layout that is based on rows and columns that can be defined in a flexible way.
HBox	All child components will be placed horizontally in a single row.
StackPane	This pane places its content nodes in a back-to-front single stack where all children will overlap each other.
TextFlow	This is a special pane to create rich text by placing all child nodes in a flow that has the same behavior as a text flow.
TilePane	All content nodes will be placed in uniformly sized layout cells or tiles.
VBox	All child components will be placed vertically in a single column.

TABLE 3-3. *Overview of Pane Classes*

Complex Nodes

All other classes that extend the Node class are components that fall into the complex node category. The largest part of this group includes the controls such as buttons, labels, and tables. These all extend the Control class. Controls have a lot of features; you can simply change their style and behavior or add a tooltip, for example. I will discuss the different features of controls in more depth in the following chapters. In addition to them, there are some other special nodes such as WebView, Canvas, and Chart. Table 3-4 describes these components.

Node	Description
MediaView	This is a component that shows multimedia content such as videos.
ImageView	This is a component that renders an image onscreen.
Canvas	This is a canvas component that provides a canvas API that matches the HTML5 canvas API. An application can paint directly into the canvas.
SwingNode	By using this node, you can add Swing components to the scene graph.
WebView	This node can show HTML content onscreen. Internally, WebKit is used to render the HTML view. By using WebKit, JavaScript and CSS are supported too.
Chart	JavaFX provides different chart types to visualize business data. The Chart class is the superclass of all these chart types. Some examples are pie and bar chart diagrams.

TABLE 3-4. *Special Components in JavaFX*

Node Basics

As mentioned, all components that can be added to a scene graph extend the Node class. This class offers a set of properties and methods. Table 3-5 contains an overview of the class properties that can be useful while working with the scene graph.

Property	Type	Description
blendMode	ObjectProperty<BlendMode>	The blend mode that defines how a node will be blended into the scene behind it. By default, the SRC_OVER mode will be used. Figure 3-7 (at the end of this table) shows a rendered outcome for some different blend modes.
boundsInLocal	ReadOnlyObjectProperty<Bounds>	Defines the bounds of the node in its untransformed local coordinate space. The layout of nodes and all specific properties will be discussed in Chapter 4.
boundsInParent	ReadOnlyObjectProperty<Bounds>	Defines the bounds of the node that includes its transformation.
cache	BooleanProperty	Defines whether bitmap caching should be used for the node.
cacheHint	ObjectProperty<CacheHint>	Defines a hint that can be used to set the bitmap-caching mechanism of a node.
cursor	ObjectProperty<Cursor>	Defines the mouse cursor of the node.
depthTest	ObjectProperty<DepthTest>	Defines whether depth testing is used. This is used for 3D rendering.
disable	BooleanProperty	Defines whether the node is disabled. Other than the disabled property, this one will contain only the state of this concrete node without its parent disabled state.

TABLE 3-5. *Properties of the Node Class*

Property	Type	Description
disabled	ReadOnlyBooleanProperty	Defines whether the node is disabled. A disabled node will normally be rendered in a different way and does not receive mouse or key events. A node is disabled if its disabled property is set to true or if its parent node in the hierarchy is disabled.
eventDispatcher	ObjectProperty<EventDispatcher>	Specifies the event dispatcher of this node.
focused	ReadOnlyBooleanProperty	Is true if the node is the focused node inside the scene.
focusTraversable	BooleanProperty	Defines whether the node is part of the focus traversal cycle. If this property is true, the focus can be moved to the node by using the default key combinations.
hover	ReadOnlyBooleanProperty	Specifies a read-only flag that defines whether the node is in hover mode. This will normally happen if the mouse cursor is over the node. This flag will normally be used for skinning issues.
id	StringProperty	Specifies the ID of the node. The ID can be used to find the node inside the scene graph and should be unique.
layoutBounds	ReadOnlyObjectProperty<Bounds>	Specifies the rectangular bounds of the node. The layout of nodes and all specific properties will be discussed in Chapter 4.
layoutX	DoubleProperty	Defines the x-coordinate of the node's translation for the purpose of layout.

TABLE 3-5. *Properties of the Node Class* (continued)

Property	Type	Description
layoutY	DoubleProperty	Defines the y-coordinate of the node's translation for the purpose of layout.
localToParentTransform	ReadOnlyObjectProperty<Transform>	Defines the affine transform that holds the computed local-to-parent transform. Transformations will be discussed in Chapter 4.
managed	BooleanProperty	Defines whether the layout of the node will be managed by its parent.
mouseTransparent	BooleanProperty	Defines whether the node is transparent to mouse events.
nodeOrientation	ObjectProperty<NodeOrientation>	Defines the orientation of the visual output. In an Arabic or Hebrew world, visual data flows from right to left, for example.
opacity	DoubleProperty	Defines the transparency of a node. If the property is set to 0, the node will be transparent.
parent	ReadOnlyObjectProperty<Parent>	Defines the parent of this node. If a node is in a scene graph, this property defines the parent node.
pickOnBounds	BooleanProperty	Defines how the picking computation is done. If set to true, picking will be computed by intersecting with the bounds of the node. Otherwise, it will be computed by intersecting with its geometric shape.
pressed	ReadOnlyBooleanProperty	Specifies the read-only flag that defines whether the node is in pressed mode. This will normally happen if this node is clicked. This flag will normally be used for skinning issues.

TABLE 3-5. *Properties of the Node Class* (continued)

Property	Type	Description
rotate	DoubleProperty	Defines the angle of rotation about the center of the node. This is part of the transformation of a node and will be discussed in Chapter 4.
rotationAxis	ObjectProperty<Point3D>	Defines the axis of rotation of this node (described in Chapter 4).
scaleX	DoubleProperty	Defines the factor by which the node is scaled along the x-axis (described in Chapter 4).
scaleY	DoubleProperty	Defines the factor by which the node is scaled along the y-axis (described in Chapter 4).
scaleZ	DoubleProperty	Defines the factor by which the node is scaled along the z-axis (described in Chapter 4).
scene	ReadOnlyObjectProperty<Scene>	Defines the scene that the node is part of. This property has read-only access.
Style	StringProperty	Defines a string representation of the used CSS style.
translateX	DoubleProperty	Defines the x-value of the translation that is added to the node transform (described in Chapter 4).
translateY	DoubleProperty	Defines the y-value of the translation that is added to the node transform (described in Chapter 4).
translateZ	DoubleProperty	Defines the z-value of the translation that is added to the node transform (described in Chapter 4).

TABLE 3-5. *Properties of the Node Class* (continued)

Property	Type	Description
visible	BooleanProperty	Defines whether the node is visible. If set to false, the node won't be rendered on the screen.
clip	ObjectProperty<Node>	Defines the clipping shape of the node. This special node is used to define the clipping region that is applied to the node.
effect	ObjectProperty<Effect>	Applies an effect on the node.

TABLE 3-5.   *Properties of the Node Class* (continued)

In addition to these properties, the Node class provides some helpful methods that can be used to manage some basic tasks when working with nodes. Some of these methods are related to the ones that are part of the Scene class. All the different methods of the Node class won't be shown here. For a complete overview, please refer to the JavaDoc or the source of the Node class.

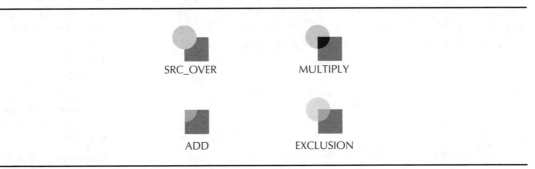

FIGURE 3-7.   *Examples for the blendMode property*

You can use the properties and methods in code to specify the characteristics of the used nodes. As an example, the following application uses several of the mentioned properties to offer some special functionality:

```java
package com.guigarage.masteringcontrols;

import javafx.application.Application;
import javafx.geometry.NodeOrientation;
import javafx.geometry.Pos;
import javafx.scene.Node;
import javafx.scene.Scene;
import javafx.scene.control.Button;
import javafx.scene.control.CheckBox;
import javafx.scene.effect.Reflection;
import javafx.scene.layout.HBox;
import javafx.stage.Stage;

public class SceneGraphApp extends Application {

    @Override
    public void start(Stage primaryStage) throws Exception {
        HBox hBox = new HBox();
        hBox.setAlignment(Pos.CENTER);
        hBox.setSpacing(12);
        Button myButton = new Button("press me!");
        myButton.setId("myButton");
        myButton.setNodeOrientation(NodeOrientation.RIGHT_TO_LEFT);
        myButton.setOnAction(e -> changeNodeVisibility(myButton.getScene(),
                        "myCheckbox"));
        CheckBox myCheckbox = new CheckBox("Hello!");
        myCheckbox.setId("myCheckbox");
        myCheckbox.setOpacity(0.7d);
        myCheckbox.setEffect(new Reflection());
        hBox.getChildren().addAll(myButton, myCheckbox);
        Scene mySceneGraph = new Scene(hBox, 800, 600);
        primaryStage.setScene(mySceneGraph);
        primaryStage.show();
    }

    private void changeNodeVisibility(Scene scene, String id)     {
        Node node = scene.lookup("#" + id);
        if(node != null) {
            node.setVisible(!node.isVisible());
        }
    }

    public static void main(String[] args) {
        launch(args);
    }
}
```

FIGURE 3-8. *The example application*

When running the application shown in Figure 3-8, a button and a check box will be part of the scene graph. Compared to the previous applications, this one is a bit different. The check box that is used has a reflection effect. Additionally, it is not completely opaque. The exclamation point of the button text is on the left side. This is the result of the different node orientation that is set on the node. In addition, both controls have a unique ID. By clicking the button, the changeNodeVisibility(...) method is called. This method uses the lookup(...) method to find the node with the given ID inside the scene graph. Because the lookup(...) method uses CSS ID specification, a hash tag must be added as a prefix to the ID. (You can read more about the specification at www.w3.org/TR/CSS21/syndata.html#value-def-identifier.) Clicking the button changes the visibility of the check box.

 NOTE
This example application has some new features that weren't mentioned until now. By calling the setOnAction(...) method on the Button instance, a special event handler is set on the button. This handler will be called whenever the button is clicked or, rather, used. This can be triggered by different input events, such as a mouse click, a pressed key, or a touch event, for example. Most of the controls that are provided by JavaFX support event handlers for common use cases. A ComboBox supports event handler instances to react to the behavior of the selection pop-up, for example.

FXML
In this chapter, most of the example applications create a scene graph with some controls. In all the examples, the layout of the application is simple and couldn't be used in a business application. In professional applications, you usually have complex layouts that need to interleave different panes and would use, for example, the AnchorPane, which is considerably more complex than the BorderPane or FlowPane. In the following code block, an AnchorPane is used to lay out two buttons. The AnchorPane class offers some static methods to affect the layout behavior of child components in an AnchorPane. Figure 3-9 shows the application view.

```
package com.guigarage.masteringcontrols;

import javafx.application.Application;
import javafx.scene.Scene;
import javafx.scene.control.Button;
```

```
import javafx.scene.layout.AnchorPane;
import javafx.stage.Stage;

public class SceneGraphApp extends Application {
    @Override
    public void start(Stage primaryStage) throws Exception {
        AnchorPane anchorpane = new AnchorPane();
        Button buttonSave = new Button("Save");
        Button buttonCancel = new Button("Cancel");

        anchorpane.getChildren().addAll(buttonSave,buttonCancel);
        AnchorPane.setBottomAnchor(buttonCancel, 6.0);
        AnchorPane.setRightAnchor(buttonCancel, 6.0);
        AnchorPane.setTopAnchor(buttonCancel, 6.0);
        AnchorPane.setBottomAnchor(buttonSave, 6.0);
        AnchorPane.setLeftAnchor(buttonSave, 6.0);
        AnchorPane.setTopAnchor(buttonSave, 6.0);

        Scene mySceneGraph = new Scene(anchorpane, 800, 600);
        primaryStage.setScene(mySceneGraph);
        primaryStage.show();
    }
    public static void main(String[] args) {
        launch(args);
    }
}
```

As you can see in the code, you need to add a number of lines to define a specific layout. The more controls and panes you need in your application, the more complex the code becomes. In Swing, this was a common problem too. By using WYSIWYG editors, developers often created source code that defined the layout of Swing applications, but this produced additional problems, including that the source code couldn't be edited by hand or the editor couldn't parse special source code.

To combat these problems, JavaFX provides FXML. As mentioned in earlier chapters, FXML is an XML-based language that can be used to provide the structure of user interfaces. You use it to define the UI layout separate from the application logic of your code. It is highly recommended

FIGURE 3-9. *The example application*

that you use FXML as often as possible. Using FXML and then using Scene Builder as a WYSIWYG editor is a best practice when developing views for a JavaFX application. Even when you want to create some modern and skinned views, you can use these tools. The following code shows the FXML that defines an `AnchorPane` with the layout that was developed in Java source earlier:

```xml
<?xml version="1.0" encoding="UTF-8"?>
<?import java.lang.*?>
<?import javafx.scene.control.*?>
<?import javafx.scene.layout.*?>
<AnchorPane xmlns="http://javafx.com/javafx/8" xmlns:fx="http://javafx.com/fxml/1">
<children>
<Button text="Save" AnchorPane.bottomAnchor="6.0" AnchorPane.leftAnchor="6.0"
   AnchorPane.topAnchor="6.0" />
<Button text="Cancel" AnchorPane.bottomAnchor="6.0" AnchorPane.rightAnchor="6.0"
   AnchorPane.topAnchor="6.0" />
</children></AnchorPane>
```

I won't discuss the definition and structure of FXML in depth, but you can see in this example that you can define the layout parameters directly in FXML. Additionally, you can define properties such as the text of buttons in FXML.

Once you create an FXML file, you need to load the file at runtime. This can be easily done by using the `FXMLLoader` class:

```java
package com.guigarage.masteringcontrols;

import javafx.application.Application;
import javafx.fxml.FXMLLoader;
import javafx.scene.Scene;
import javafx.scene.layout.Pane;
import javafx.stage.Stage;

public class SceneGraphApp extends Application {

    @Override
    public void start(Stage primaryStage) throws Exception {
        Pane myPane = (Pane) FXMLLoader.load(getClass().getResource("layout.fxml"));
        Scene mySceneGraph = new Scene(myPane, 800, 600);
        primaryStage.setScene(mySceneGraph);
        primaryStage.show();
    }

    public static void main(String[] args) {
        launch(args);
    }
}
```

In the code, note that `getClass().getResource(...)` is used to load the FXML file. This is a best practice to load resources in Java. To do this, you need to place the `layout.fxml` file in the same package as the class file, `SceneGraphApp.class` in this case. Incidentally, most modern Java applications use a setup that was defined by Maven some years ago where all Java code is placed in an `src/main/java` subfolder. It is recommend that you use this structure and don't put any resource files such as images, XML, or CSS files in this folder. For those resources, create an `src/main/resources` folder. The `getResource(...)` method will still work if the resource is located in the same package as the class but in a resources folder. Here is a working folder tree for the given example:

```
project/
    src/
        main/
            java/
                com/
                    guigarage/
                        masteringcontrols/
                            SceneGraphApp.java
            resources/
                com/
                    guigarage/
                        masteringcontrols/
                            layout.fxml
```

Once this structure is created, most modern IDEs will identity the setup and add `src/main/java` and `src/main/resources` automatically to the classpath. Sometimes, you need to set up your environment by hand and add these folders to the classpath.

In addition to these features, FXML provides a way to interact with the UI and bind a controller to the view. When defining an FXML file, you can define a controller class. The following snippet shows how a controller can be specified in FXML:

```
...
<AnchorPane fx:controller="com.guigarage.masteringcontrols.ViewController"
    xmlns="http://javafx.com/javafx/8" xmlns:fx="http://javafx.com/fxml/1">
<children>
<Button fx:id="saveButton" onAction="#save" text="Save" AnchorPane.bottomAnchor="6.0"
    AnchorPane.leftAnchor="6.0" AnchorPane.topAnchor="6.0" />
<Button fx:id="cancelButton" text="Cancel" AnchorPane.bottomAnchor="6.0" AnchorPane.
    rightAnchor="6.0" AnchorPane.topAnchor="6.0" />
</children></AnchorPane>
```

In addition to the controller class that was added as a parameter to the `AnchorPane`, new parameters are defined for the buttons in the FXML. The `fx:id` parameters define unique IDs for the two buttons. By using these IDs, the buttons can be accessed in the controller class. This can be done by using special annotations. Event handlers can be defined in FXML too. In the definition of the save button, for example, an additional parameter is added. This `onAction` parameter links to a method that is part of the controller. When the button is clicked, the `save` method will be triggered. Furthermore, each controller class can define an `initialize()` method. This method will be called when the controller is created and all annotated values are injected. The following code shows how a controller that matches the FXML file may look:

```
package com.guigarage.masteringcontrols;

import javafx.event.ActionEvent;
import javafx.fxml.FXML;
import javafx.scene.control.Button;
```

```
public class ViewController {

    @FXML
    private Button saveButton;

    @FXML
    private Button cancelButton;

    @FXML protected void save(ActionEvent event) {
        //TODO...
    }
    public void initialize() {
        //TODO...
    }

}
```

When the FXML file is loaded, a new instance of the controller class will be created automatically, and all fields that have the @FXML annotation will be filled by injection. Additionally, the save (...) method will be bound to the onAction event of the save button.

Summary

This chapter showed all the basic functionality of the scene graph. It covered the different types of nodes and the basic usage of event handling, and it introduced FXML. Some of the basic features of JavaFX were only briefly mentioned. For further information on the basics of JavaFX, review a beginner's guide to learning JavaFX, such as *Quick Start Guide to JavaFX* (McGraw-Hill, 2014).

After reading the chapter, you should now understand all the basic technologies and methods for creating a simple JavaFX application with a default layout. The next chapters will define special features such as the internal layout mechanism of JavaFX, which will help you create special layout panes for applications.

CHAPTER

4

Laying Out and Transforming Nodes in the Scene Graph

A s shown in the previous chapter, the UI of a JavaFX application is based on a hierarchy of nodes laid out and rendered in the scene graph. By using different interleaved panes, you can create a custom layout. In this chapter, you will take a deeper look at how panes, such as the FlowPane control, work internally. Additionally, you will learn about the different transformation possibilities of JavaFX.

Adding Some Transformations

The scene graph API offers the ability to transform a node or a group of nodes in a user interface. JavaFX supports a set of transformations that can manipulate the position of node pixels in the internal coordination system. For example, scaling a node will not change the defined location of the node, but all the pixels will be *transformed* to the new position. If the scaling enlarges, node pixels will be added. Internal algorithms are used to calculate the transformed pixels. JavaFX supports five transformations, as listed here:

- Scaling
- Rotation
- Translation
- Shearing
- Affine

Figure 4-1 shows samples of the first four transformation types. The Affine transformation is a more general type that can be used to define any transformation between two affine spaces. The Node class has some methods that can be used to define a transformation on it, and you can combine transformations to rotate and scale a node, for example. Table 4-1 contains an overview of the methods that can be used to define transformations on a node.

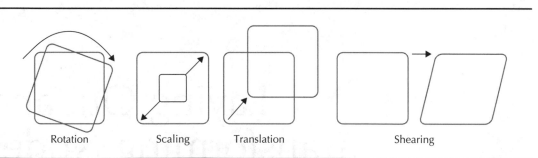

Rotation   Scaling   Translation   Shearing

FIGURE 4-1. *Transformation types*

Method	Description
`ObservableList<Transform>` `    transformsProperty()`	Defines a list of transform objects that will be applied to the node
`DoubleProperty translateXProperty()`	Defines the x-coordinate of the translation that is added to the node transform
`DoubleProperty translateYProperty()`	Defines the y-coordinate of the translation that is added to the node transform
`DoubleProperty translateZProperty()`	Defines the z-coordinate of the translation that is added to the node transform
`DoubleProperty scaleXProperty()`	Defines the factor by which the node and its content is scaled about the center along the x-axis
`DoubleProperty scaleYProperty()`	Defines the factor by which the node and its content is scaled about the center along the y-axis
`DoubleProperty scaleZProperty()`	Defines the factor by which the node and its content is scaled about the center along the z-axis
`DoubleProperty rotateProperty()`	Defines the angle of rotation around the node's center in degrees
`ObjectProperty<Point3D>` `    rotationAxisProperty()`	Defines the axis of rotation of the node
`ReadOnlyObjectProperty<Transform>` `    localToParentTransformProperty()`	A concatenation of all transforms in this node
`ReadOnlyObjectProperty<Transform>` `    localToSceneTransformProperty()`	A concatenation of all transforms in this node's parents and in the node

TABLE 4-1.   *Overview of Methods of the Node Class to Handle Transformations*

The following example, a pane wrapping two buttons, uses gesture events to apply different transformations to an HBox. Because in the scene graph a transformation affects all nodes under the transformed one, the buttons in this application will be transformed as well.

```
package com.guigarage.masteringcontrols;
import javafx.application.Application;
import javafx.geometry.Pos;
import javafx.scene.Scene;
import javafx.scene.control.Button;
import javafx.scene.layout.HBox;
import javafx.stage.Stage;

public class SceneGraphApp extends Application {

    @Override
    public void start(Stage primaryStage) throws Exception {
        HBox hBox = new HBox();
        hBox.setAlignment(Pos.CENTER);
```

```
        hBox.getChildren().add(new Button("Button 1"));
        hBox.getChildren().add(new Button("Button 2"));

        hBox.setOnZoom(e -> {hBox.setScaleX(hBox.getScaleX() * e.getZoomFactor());
        hBox.setScaleY(hBox.getScaleY() * e.getZoomFactor());});
        hBox.setOnRotate(e -> hBox.setRotate(hBox.getRotate() + e.getAngle()));

        Scene mySceneGraph = new Scene(hBox, 800, 600);
        primaryStage.setScene(mySceneGraph);
        primaryStage.show();
    }

    public static void main(String[] args) {
        launch(args);
    }
}
```

Once you start the demo, you can transform the objects onscreen by simply using your fingers. Most people will be familiar with this behavior from mobile devices. iOS, for example, heavily uses this same behavior. Figure 4-2 shows an application after a gesture has occurred.

By zooming in on the buttons, you can see that the resolution of the controls won't become pixelated. All controls are composed of a set of primitives such as shapes and CSS information, and since all these primitives are vector based, a control in JavaFX is scalable without any loss of quality.

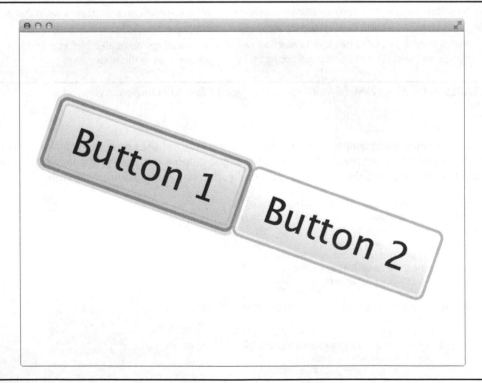

FIGURE 4-2. *Transformed nodes*

Running the Sample Without Gesture Support

The demo should be run on a device that supports gesture events. At the time of writing this book, the Microsoft Surface tablet and MacBook will successfully run the demo. If you don't have a device that supports gestures and can run JavaFX, simply change the demo to create a transformation experience that can be handled by using only the mouse. To do so, add two sliders to the scene that will change the transformation values. (A slider is a default JavaFX control that will be covered later in the book.) The following code snippet contains a refactored application without gesture events:

```
package com.guigarage.masteringcontrols;
import javafx.application.Application;
import javafx.scene.Scene;
import javafx.scene.control.Button;
import javafx.scene.control.Slider;
import javafx.scene.layout.BorderPane;
import javafx.scene.layout.VBox;
import javafx.scene.paint.Color;
import javafx.stage.Stage;
public class TransformApp extends Application {
    public static void main(String[] args) {
        launch(args);
    }
    @Override
    public void start(Stage primaryStage) throws Exception {
        Button button = new Button("Hello World");
        BorderPane myPane = new BorderPane();
        myPane.setCenter(button);
        VBox menu = new VBox();
        Slider zoomSlider = new Slider(0.2, 4, 1);
        zoomSlider.valueProperty().addListener(e -> {button.setScaleX(zoomSlider.
                                                getValue());
            button.setScaleY(zoomSlider.getValue());});
        Slider rotateSlider = new Slider(-180, 180, 0);
        rotateSlider.valueProperty().addListener(e -> {
            button.setRotate(rotateSlider.getValue());
        });
        menu.getChildren().addAll(zoomSlider, rotateSlider);
        myPane.setBottom(menu);
        myPane.setBackground(null);
        Scene myScene = new Scene(myPane);
        myScene.setFill(Color.DARKORANGE);
        primaryStage.setScene(myScene);
        primaryStage.setTitle("App");
        primaryStage.setWidth(300);
        primaryStage.setHeight(200);
        primaryStage.show();
    }
}
```

Once the application is running, you can change the value of the sliders to create the transformations that will affect the location of the HBox and the buttons in the scene graph.

Adding a Third Dimension

The first demo shown earlier in the chapter transforms the components along the x-axis and y-axis of the scene graph. You might be familiar with this behavior from some other toolkits; even with Swing, you can create this effect by using some special Java2D classes. But JavaFX supports the z-axis too. If you have never worked with a 3D system, you can think about this axis as a third dimension that adds depth to the surface. JavaFX's `Shape3D` class is the base class for three-dimensional nodes. By using these nodes, you can create a three-dimensional view, as shown in Figure 4-3.

The 3D support of JavaFX won't be part of this book. For more information about the different 3D features of JavaFX (2D shapes, lights, textures) you should read the JavaDoc.

Extended Transformation APIs

As you have already seen, it's easy to define some transformations for a node. As a next step, you'll look at the classes in the `javafx.scene.transform` package. These classes define the different transformation types that can be applied to a node. As a base class, the abstract class `Transform` defines the complete logic and mathematical material that is needed to render a

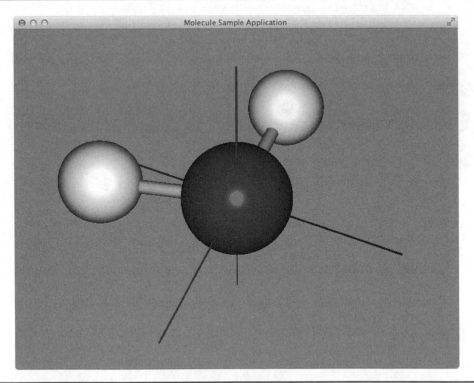

FIGURE 4-3. *An application with three-dimensional elements*

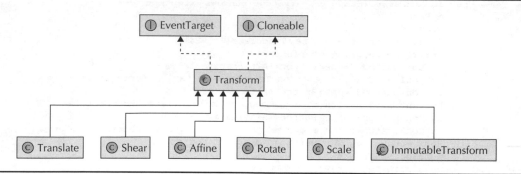

FIGURE 4-4.   *Class hierarchy of all transformation classes*

transformation. You'll also find a set of classes that derive the Transform class in the javafx
.scene.transform package. These classes define different transformation types. Figure 4-4
shows an overview of the class hierarchy.

The Translate, Shear, Rotate, and Scale classes should be used when a simple
transformation will be executed. These classes are designed for the special requirements of the
different transformation types. If you want to create a general affine transformation, you can use
the Affine class. This class defines a general affine transformation, and all the other mentioned
transformations are special types of an affine transformation. An affine transformation can be
generally described as a transformation between two affine spaces that preserves points, straight
lines, and planes. Matrix operations can be performed on instances of the Affine class, allowing
this class to provide a better fit for complex transformations.

You can apply a transformation that is defined by the given classes to any node. The following
demo application shows the classes you can use:

```
package com.guigarage.masteringcontrols;
import javafx.application.Application;
import javafx.collections.FXCollections;
import javafx.geometry.Insets;
import javafx.geometry.Pos;
import javafx.scene.Scene;
import javafx.scene.control.Button;
import javafx.scene.layout.BorderPane;
import javafx.scene.layout.HBox;
import javafx.scene.layout.StackPane;
import javafx.scene.shape.Rectangle;
import javafx.scene.transform.Rotate;
import javafx.scene.transform.Shear;
import javafx.scene.transform.Transform;
import javafx.scene.transform.Translate;
import javafx.stage.Stage;
import java.util.List;
public class TransformDemo  extends Application {
    private StackPane myPane;
    @Override
```

```java
public void start(Stage primaryStage) throws Exception {
    myPane = new StackPane();
    Transform rotation = new Rotate(45);
    Transform translate = new Translate(24, 24);
    Transform shearing = new Shear(0, 1);
    Button button1 = new Button("Alternative 1");
    button1.setOnAction(e -> useTransforms(rotation, translate));
    Button button2 = new Button("Alternative 2");
    button2.setOnAction(e -> useTransforms(translate, rotation));
    Button button3 = new Button("Alternative 3");
    button3.setOnAction(e -> useTransforms(rotation, shearing, translate));
    HBox menu = new HBox(button1, button2, button3);
    menu.setSpacing(6);
    menu.setAlignment(Pos.CENTER);
    menu.setPadding(new Insets(12));
    BorderPane mainPane = new BorderPane();
    mainPane.setCenter(myPane);
    mainPane.setBottom(menu);
    Scene myScene = new Scene(mainPane);
    primaryStage.setScene(myScene);
    primaryStage.setTitle("App");
    primaryStage.setWidth(300);
    primaryStage.setHeight(200);
    primaryStage.show();
}

public void useTransforms(Transform... transforms) {
    myPane.getChildren().clear();
    Rectangle origin = new Rectangle(40, 40);
    origin.setStyle("-fx-stroke: blue;" +
            "-fx-fill: darkgrey;");
    origin.setOpacity(0.5d);
    myPane.getChildren().addAll(origin);
    List<Transform> usedTransforms = FXCollections.observableArrayList();
    for(Transform transform : transforms) {
        usedTransforms.add(transform);
        Rectangle r = new Rectangle(40, 40);
        r.setStyle("-fx-stroke: blue;" +
                "-fx-fill: transparent;");
        r.setOpacity((double) usedTransforms.size() / (double) transforms.length);
        r.getTransforms().addAll(usedTransforms);
        myPane.getChildren().addAll(r);
    }
}
public static void main(String[] args) {
    launch(args);
}
}
```

In the given example, three transforms (rotation, translate, and shearing) will be used to transform a rectangle. The code is a little more complex than the demos shown earlier, so let's look at it in further depth.

The application consists of two panes. The first pane is a `StackPane` control that will be used to visualize different transforms. The second pane is an `HBox` called menu. This pane contains buttons that will handle the action of the application. Whenever one of these buttons is clicked, a list of

`Transform` instances will be executed on a rectangle, which will be shown in the `StackPane` node. Each button defines a different order of the transforms, and the result of the rectangle will be completely different. This depends on the order in which the transforms are executed on the rectangle. To visualize the steps of transformations, the `useTransform(...)` method is used. This method adds a rectangle for each transformation step onscreen. Figure 4-5 shows the different results of the transforms. In the screen on the left, the rectangle is rotated, and after the rotation, it is translated. The rotation always has the top-left corner of the rectangle as its center. A rotation of a node affects its complete coordination system. Therefore, the translation in the left screen is executed on a rotated coordination system. In the screen in the middle, the translation is performed before the rotation of the rectangle. In both examples, the same transforms are executed on the rectangle, but the resulting location of the rectangle is different because of the changed order of the transforms. The rightmost screen adds a shearing to the list of transforms.

NOTE
In JavaFX, each transformation is represented by a matrix. Each point in the node is multiplied by the matrix to determine its new position. Matrix multiplication is not associative, so changing the order in which the transforms are applied will produce different results, as shown in Figure 4-5.

In most cases, a developer will use the transform methods that the `Node` class provides directly. It is important to know that the transforms defined by these methods are executed in a given order: translate, scale, and rotate. Additionally, it is important that the pivot of the rotation is not the top-left corner of a node. When using the internal rotation of a node, the pivot point is computed as the center of the node. Figure 4-6 shows an example of a node that is rotated by using the `setRotate(45)` method. As you can see, the rotation pivot is a different one from in the previous example. All additional transformations that are set on a node by using the transforms property will be applied before the inner transforms of the node are executed. Whenever both types of transformation are mixed, developers have to know this order to avoid any unwanted behavior. It is not necessary to mix the different approaches. As already mentioned, it is a best practice to use the internal methods of a node to transform it.

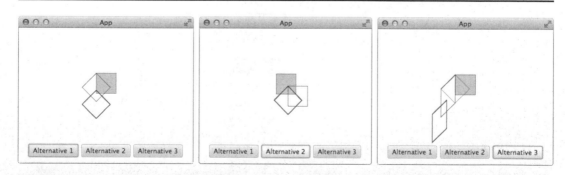

FIGURE 4-5. *Different transformation orders*

FIGURE 4-6. *A simple rotation*

Laying Out Nodes

The earlier examples used panes to lay out groups of nodes in the scene graph. You can also use the transformation of nodes to lay out nodes; however, as a best practice, you should use panes to lay out all the nodes of an application. The transform features are best for defining special behavior, such as that used in animations, for example. Or, an important control can scale or rotate when the mouse button hovers above it to create a better user experience. Still, all these nodes need to be laid out in a pane before a transformation affects them.

In the previous chapters, the `Pane` class and some concrete implementations such as the `StackPane` were shown. Figure 4-7 shows a short overview of the class hierarchy. The four

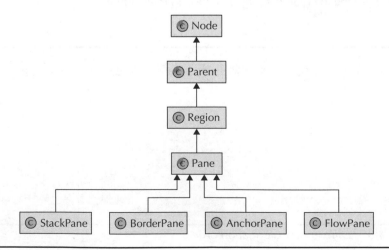

FIGURE 4-7. *Class hierarchy of panes*

pane types (StackPane, BorderPane, AnchorPane, and FlowPane) that are shown in the figure are only examples.

JavaFX provides a large set of default implementations that can be used to lay out an application. While these default implementations meet many needs, developers may require a special layout that can't be created by using these default implementations. In these situations, you can create a custom pane. The following examples show how to define a custom layout with JavaFX and how the layout algorithms of JavaFX behave internally.

Creating a Custom Pane

To create a pane that lays out its children with a special algorithm, you need a new class that is a subclass of the Pane class. In the following example, a special layout is needed that sorts all child nodes by the preferred width of the node. It should act like an HBox, but all nodes should appear in order of their width instead of the default child order. The following code block shows how a custom pane that implements this feature should look in a first iteration:

```java
package com.guigarage.masteringcontrols;
import javafx.geometry.HPos;
import javafx.geometry.VPos;
import javafx.scene.Node;
import javafx.scene.layout.Pane;
import java.util.ArrayList;
import java.util.Collections;
import java.util.List;
public class SortedPane extends Pane {
    @Override
    protected void layoutChildren() {
        List<Node> sortedChildren = new ArrayList<>(getChildren());
        Collections.sort(sortedChildren, (c1, c2) -> new Double(c1.prefWidth(-1)).
            compareTo(new Double(c2.prefWidth(-1))));
        double currentX = 0;
        for(Node c : sortedChildren) {
            double width = c.prefWidth(-1);
            double height = c.prefHeight(-1);
            layoutInArea(c, currentX, 0, width, height, 0,HPos.CENTER, VPos.CENTER);
            currentX = currentX + width;
        }
    }
    @Override
    protected double computePrefHeight(double width) {
        double maxHeight = 0;
        for(Node c : getChildren()) {
            maxHeight = Math.max(c.prefHeight(-1), maxHeight);
        }
        return maxHeight;
    }
    @Override
    protected double computePrefWidth(double height) {
        double width = 0;
        for(Node c : getChildren()) {
            width = width + c.prefWidth(-1);
        }
        return width;
    }
```

```
    @Override
    protected double computeMaxHeight(double width) {
        return computePrefHeight(width);
    }
    @Override
    protected double computeMaxWidth(double height) {
        return computePrefWidth(height);
    }
    @Override
    protected double computeMinHeight(double width) {
        return computePrefHeight(width);
    }
    @Override
    protected double computeMinWidth(double height) {
        return super.computePrefWidth(height);
    }
}
```

As you can see, there are two kinds of methods that need to be overridden: the `layoutChildren(...)` method and all the methods that compute the size of the pane. Let's take a look at all the `compute...(...)` methods first. Most developers who have worked with UI toolkits know the three different sizes that can be defined for a component: minimum, maximum, and preferred. In JavaFX, all of these types are supported, and the scene graph API offers methods to calculate the width and height of these sizes. A great benefit of these methods is that you can calculate the width depending on the height, and vice versa. I'll cover this further a bit later, but let's first consider the simple calculations that don't depend on each other. All the nodes that are wrapped in the pane should fit in its bounds. To do so, you calculate the preferred width and height of the pane using the methods `computePrefHeight(...)` and `computePrefWidth(...)`. Because all child nodes should be ordered in a horizontal direction, the preferred height of the pane is equal to the height of the highest child node. This is done in the `computePrefHeight(...)` method by simply iterating over all the children and finding the maximum height with the help of `Math.max(...)`. The preferred width of the pane is equal to the sum of all the child nodes' widths. By calculating this, the preferred height of the pane is also calculated. These values are needed to lay out the parent region of the pane once it is added to a scene graph. Each pane in JavaFX should use the calculated sizes (maximum, minimum, and preferred) to calculate its own size. In the given example, you want the pane to always be as big as its children. To achieve this, you can simply override the `computeMin...(...)` and `computeMax...(...)` methods by returning the preferred size. Other pane implementations, such as the `StackPane`, use `Double.MAX_VALUE` to define the maximum size. Here, the pane can be bigger than its children, for example.

Once all these sizes are calculated, you need the layout of the child nodes. This happens in the `layoutChildren()` methods that can be overridden by a custom pane. In this example, you create a sorted list of all child nodes and then define the bounds of them. Here, you use the preferred size of a child node and calculate only the X position of the nodes. By doing this, all nodes will appear in a sorted line. To place a node in a pane or region, you can use the `layoutInArea(...)` method, which has a default implementation to define the bounds of a child. You will take a deeper look at this mechanism later in the chapter. First, you need to know only the first five parameters of this method: the child nodes and its calculated bounds that are defined by its x-position, y-position, width, and height. For the last three parameters, default values are used here.

After you define the `SortedPane` class, you can simply use it in an application. The following code defines a demo application that uses the `SortedPane` class. Figure 4-8 shows how the example should look onscreen.

```java
package com.guigarage.masteringcontrols;
import javafx.application.Application;
import javafx.geometry.Insets;
import javafx.scene.Scene;
import javafx.scene.control.Button;
import javafx.stage.Stage;
public class LayoutDemo  extends Application {
    @Override
    public void start(Stage primaryStage) throws Exception {
        SortedPane myPane = new SortedPane();
        myPane.getChildren().add(new Button("Hello World"));
        myPane.getChildren().add(new Button("Long Text.............."));
        myPane.getChildren().add(new Button("short"));
        Scene myScene = new Scene(myPane);
        primaryStage.setScene(myScene);
        primaryStage.show();
    }
    public static void main(String[] args) {
        launch(args);
    }
}
```

As you can see in Figure 4-8, all child nodes of the `SortedPane` appear in a sorted order depending on its visual width. The given example contains a good overview of the basic methods that need to be known to create a custom `Pane` class, but the layout API of JavaFX offers many more possibilities. In a professional application, the shown mechanisms are not enough to define a pane that fits completely into any JavaFX application. By default, JavaFX provides properties to define the padding and insets of a pane. Additionally, a border can be set to a pane. This border should not hide the underlying child nodes. To strictly follow all the given definitions that are part of the JavaFX layout API, you will need the information in the next section.

FIGURE 4-8. *Visual result of the SortedPane demo*

Floating-Point Bounds

Developers who have worked with the Swing or AWT toolkit should notice one big difference in JavaFX: All properties that define the bounds of a node are defined as double. The methods of JComponent have their historical background in AWT. At the time of implementation, no one thought about rectangles that were arranged between pixels and were drawn with antialiasing. The JavaFX method provides this functionality, and once transformation comes into play, everyone should understand why this is essential. By using double values, you can define bounds that don't fit into the pixel-based grid that is forced by a monitor, for example. In JavaFX, the size of a component can be defined by using floating-point bounds, as shown in this illustration.

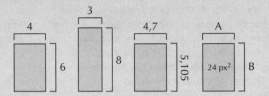

All the rectangles that are shown in the image have a region of 24 pixels when they are rendered onscreen without a scaling transform. The first two rectangles could be defined in Swing too. But the third rectangle is defined with floating-point values. This can be done only in JavaFX.

When a node is rendered, the bound will snap to pixels. This is handled by the `snapToPixel` property that is defined in the `Region` class. This `Boolean` property is set true by default and will adjust the position, spacing, and size of all children of the node to pixel boundaries. Once this property is set to false, a fractional alignment is used, which may lead to "fuzzy-looking" borders.

The Visual Structure of a Region

As stated earlier, each pane and control in JavaFX extend the `Region` class. This class defines some special properties and behaviors of how it appears onscreen. You need to know these features to lay out custom controls and panes in the right way. These definitions are not reinvented by JavaFX, though. The CSS3 specification of the World Wide Web Consortium (W3C) for backgrounds and borders is used internally. You can find the complete specification at www.w3.org/TR/2012/CR-css3-background-20120724/.

As defined in the specification, a region contains a border area and a padding area for decoration, as shown in Figure 4-9. The insets of a region are defined as a union of these two areas. All child nodes of a region should be laid out inside the content area. The margin that is shown in Figure 4-9 can be used by panes. The HBox, for example, has the static method setMargin(...) to define a margin for a child node inside an HBox instance.

All custom panes and controls should use this specification. If you provide custom panes in a third-party library, for example, developers who use the panes normally will expect the described behavior. The SortedPane class that was created earlier doesn't use the given insets when laying

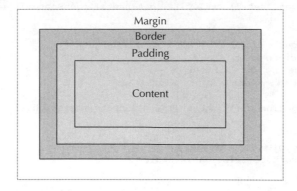

FIGURE 4-9. *Areas of a region*

out all child nodes or computing the size of the pane. To fit in the defined specifications, some additions are needed. The following code contains a new version of the SortedPane that internally uses the border and padding insets for calculation:

```java
package com.guigarage.masteringcontrols;
import javafx.beans.property.DoubleProperty;
import javafx.beans.property.SimpleDoubleProperty;
import javafx.geometry.HPos;
import javafx.geometry.VPos;
import javafx.scene.Node;
import javafx.scene.layout.Pane;
import java.util.ArrayList;
import java.util.Collections;
import java.util.List;

public class SortedPane extends Pane {

    @Override
    protected void layoutChildren() {
        List<Node> sortedChildren = new ArrayList<>(getChildren());
        Collections.sort(sortedChildren, (c1, c2) -> new Double(c1.prefWidth(-1)).
                    compareTo(new Double(c2.prefWidth(-1))));
        double currentX = getInsets().getLeft();
        for(Node c : sortedChildren) {
            double width = c.prefWidth(-1);
            double height = c.prefHeight(-1);
            layoutInArea(c, currentX, getInsets().getTop(), width, height, 0,HPos.
                    CENTER, VPos.CENTER);
            currentX = currentX + width;
        }
    }

    @Override
    protected double computePrefHeight(double width) {
        double maxHeight = 0;
        for(Node c : getChildren()) {
            maxHeight = Math.max(c.prefHeight(-1), maxHeight);
```

```
        }
        return getInsets().getTop() + getInsets().getBottom() + maxHeight;
    }
    @Override
    protected double computePrefWidth(double height) {
        double width = 0;
        for(Node c : getChildren()) {
            width = width + c.prefWidth(-1);
        }
        return getInsets().getLeft() + getInsets().getRight() + width;
    }
    @Override
    protected double computeMaxHeight(double width) {
        return computePrefHeight(width);
    }
    @Override
    protected double computeMaxWidth(double height) {
        return computePrefWidth(height);
    }
    @Override
    protected double computeMinHeight(double width) {
        return computePrefHeight(width);
    }
    @Override
    protected double computeMinWidth(double height) {
        return computePrefWidth(height);
    }
}
```

As mentioned earlier, the `insets` property of a region is a union of the border area and the padding area. Therefore, this property can be used to calculate the content area of the `SortedPane`. All child nodes of the pane will now be rendered inside this area. The size of the border and the custom padding of the pane are added to the calculation. In the `computePrefHeight(...)` and `computePrefWidth(...)` methods, the `insets` property is used to calculate the preferred size. The particular values of the property (top/bottom for the height and left/right for the width) are added to the earlier calculated values. As a result, the pane will be as big is its content in union with the border and padding. In the `layoutChildren()` method, the `insets` property is used too. The y-position of all components is equal to the height of the insets area, and the x-position of the first child node is equal to the width of the left insets. In JavaFX, different values can be defined for the top, bottom, right, and left of the padding or the border. You can have a border that has a thickness of 3 pixels on the left side and 20 pixels on the right side, for example.

Before you look at the visual result of the `SortedPane`, you need to implement one additional feature. In the first demo, all child nodes are rendered without any spacing between them. This should be variable. To do so, a spacing property is needed. The property API was mentioned earlier in this book, and some properties have already been used in the examples, but this is the first point where a custom property is added to a class. The following example shows the final version of the `SortedPane`. Here, a `DoubleProperty` is added to define the spacing between all child components. The property is defined because it is a best practice in JavaFX. All internal classes of JavaFX define properties, as shown in this example.

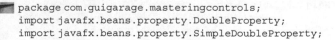

```
package com.guigarage.masteringcontrols;
import javafx.beans.property.DoubleProperty;
import javafx.beans.property.SimpleDoubleProperty;
```

```java
import javafx.geometry.HPos;
import javafx.geometry.VPos;
import javafx.scene.Node;
import javafx.scene.layout.Pane;
import java.util.ArrayList;
import java.util.Collections;
import java.util.List;
public class SortedPane extends Pane {
    public SortedPane() {
        super();
    }
    public SortedPane(double spacing) {
        this();
        setSpacing(spacing);
    }
    public final DoubleProperty spacingProperty() {
        if (spacing == null) {
            spacing = new SimpleDoubleProperty(0);
        }
        return spacing;
    }
    private DoubleProperty spacing;
    public final void setSpacing(double value) { spacingProperty().set(value); }
    public final double getSpacing() { return spacing == null ? 0 : spacing.get(); }
    @Override
    protected void layoutChildren() {
        List<Node> sortedChildren = new ArrayList<>(getChildren());
        Collections.sort(sortedChildren, (c1, c2) -> new Double(c1.prefWidth(-1)).
                        compareTo(new Double(c2.prefWidth(-1))));
        double currentX = getInsets().getLeft();
        for(Node c : sortedChildren) {
            double width = c.prefWidth(-1);
            double height = c.prefHeight(-1);
            layoutInArea(c, currentX, getInsets().getTop(), width, height, 0,HPos.
                        CENTER, VPos.CENTER);
            currentX = currentX + width + getSpacing();
        }
    }
    @Override
    protected double computePrefHeight(double width) {
        double maxHeight = 0;
        for(Node c : getChildren()) {
            maxHeight = Math.max(c.prefHeight(-1), maxHeight);
        }
        return getInsets().getTop() + getInsets().getBottom() + maxHeight;
    }
    @Override
    protected double computePrefWidth(double height) {
        double width = 0;
        for(Node c : getChildren()) {
            width = width + c.prefWidth(-1);
        }
        double cumulatedSpacing = 0;
        if(getChildren().size() > 1) {
            cumulatedSpacing =  (getChildren().size() - 1) * getSpacing();
```

```
            }
            return getInsets().getLeft() + getInsets().getRight() + width +
                cumulatedSpacing;
        }
        @Override
        protected double computeMaxHeight(double width) {
            return computePrefHeight(width);
        }
        @Override
        protected double computeMaxWidth(double height) {
            return computePrefWidth(height);
        }
        @Override
        protected double computeMinHeight(double width) {
            return computePrefHeight(width);
        }
        @Override
        protected double computeMinWidth(double height) {
            return computePrefWidth(height);
        }
    }
}
```

In addition to the property that is defined, getter and setter methods are defined to access the double value of the property. The spacing value is used in the different methods just as when the insets were added. The following application uses the final version of the `SortedPane` and adds padding and spacing to the pane. Figure 4-10 shows how the application will look onscreen.

```
package com.guigarage.masteringcontrols;
import javafx.application.Application;
import javafx.geometry.Insets;
import javafx.scene.Scene;
import javafx.scene.control.Button;
import javafx.stage.Stage;
public class LayoutDemo  extends Application {
    @Override
    public void start(Stage primaryStage) throws Exception {
        SortedPane myPane = new SortedPane();
        myPane.setPadding(new Insets(24,24,24,24));
        myPane.setSpacing(12);
        myPane.getChildren().add(new Button("Hello World"));
```

FIGURE 4-10. *SortedPane with padding and spacing*

```
        myPane.getChildren().add(new Button("Long Text.............."));
        myPane.getChildren().add(new Button("short"));
        Scene myScene = new Scene(myPane);
        primaryStage.setScene(myScene);
        primaryStage.show();
    }
    public static void main(String[] args) {
        launch(args);
    }
}
```

Using Default Values for Size Calculation

In the demo, all methods to compute the minimum, maximum, and preferred sizes are overwritten. However, this doesn't need to be done in all cases. You can set a default value to all the shown values by using methods such as `setPrefHeight(…)` or `setMinWidth(…)`. Once a value is set, it will be used instead of calculating a value with the help of the shown methods. In addition, you can use constants to add flexibility: If the preferred width is set by using the `setPrefWidth(…)` method, it can be simply unset by using the `Region.USE_COMPUTED_SIZE` constant. After calling `setPrefWidth(USE_COMPUTED_SIZE)`, the layout mechanism will use the `computePrefWidth(…)` method again. If the minimum or maximum value should be equal to the preferred one, you can use the `Region.USE_PREF_SIZE` flag. By passing this flag to `setMinWidth(…)`, the layout mechanism will never call `computeMinWidth(…)`. Instead, `computePrefWidth(…)` will be used. By using these flags, some of the methods of the `SortedPane` class don't need to be overwritten. The constructor of the class should simply include the following code snippet:

```
setMaxWidth(USE_PREF_SIZE);
setMinWidth(USE_PREF_SIZE);
setMaxHeight(USE_PREF_SIZE);
setMinHeight(USE_PREF_SIZE);
```

Once this is done, you no longer need to overwrite the `computeMinWith(…)`, `computeMinHeight(…)`, `computeMaxWidth(…)`, and `computeMaxHeight(…)` methods. As a result, the code will be much smaller. This effect can simply be negated by using the `Region.USE_COMPUTED_SIZE` flag.

Using Properties in Custom Classes

In all custom classes, you should use the JavaFX property API. By doing this, developers get the benefit of all the features, such as binding, that are part of the property API. At first sight, it is a lot of code that needs to be added to a class, but when CSS or other special APIs come into play, properties are needed. Also, in other UI toolkits such as Swing, a lot of code is added if developers want to use values the right way. For example, if property change support is needed in Swing, a `PropertyChangeEvent` needs to be fired in each setter. This isn't needed in JavaFX, thanks to the property API, which offers a complete set of default properties.

In the example, the `SimpleDoubleProperty` class is used. This class is the default implementation for a property that holds a double value. The property instance offers read and write access to the property. In addition to this class, a complete set of default implementations is part of the API, such as `SimpleStringProperty`. JavaFX contains property classes for all primitive data types. For all value types where no default implementation is defined, the

`SimpleObjectProperty<T>` class can be used. This class uses generics to define the type of its content. If only read access is allowed for a value, developers can use the `ReadOnlyProperty` classes such as `ReadOnlyStringProperty`. To add perfect property support to the `SortedPane` class, some additional changes are needed. Whenever the spacing property is set, the pane will not automatically re-layout its content. To do so, the `requestLayout()` methods that start a redo need to be called. This could be done by adding a listener to them, as shown in the following code:

```
public SortedPane() {
        super();
        spacingProperty().addListener(e -> requestLayout());
    }
```

As a first step, this is okay and will work in all cases. But if you want to develop custom panes and controls that follow all the best practices set by the default classes of JavaFX, you need to do this in another way. As you can see in the `spacingProperty()` method, the instance of the property will be created only when it is needed. As long as only the `getSpacing()` method is called, for example, the property instance will never be created. This is done to protect resources. A property instance contains some fields that will need memory when a new instance is created. Additionally, a listener is created in the code snippet. This will allocate memory too. This can be avoided by using the `invalidated()` method of the `SimpleDoubleProperty` class. This method will be called whenever a new value is set to the property. By overwriting this method as shown in the following code snippet, the `requestLayout()` method will be called whenever a new spacing value is set. As a result, the property will be created only when it is needed.

```
public final DoubleProperty spacingProperty() {
        if (spacing == null) {
            spacing = new SimpleDoubleProperty(0) {
                @Override
                protected void invalidated() {
                    super.invalidated();
                    requestLayout();
                }
            };
        }
        return spacing;
    }
```

You can test the new behavior and the automatically reformatted layout with the following demo. Here a slider control is added to change the spacing of the `SortedPane` instance at runtime. Changing the value of the slider will have direct visual feedback because the spacing between the child nodes of the `SortedPane` will change onscreen.

```
package com.guigarage.masteringcontrols;
import javafx.application.Application;
import javafx.geometry.Insets;
import javafx.scene.Scene;
import javafx.scene.control.Button;
import javafx.scene.control.Slider;
import javafx.scene.layout.VBox;
```

```
import javafx.stage.Stage;
public class LayoutDemo  extends Application {
    @Override
    public void start(Stage primaryStage) throws Exception {
        SortedPane myPane = new SortedPane();
        myPane.setPadding(new Insets(24,24,24,24));
        myPane.setSpacing(12);
        myPane.getChildren().add(new Button("Hello World"));
        myPane.getChildren().add(new Button("Long Text.............."));
        myPane.getChildren().add(new Button("short"));
        Slider slider = new Slider();
        slider.valueProperty().bindBidirectional(myPane.spacingProperty());
        VBox box = new VBox();
        box.getChildren().addAll(myPane, slider);

        Scene myScene = new Scene(box);
        primaryStage.setScene(myScene);
        primaryStage.show();
    }
    public static void main(String[] args) {
        launch(args);
    }
}
```

Extended Internal Layout Mechanisms

The methods that compute the desired size of a region can handle the width-to-height ratio. Additionally, the layoutInArea(…) method is used internally in the SortedPane example and wasn't described until now. Since I described the basic mechanisms of layout, I'll discuss these more specific aspects now. These mechanisms will help to create complex custom layout algorithms in JavaFX.

Handling the Aspect Ratio of a Region

You will sometimes have a control or pane where the width depends on the height of the node, or vice versa. This was a sorely missed feature in the Swing UI toolkit; in Swing, it was difficult to create a dynamic label with line wrap. In a label that supports this behavior, the text will automatically add a page whenever the maximum width of the label is reached. As a result, the height of the label depends on its width. All text components in JavaFX support this behavior because the JavaFX layout can handle the aspect ratio. This can be defined by adding more logic to the methods that will calculate the minimum, maximum, and preferred sizes of a Region instance. To do so, a parameter is defined in the method header. The computePrefWidth(double height) method, for example, adds a height parameter. The method can then be used to calculate a width that depends on the given height. The size of a region can have only one dependency, of course. The height will depend on the width, or the width will depend on the height. Both dependencies can't logically be handled. To do that, you must define an additional value in the Node class: content bias. This value defines the node's resizing bias for layout purposes. By default, the getContentBias() method returns null. This means there is no defined ratio; –1 will be used for all parameters of the compute…(…) methods in this case. If the getContentBias() method returns a vertical or horizontal orientation, a ratio is defined, and concrete values are passed to the compute…(…) methods.

Let's think about a content bias that is defined as a horizontal orientation. In this case, the height of a node depends on its width. When the node needs to have its layout updated, the `computePrefWidth(...)` method will be called first. Here, −1 is passed to the method, and a default width will be calculated. Based on the maximum, minimum, and preferred widths of the node, the parent region will set a width that will be used. This calculated width will now be used to define the height of the node. To do so, the `computePrefHeigth(...)` method is called with the calculated width. The implementation of the method can calculate a preferred width that fits the given height. This described behavior is used in the `Label` control of JavaFX to add page layout, for example. To gain a better understanding of the mechanism, the following example will use aspect ratio.

To show the usage of the content bias value, you will create a custom node. This class extends the `Region` class and will always have a surface area of a given value. Because the surface area is given, the width of the node depends on its height, or vice versa, depending on its content bias. To show all different variations, the content bias of the node needs to be changeable too. The following class implements the `Region` class that supports all the necessary features:

```java
package com.guigarage.masteringcontrols;
import javafx.beans.property.DoubleProperty;
import javafx.beans.property.ObjectProperty;
import javafx.beans.property.SimpleDoubleProperty;
import javafx.beans.property.SimpleObjectProperty;
import javafx.geometry.Orientation;
import javafx.scene.layout.Region;

public class AreaRegion extends Region {

    private ObjectProperty<Orientation> contentBias;

    public final ObjectProperty<Orientation> contentBiasProperty() {
        if (contentBias == null) {
            contentBias = new SimpleObjectProperty<Orientation>(null) {
                @Override
                protected void invalidated() {
                    super.invalidated();
                    requestParentLayout();
                }
            };
        }
        return contentBias;
    }

    public final void setContentBias(Orientation value) { contentBiasProperty().
        set(value); }
    @Override
    public Orientation getContentBias() {
        return contentBias == null ? null : contentBias.get();
    }

    private DoubleProperty surfaceArea;

    public final DoubleProperty surfaceAreaProperty() {
        if (surfaceArea == null) {
            surfaceArea = new SimpleDoubleProperty(64000.0) {
                @Override
```

```
                    protected void invalidated() {
                        super.invalidated();
                        requestLayout();
                    }
                };
            }
        return surfaceArea;
    }
    public final void setSurfaceArea(double value) { surfaceAreaProperty().set(value);
}
    public final double getSurfaceArea() { return surfaceArea == null ? 64000.0 :
surfaceArea.get(); }
    @Override
    protected double computeMaxHeight(double width) {
        if (width < 0) {
            return Double.MAX_VALUE;
        } else {
            return getSurfaceArea() / width;
        }
    }
    @Override
    protected double computeMaxWidth(double height) {
        if (height < 0) {
            return Double.MAX_VALUE;
        } else {
            return getSurfaceArea() / height;
        }
    }
    @Override
    protected double computeMinHeight(double width) {
        if (width < 0) {
            return Double.MIN_VALUE;
        } else {
            return getSurfaceArea() / width;
        }
    }
    @Override
    protected double computeMinWidth(double height) {
        if (height < 0) {
            return Double.MIN_VALUE;
        } else {
            return getSurfaceArea() / height;
        }
    }
    @Override
    protected double computePrefHeight(double width) {
        if (width < 0) {
            return Math.sqrt(getSurfaceArea());
        } else {
            return getSurfaceArea() / width;
        }
    }
    @Override
    protected double computePrefWidth(double height) {
        if (height < 0) {
            return Math.sqrt(getSurfaceArea());
```

```
        } else {
            return getSurfaceArea() / height;
        }
    }
}
```

With `contentBias` and `surfaceArea`, two additional properties are added to the class by using the property API. The `AreaRegion` class overrides the `getContentBias()` methods and returns the content bias that is defined by the included property. All `compute...(...)` methods that are needed to calculate the size of the node are overridden. In this method, the aspect ratio is defined. This can be easily done by adding an if-else statement to the code. When the internal content bias is set to `Orientation.VERTICAL`, all methods that compute a width will be called with a given height. Otherwise, the height is −1, and a default value can be used. Whenever the content bias or the surface area is set, the parent region of the instance needs to be laid out. To do this, the `requestLayout()` method is called in the `invalidated()` method of the properties.

The following application uses the `AreaRegion` class and adds some controls to change its behavior:

```
package com.guigarage.masteringcontrols;
import javafx.application.Application;
import javafx.geometry.Insets;
import javafx.geometry.Orientation;
import javafx.scene.Scene;
import javafx.scene.control.Button;
import javafx.scene.control.Slider;
import javafx.scene.layout.HBox;
import javafx.scene.layout.StackPane;
import javafx.scene.layout.VBox;
import javafx.stage.Stage;
public class AspectRatioDemo  extends Application {
    @Override
    public void start(Stage primaryStage) throws Exception {
        AreaRegion region = new AreaRegion();
        region.setContentBias(Orientation.VERTICAL);
        region.setStyle("-fx-border-width: 3;" +
                "-fx-border-color: black;" +
                "-fx-background-color: lightblue;");
        StackPane myPane = new StackPane();
        myPane.setPadding(new Insets(24));
        myPane.getChildren().add(region);
        Button verticalButton = new Button("Vertical");
        verticalButton.setOnAction(e -> region.setContentBias(Orientation.VERTICAL));
        Button horizontalButton = new Button("Horizontal");
        horizontalButton.setOnAction(e -> region.setContentBias(Orientation.
                            HORIZONTAL));
        HBox buttonPane = new HBox(verticalButton, horizontalButton);
        buttonPane.setSpacing(12);
        Slider surfaceAreaSlider = new Slider(0, 640000.0, 64000.0);
        region.surfaceAreaProperty().bind(surfaceAreaSlider.valueProperty());
        VBox mainPane = new VBox(myPane, buttonPane, surfaceAreaSlider);
        Scene myScene = new Scene(mainPane);
        primaryStage.setScene(myScene);
        primaryStage.setWidth(800);
```

```
        primaryStage.setHeight(600);
        primaryStage.show();
    }
    public static void main(String[] args) {
        launch(args);
    }
}
```

CSS is used in this example to define attributes that specify the way the `AreaRegion` is displayed. The CSS string defines a black border and a blue background for the node. This is done here only to render the `AreaRegion` onscreen in a special color. CSS will be explained later in the book.

When the application is started, the content bias of the `AreaRegion` can be changed by two buttons. Additionally, the surface area can be set by a slider. Here, the application takes advantage of the property API's benefits by simply binding the surface area to the value of the slider. Because this is a dynamic example, no screenshot is shown here. When running the demo and changing some of its input values, you can see how the different content bias will affect the layout of the `AreaRegion` inside the `StackPane`. By simply changing the size of the application window, the bounds of the `AreaRegion` will change by always fitting the given surface area.

Additional Layout Mechanisms

All the mechanisms that decide which compute method will be used and how the content bias will be interpreted are hidden by the `layoutInArea(...)` method. By using the method inside the `layoutChildren()` method, developers can simply define an area in which a defined child component should be laid out. Internally, the method will set the bounds of the child node by calling `Node.resize(double width, double height)` and `Node.relocate(double x, double y)`. In most cases, a developer should use either the `layoutInArea(...)` or `positionInArea(...)` method of the `Region` class. The difference between these two methods is simple: `positionInArea(...)` never changes the size of a child node; it only sets the location. In most cases, `layoutInArea(...)` will be used. To prevent the resizing of a node, the `Node.isResizable()` method can be overwritten. As a result, a node can control this behavior by itself. A button returns `true` here because the size of a button can change. A rectangle returns `false` here. If a rectangle is defined with a given size, such as is done with `new Rectangle(40,40)`, it should not change its size.

The javafx.geometry Package

In older Java-based UI toolkits, geometrical definitions such as alignments or orientations were defined by static constants in the code. Often, integer values were used. All these toolkits were created before enumerations were added to the Java language. In JavaFX, all these definitions are defined by enums in the `javafx.geometry` package. Some of them, such as the `Orientation` enum, have already been used in the demo applications in this chapter. Table 4-2 describes the enums that are part of this package.

In addition to the enums, this package defines some helper classes such as `Dimension2D` or `Point3D`. Whenever it makes sense, these classes should be used in code.

Working with Constraints

When creating a more complex custom `Pane` class, as shown in the previous example, constraints can be useful. Constraints describe the layout properties of a child node inside a specific pane in order to define a more specialized layout of the node's children. More complex panes such as the `GridPane` make extensive use of this feature. A simpler example is the margin inside an

Enum	Description	States
HorizontalDirection	Represents a horizontal direction	LEFT, RIGHT
HPos	Represents horizontal positioning and alignment	LEFT, CENTER, RIGHT
NodeOrientation	Represents the flow of visual data	LEFT_TO_RIGHT, RIGHT_TO_LEFT, INHERIT
Orientation	Represents an orientation	HORIZONTAL, VERTICAL
Pos	Represents vertical and horizontal positioning and alignment	TOP_LEFT, TOP_CENTER, TOP_RIGHT, CENTER_LEFT, CENTER, CENTER_RIGHT, BOTTOM_LEFT, BOTTOM_CENTER, BOTTOM_RIGHT, BASELINE_LEFT, BASELINE_CENTER, BASELINE_RIGHT
Side	Represents a side of a rectangle	TOP, BOTTOM, LEFT, RIGHT
VerticalDirection	Represents a vertical direction	UP, DOWN
VPos	Represents a vertical positioning and alignment	TOP, CENTER, BASELINE, BOTTOM

TABLE 4-2. *Geometrical Enums*

HBox. To apply a custom margin on a child node of an HBox, you can call the static method setMargin(Node child, Insets value) and define the child node and its special margin. An instance of HBox will use this margin whenever the child node is laid out. Custom constraints can be easily added to a pane by using the two static methods: Pane.setConstraint(Node node, Object key, Object value) and Pane.getConstraint(Node node, Object key).

Combining Transforms and Layout

This chapter has shown two different JavaFX APIs to render nodes in the defined bounds on the screen. Usually, the complete layout of nodes inside the scene graph is done by using the Region and Pane classes. Additionally, transforms can be applied to a node. Furthermore, you can mix these two APIs without any problems. The following example shows how a child of the SortedPane can be transformed:

```
package com.guigarage.masteringcontrols;
import javafx.application.Application;
import javafx.geometry.Insets;
import javafx.scene.Scene;
import javafx.scene.control.Button;
import javafx.scene.layout.StackPane;
```

```
import javafx.stage.Stage;
public class LayoutDemo  extends Application {
    @Override
    public void start(Stage primaryStage) throws Exception {
        SortedPane myPane = new SortedPane();
        myPane.setPadding(new Insets(12,12,12,12));
        myPane.setSpacing(8);
        myPane.setStyle("-fx-border-width: 3;" +
                "-fx-border-color: black;" +
                "-fx-background-color: lightblue;");
        Button transformedButton = new Button("Hello World");
        transformedButton.setTranslateX(24);
        transformedButton.setTranslateY(24);
        transformedButton.setRotate(12);
        myPane.getChildren().add(transformedButton);
        myPane.getChildren().add(new Button("Long Text.............."));
        myPane.getChildren().add(new Button("short"));
        StackPane pane = new StackPane();
        pane.getChildren().add(myPane);
        Scene myScene = new Scene(pane);
        primaryStage.setScene(myScene);
        primaryStage.setWidth(400);
        primaryStage.setHeight(140);
        primaryStage.show();
    }
    public static void main(String[] args) {
        launch(args);
    }
}
```

In this application, a translation and rotation transform is defined for one of the buttons that is wrapped in the SortedPane. Figure 4-11 shows how the application will be rendered onscreen. As you can see, the Hello World button is transformed after the layout of the SortedPane is done. Additionally, another feature of the scene graph is shown here: A child node can be rendered outside the bounds of its parent. This isn't possible in older UI toolkits such as Swing where each container has a defined canvas and can't render any content outside this canvas.

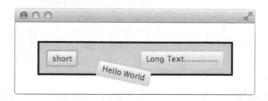

FIGURE 4-11. *Mixing layout and transformations*

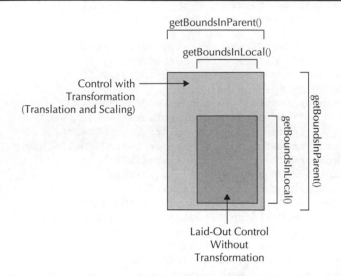

FIGURE 4-12. *Difference between getBoundsInParent() and getBoundsInLocal()*

Because a container renders all its child components in Swing, any content that is not inside the area of the canvas will be cut off on the screen because it is never rendered on it.

Accessing the Bounds of a Node

The bounds of a node are normally set by its parent. You can easily access these bounds by using the getBoundsInLocal() method. Once a transform is applied on the node, the bounds onscreen will change, but sometimes you want to access the bounds of a transformed node, so you can use the getBoundsInParent() method. Figure 4-12 shows an example of a rectangle that is transformed and the different results of the two methods.

Summary

Earlier chapters described the basic mechanism of node hierarchies in the scene graph, as well as how simple applications can be created by using Scene Builder and default Pane classes. This chapter went one step further and showed how you can create custom transformations and layout. Most of the time, developers don't need to create custom panes to lay out controls onscreen, but it is important to know at least the basic mechanism of layout and how padding and the border area can affect the bounds of nodes. Additionally, transformations can be helpful when you need a special user experience or better feedback. Combined with animations, transformations will help you create awesome applications with modern interactions. In addition, the chapter described the internal mechanism of layout in JavaFX that you will need whenever you create a custom pane or control. When custom controls are discussed later in this book, all the content of this chapter will be important to understand.

CHAPTER
5

JavaFX Basic Controls

J avaFX 8 provides a huge set of default controls that you can use to create modern desktop applications. Because there are so many, it will take two chapters to cover all of them. This chapter will cover the Control class and the basic controls that are part of JavaFX 8. In addition, the chapter will demonstrate how the controls can be used and combined to create an application. Lastly, the chapter will look at how to start changing the UI and behavior of these controls. In Chapter 6, I'll cover the more advanced controls.

The Control Class

All controls in JavaFX extend the abstract Control class. This class provides some default features that are part of each control. For example, each control is a node, so each control can be part of the scene graph. Figure 5-1 shows the dependency hierarchy of the Control class. The diagram is not a comprehensive list of all the controls that extend the Control class; in addition to the Button class shown here, several abstract classes extend the Control class and provide basic functionality for special types of controls. The ButtonBase class is one example; it defines basic functionality for a button-based control.

As you can see in Figure 5-1, the Control class extends the Region class. Because of the class hierarchy, the Control class can control all the properties, such as the padding, of the Region class. Each JavaFX control is composed of a set of nodes, so each control internally holds a set of child nodes. When using default controls, developers don't need to be aware of this behavior, but a custom control often uses a set of shapes or other nodes. You will look at this in more detail when I discuss custom controls in Chapter 10.

The Control class offers some properties that you can use to configure each control. Table 5-1 contains an overview of these properties. Some of them, like the skin property, are useful only when you need a custom control or a special behavior. I will discuss these properties in more detail later in the following chapters, but take a minute to review them now.

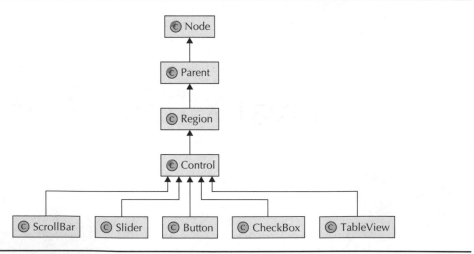

FIGURE 5-1. *Simplified dependency hierarchy of controls*

Property	Type	Description
contextMenu	ObjectProperty<ContextMenu>	Defines the context menu of the control.
skin	ObjectProperty<Skin<?>>	Defines the skin of the control. This is needed to create custom controls and will be discussed in Chapter 6.
tooltip	ObjectProperty<Tooltip>	Defines the tooltip for this control.

TABLE 5-1. *Properties of the Control Class*

Controls in JavaFX are classified in two types: basic controls (for example, a button or a text field) and complex controls (for example, a table or a tree). For now, it's important to understand basic controls before moving on to more complex commands in the next chapter.

Basic Controls

Most developers will be familiar with basic controls because most UI toolkits rely on these controls. The basic controls in JavaFX include the following:

- Button
- CheckBox
- Hyperlink
- ToggleButton
- RadioButton
- Label
- TextField
- PasswordField
- TextArea
- ProgressIndicator
- ProgressBar
- Slider

Figure 5-2 shows a window that includes a sample of each of these Control classes. The controls in JavaFX offer much greater potential than most other available toolkits such as Swing. All Control classes contain properties that can be used to create individual forms of these controls, and by setting these properties, you can easily change the font of a button or its text alignment, for example. In addition, you can style the controls using CSS. These features allow you to create a modern and interactive application with a custom look.

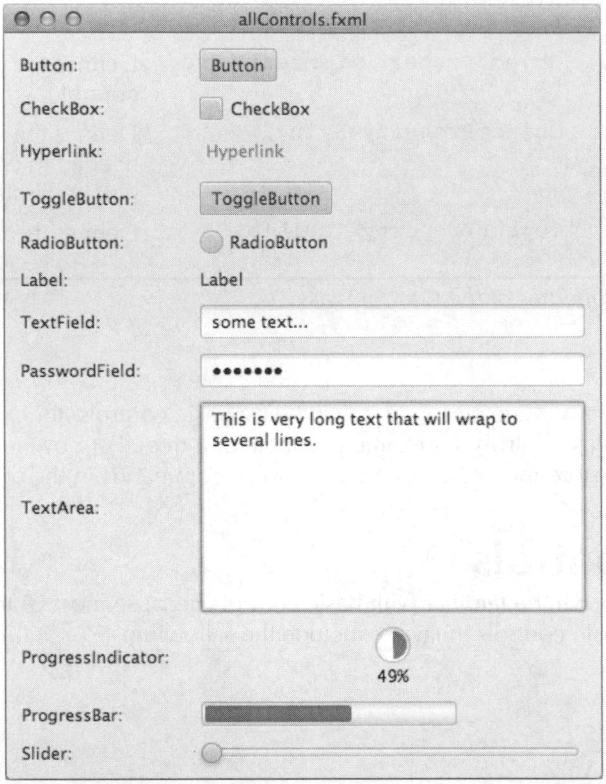

FIGURE 5-2. *Basic controls*

Let's first look at the interaction between controls by creating a demo application. The following class defines the complete application:

```
package com.guigarage.masteringcontrols;
import javafx.application.Application;
import javafx.geometry.HPos;
import javafx.geometry.Insets;
import javafx.scene.Scene;
import javafx.scene.control.Button;
import javafx.scene.control.Label;
import javafx.scene.control.PasswordField;
import javafx.scene.control.TextField;
import javafx.scene.layout.GridPane;
import javafx.stage.Stage;
```

```
public class SimpleControls  extends Application {
    @Override
    public void start(Stage primaryStage) throws Exception {
        Label userLabel = new Label("User:");
        Label passwordLabel = new Label("Password:");
        TextField userNameField = new TextField();
        userNameField.setPromptText("username");
        PasswordField passwordField = new PasswordField();
        passwordField.setPromptText("password");
        Button button = new Button("Login");
        GridPane gridPane = new GridPane();
        gridPane.setHgap(6);
        gridPane.setVgap(6);
        gridPane.setPadding(new Insets(6));
        gridPane.add(userLabel, 0, 0);
        gridPane.add(userNameField, 1, 0);
        gridPane.add(passwordLabel, 0, 1);
        gridPane.add(passwordField, 1, 1);
        gridPane.add(button, 0, 2, 2, 1);
        GridPane.setHalignment(button, HPos.CENTER);
        Scene myScene = new Scene(gridPane);
        primaryStage.setScene(myScene);
        primaryStage.setTitle("Login");
        primaryStage.show();
    }
    public static void main(String[] args) {
        launch(args);
    }
}
```

Most of the functions used in this application were covered in earlier chapters, but let's take a more detailed look at what is happening here: A GridPane is created as the root node of the scene graph. This pane contains all the controls that are used in the application as child nodes. To define a more professional look and give you a better understanding of the application, I used a special property for the TextField instances, shown in Figure 5-3. Specifically, by using the promptText property, I added a text hint to the text fields. This text will be shown when the fields contain no custom text.

FIGURE 5-3.   *Login dialog created by basic controls*

With JavaFX, you can use the property API to add interactions to this application using a few simple lines of code. Most attributes of the different `Control` classes are implemented as properties, and therefore, you can create bindings between these properties. Let's apply three behaviors to this application: I'll show how to disable the `PasswordField` until a username is entered, disable the Login button until text is entered in both text fields, and display a short login message after the Login button is clicked. The following code snippet implements the complete behavior in only three lines of code:

```
passwordField.disableProperty().bind(userNameField.textProperty().isEmpty());

button.disableProperty().bind(userNameField.textProperty().isEmpty().
    or(passwordField.textProperty().isEmpty()));

button.setOnAction(event -> System.out.println("Login: " + userNameField.
    getText() + " / " + passwordField.getText()));
```

In the first line, the `disable` property of the `PasswordField` is bound to a `Boolean` property that defines whether the `TextField` for the username is empty. Here, I use the `isEmpty()` method of the `StringProperty` class. Most of the property classes in JavaFX provide helpful methods like this one. The method creates a `Boolean` property that wraps the empty state of the `StringProperty`. Whenever the internal string of the property is null or empty, the created `BooleanProperty` will contain the `Boolean` value true. Otherwise, it will contain false. The second line shows another feature of the property API. With the internal fluent API, you can create a concatenation of two different `Boolean` properties by using the `or(...)` method. This method is part of the `BooleanProperty` and can be used to combine different `Boolean` properties. Additionally, the class offers functions such as `not()` or `and(...)`. You can find comparable methods in all property types in JavaFX. In the last line, I add an event handler to the `Button` control. Once text is entered in both fields, the button can be clicked. With each click, the event handler will handle the event and print the entered login information on the console. The handler is defined as a lambda expression, so it can be written in one line of code.

NOTE
The helpful methods used in the code snippet to concatenate `Boolean` properties or define properties that wrap the empty state of a `StringProperty` are defined in the expression classes. JavaFX contains these abstract classes for the data types `Boolean`, `Double`, `Float`, `Integer`, `List`, `Long`, `Map`, `Number`, `Object`, `Set`, and `String`. The specific property classes such as `StringProperty` extend the corresponding expression class to provide these functionalities. You can find all the expression classes in the `javafx.beans.binding` package. In addition to these classes, the `When` class and a set of binding classes for all given data types are part of this package. With the use of these classes, JavaFX provides a fluent API that can be used to create really complex and flexible bindings with only a few lines of code.

The following sections explain the specific properties and characteristics of the controls I identified as basic controls. The examples are intended to provide a general understanding of the power of JavaFX controls. An exhaustive list of properties and methods is beyond our scope, but can be found in the complete documentation available in the JavaDoc of JavaFX.

Labeled Controls

All control types that can render labeled text on their surface extend the `Labeled` class. This class defines properties that can be used to influence the rendering of text onscreen. The basic controls that extend the `Labeled` class include the following:

- `CheckBox`
- `Hyperlink`
- `ToggleButton`
- `RadioButton`
- `Button`
- `Label`

Figure 5-4 shows the class hierarchy of these classes. Controls such as menu items and table cells also extend the `Labeled` class, but are considered advanced controls. I'll discuss these further in Chapter 6.

You may have noticed that `Labeled` controls have been used in many of the examples so far. Whenever I created a button or a label, I defined text for these controls. The String that was passed to the controls as the visible text is used for the `text` property internally. In most cases, the String was passed as a parameter of the constructor of these controls, but it can be easily changed at any time by calling `setText(…)` or `textProperty().set(…)`. Besides the `text` property, the `Labeled` class defines a lot of properties to style the look of the text and the complete control. Table 5-2 describes the properties that are part of the `Labeled` class.

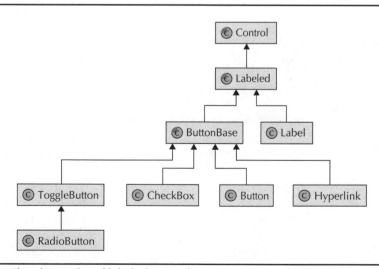

FIGURE 5-4. *Class hierarchy of labeled controls*

Property	Type	Description
contentDisplay	ObjectProperty<ContentDisplay>	Defines the positioning of the graphic node relative to the text. A Labeled control can contain a graphic node to render, such as an icon next to the text.
alignment	ObjectProperty<Pos>	Specifies how the text and graphic node should be aligned.
ellipsisString	StringProperty	Specifies the String that is displayed for the ellipsis when text is truncated. (... is the default value.)
font	ObjectProperty<Font>	Specifies the font to use for the text in the control.
graphic	ObjectProperty<Node>	Specifies a node that is wrapped in the control. This can be used to show an icon or image, for example.
graphicTextGap	DoubleProperty	Specifies the space between the graphic and text.
labelPadding	ReadOnlyObjectProperty<Insets>	Specifies the padding around the Labeled class's text and graphic content. This property can be set only with CSS.
lineSpacing	DoubleProperty	Specifies the space in pixels between the lines of the text if wrapping is activated.
mnemonicParsing	BooleanProperty	Activates text parsing for a mnemonic character and determines a key combination.
text	StringProperty	Specifies the text that is displayed in the control.
textAlignment	ObjectProperty<TextAlignment>	Specifies the behavior for lines of a multiline text.
textFill	ObjectProperty<Paint>	Specifies the paint object that is used to fill the rendered text.
textOverrun	ObjectProperty<OverrunStyle>	Specifies the behavior to use if the text exceeds the available space.
underline	BooleanProperty	Defines whether the text is underlined.
wrapText	BooleanProperty	Defines whether a text that exceeds the width of the control will be wrapped in another line.

TABLE 5-2. *Properties of the Labeled Class*

The following code snippet uses a handful of these properties to define a custom button:

```
Button button = new Button("This is a long text");
        button.setAlignment(Pos.BOTTOM_LEFT);
        button.setWrapText(true);
        button.setUnderline(true);
        button.setLineSpacing(12);
        button.setFont(new Font(24));
        button.setTextFill(Color.GREEN);

Rectangle rect = new Rectangle(24,24);
        rect.setFill(Color.BROWN);
        button.setGraphic(rect);
        button.setGraphicTextGap(42);
        button.setContentDisplay(ContentDisplay.RIGHT);
```

The button that is defined by the snippet can be used in any scene graph as shown in earlier examples. As you can see in Figure 5-5, the button looks different from any buttons shown previously. Both the font and the position of the text in the control have changed. I used the `wrapText` property to split the text into two lines dynamically, showing the complete text within a given width. The `lineSpacing` property defines the space between the lines, and the `textFill` property defines a color to render the text onscreen. In Table 5-2, notice that the `textFill` property is defined as `ObjectProperty<Paint>`. The `Paint` class is the superclass for colors, gradients, or patterns that can be used in JavaFX to fill or draw a section.

Besides custom alignment and text style, the `graphic` property is used as an easy way to define an icon or a custom visual representation of any state or data in a control. The `graphic` property can hold any `Node` object. This node will be added to the `Labeled` control and rendered in it. You can define the position of the graphic node with a set of properties, as already mentioned in Table 5-2. In the example, I use a simple static rectangle as the graphic node of the button, but thanks to JavaFX, there no limits here; each class that extends the `Node` class can be used for the `graphic` property. For example, you could instead choose a custom image or even an MP4 movie as the graphic object onscreen.

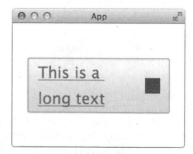

FIGURE 5-5.   *Customized button control*

NOTE
Most of the nodes in JavaFX are resolution independent and can be scaled without a loss of information or pixelation. Whenever a pixel-based image is used in JavaFX, though, this benefit is destroyed. Think about an icon that has a size of 32×32 pixels, for example. When this icon is defined as an image for the graphic *property of a button, it will be shown onscreen. When the button is scaled up by a transform, the icon can look pixelated. Therefore, to avoid this behavior, you need to use a vector-based icon. You could use the* SVGPath *class, which is a node that extends the* Shape *class and renders a Scalable Vector Graphic (SVG) path onscreen. (SVG is a standard specification to define vector-based graphics.) With the help of this class, you can create an icon as an SVG path that can easily be used in JavaFX.*

Label

The Label class encapsulates text and shows it onscreen. Most of the functionality of the Label control is implemented in the Labeled class, which is the superclass of the Label control. Thus, the Label contains only one additional property: labelFor. The labelFor property is an ObjectProperty<Node>, where the node can utilize the label to show its mnemonics.

ButtonBase and Button

The ButtonBase class provides basic functionality for all controls that act like buttons. This means that a control can be in an "armed," (or "pressed") state and fire an event. A button will be armed when the mouse is pressed on it and will fire when the mouse is released. This abstract class includes two properties: armed, which is a ReadOnlyBooleanProperty that indicates the button has been armed, and onAction, which is an ObjectProperty<EventHandler<Action Event>> that invokes the event handler when the button is fired. The following are the most important methods:

- void arm() Arms the button
- void disarm() Disarms the button
- void fire() Fires the button

Because the ButtonBase class extends Labeled, the text that is part of each control that extends this class can be styled as mentioned earlier.

The most common implementation of the ButtonBase class is the Button control. This control behaves exactly as you would expect and is well known to most developers. The button is armed by pressing a mouse or a key, and it will fire an action whenever the mouse or key is released. All this functionality is already implemented in the ButtonBase class, and the Button class offers two additional Boolean properties:

- cancelButton If cancelButton is set to true, the Button class will handle a keyboard VK_ESC press if no other node in the scene consumes it. In this case, the onAction event handler will be called.
- defaultButton If defaultButton is set to true, the Button class will handle a keyboard VK_ENTER press if no other node in the scene consumes it. In this case, the onAction event handler will be called.

CheckBox   In most UI toolkits, a CheckBox control has a checked state and can be checked or unchecked. Normally, this is shown with a tick mark. In JavaFX, a CheckBox control can have two or three different states. The class provides a selected property that behaves exactly as in other UI toolkits, but also contains an indeterminate property, which is the property that can be used to define a third state of the CheckBox control. Table 5-3 shows the impact on the visual representation of the control.

The CheckBox class extends the ButtonBase class, and therefore, an event handler for action events can be added to it. This handler will be called whenever the state of the CheckBox changes. The CheckBox class provides three Boolean properties to define its behavior and state, shown here:

- selected   Indicates whether this CheckBox is checked
- indeterminate   Determines whether the CheckBox is in the indeterminate state
- allowIndeterminate   Defines whether indeterminate is used

Hyperlink   The Hyperlink control is like a Label control that adds action support. Everyone knows hyperlinks on the Web link one page to another. In JavaFX, the Hyperlink control looks like an HTML hyperlink. It appears like a label that can be pressed and will become underlined whenever the mouse is over it. Likewise, the JavaFX Hyperlink control changes its color after it is pressed the first time. To do so, the control offers the visited property. This is the only property that is implemented by the class. The Hyperlink control extends the ButtonBase class.

RadioButton and ToggleButton   Besides the RadioButton control that most developers should know from other UI toolkits, such as Swing, the ToggleButton is an alternative control in JavaFX that can be used to define toggleable controls in an application. The RadioButton class extends the ToggleButton class that inherits from the Control class. Both controls should be used when a series of items is needed where only one item can be selected. Instances of ToggleButton and RadioButton can be placed in groups. A group is represented by the ToggleGroup class and needs to be created; by default, the controls are not in a group. You can define a toggleable

selected	indeterminate	Visual Representation
true	false	☑ CheckBox
false	false	☐ CheckBox
false	true	▬ CheckBox
true	true	▬ CheckBox

TABLE 5-3.   *States of a CheckBox*

control to a group by calling the `setToggleGroup(...)` method on the `ToggleButton` or `RadioButton`. Whenever one control in a group is selected, all other controls will be automatically deselected. Each of these two control types can hold custom user data. The user data of the selected control can be received by the group. Here is a small example that shows how to create a group with a `RadioButton` and a `ToggleButton`:

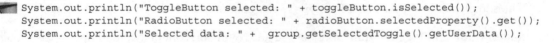

```
ToggleButton toggleButton = new ToggleButton("big value");
toggleButton.setUserData(1000.0d);


RadioButton radioButton = new RadioButton("small value");
radioButton.setUserData(0.1d);

ToggleGroup group = new ToggleGroup();
toggleButton.setToggleGroup(group);
radioButton.setToggleGroup(group);
```

Because both controls are part of the same group, only one of them can be selected. The `Control` classes and the `ToggleGroup` provide properties to check the selection state and to receive the user data of the selected control. The following code snippet shows how this can be done in different ways:

```
System.out.println("ToggleButton selected: " + toggleButton.isSelected());
System.out.println("RadioButton selected: " + radioButton.selectedProperty().get());
System.out.println("Selected data: " + group.getSelectedToggle().getUserData());
```

NOTE
The `ToggleGroup` uses internally the `javafx.scene.control`
`.Toggle` interface. This interface defines all methods that are needed
to use a toggleable control in a `ToggleGroup`. `ToggleButton` and
`RadioButton` implement this interface. Besides these two controls,
some special controls for menus such as the `RadioMenuItem` class
implement this interface, too. If a custom control should be used
inside a `ToggleGroup`, the `Control` class needs to implement this
interface. By doing so, the control can be combined with any other
toggleable control in a `ToggleGroup`.

The `RadioButton` and `ToggleButton` have some differences in look and behavior. You can see both controls in Figure 5-2 shown earlier. Unlike the `RadioButton`, the `ToggleButton` is rendered like a button, but it's not a command button like the `Button` control. When a `ToggleButton` is selected, it is rendered like an armed button. The next difference between these two controls is that a `ToggleButton` can be deselected. Unlike the `RadioButton`, a `ToggleButton` can be unselected, which allows you to create a `ToggleGroup` where no item needs to be selected. There are two properties implemented by the `ToggleButton` class: `selectedProperty`, which is a `Boolean` property that indicates whether the toggle button is selected, and `toggleGroupProperty`, which is an `ObjectProperty<ToggleGroup>` that defines the `ToggleGroup` to which the `ToggleButton` belongs.

Controls for Text Input

JavaFX contains a set of controls that can be used to enter text on the screen. These controls extend the abstract class TextInputControl, which is the class that defines the basic properties and functionalities for all controls that offer text input. All these controls support the possibility of text selection, editing, and a caret. A caret is an indicator that is used to show the current position within the text. Normally, a caret will be shown when the text input control is the one in focus, and the position of the caret can usually be changed by the mouse or the arrow keys. Table 5-4 shows the properties that are offered by the TextInputControl class.

Using the caret allows you to position text within the containing text. To set the position of the caret, the TextInputControl offers a number of methods. In addition, the basic class includes methods for editing the contained text or selecting a sequence of the text. Table 5-5 gives an overview of these methods.

The most common implementation of the TextInputControl class is the TextField class. This control can wrap one line of text. The TextField control was used in earlier examples, including the login sample at the beginning of this chapter (shown in Figure 5-2). The control adds some properties to the basic ones that are defined in its superclass. Table 5-6 describes these properties.

The PasswordField class extends TextField. A PasswordField masks the entered input and can be used for login dialogs, among other things. In addition, cut and copy can't be used in a PasswordField. The PasswordField introduces no additional properties or methods.

Property	Type	Description
anchor	ReadOnlyIntegerProperty	This specifies the anchor position of the text selection.
caretPosition	ReadOnlyIntegerProperty	This specifies the current position of the caret.
editable	BooleanProperty	If this is false, the TextInputControl cannot be edited by a user.
font	ObjectProperty<Font>	This specifies the font of the TextInputControl.
length	ReadOnlyIntegerProperty	This specifies the length in characters of the text.
promptText	StringProperty	This specifies the prompt text to display if no text is defined.
selectedText	ReadOnlyStringProperty	This defines the characters in the TextInputControl that are selected.
selection	ReadOnlyObjectProperty<IndexRange>	This specifies the current selection.
text	StringProperty	This specifies the textual content of this TextInputControl.

TABLE 5-4. *Properties of the TextInputControl Class*

Method	Description
`void appendText(String text)`	Appends a sequence of characters to the content.
`void backward()`	Moves the caret position backward.
`void clear()`	Clears the text.
`void copy()`	Copies the selected text to the system clipboard.
`void cut()`	Cuts the selected text and copies it to the system clipboard.
`boolean deleteNextChar()`	Deletes the character that follows the current caret position.
`boolean deletePreviousChar()`	Deletes the character that precedes the current caret position.
`void deleteText(IndexRange range)`	Removes a range of characters from the content.
`void deleteText(int start, int end)`	Removes a range of characters from the content.
`void deselect()`	Clears the selection.
`void end()`	Moves the caret to after the last character of the text.
`void endOfNextWord()`	Moves the caret to the end of the next word.
`void extendSelection(int pos)`	Extends the selection to include the specified position.
`void forward()`	Moves the caret one position forward.
`void home()`	Moves the caret to the beginning of the text.
`void insertText(int index, String text)`	Inserts a sequence of characters into the content.
`void nextWord()`	Moves the caret to the beginning of the next word.
`void paste()`	Copies the content of the system clipboard at the caret position or replaces the selected text.
`void positionCaret(int pos)`	Positions the caret to a specific position.
`void previousWord()`	Moves the caret to the beginning of the previous word.
`void replaceSelection(String replacement)`	Replaces the selection with the given String. If there is no selection, the text is inserted at the caret position.
`void replaceText(IndexRange range, String text)`	Replaces a range of characters with the given text.
`void replaceText(int start, int end, String text)`	Replaces a range of characters with the given text.
`void selectAll()`	Selects all text in the text input.

TABLE 5-5. *Methods of the TextInputControl Class*

Method	Description
`void selectBackward()`	Moves the selection backward one character in the text.
`void selectEnd()`	Moves the caret to after the last character of text.
`void selectEndOfNextWord()`	Moves the caret to the end of the next word.
`void selectForward()`	Moves the selection forward one character in the text.
`void selectHome()`	Moves the caret to before the first character of text.
`void selectNextWord()`	Moves the caret to the beginning of the next word.
`void selectPositionCaret(int pos)`	Sets the caret to the given position.
`void selectPreviousWord()`	Moves the caret to the beginning of the previous word.
`void selectRange(int anchor, int caretPosition)`	Positions the anchor and caret.

TABLE 5-5. *Methods of the TextInputControl Class* (continued)

The next text input control is the `TextArea`. This control can be used to enter multiple lines of plain text; it is specially designed to render long text that can be wrapped in multiple lines. If the text is too long to fit in the `TextArea`, a scroll bar will be added automatically to the control so users can scroll through the whole text. In addition, you can define the preferred count of characters in a line and the preferred number of lines. This will internally be used to define the preferred size of the `TextArea`. By default, the text wrap is not active in a `TextArea`. If the entered text will exceed the width of the `TextArea`, a horizontal scroll bar will be shown. Once wrapping is activated, the text will wrap in multiple lines. In this case, a vertical scroll bar will be shown when the text extends the `TextArea`. Table 5-7 describes all the properties defined in the `TextArea` class.

Property	Type	Description
`alignment`	`ObjectProperty<Pos>`	Specifies how the text should be aligned.
`onAction`	`ObjectProperty<EventHandler <ActionEvent>>`	Specifies the handler that will receive event action events. This will normally happen when the ENTER key is pressed.
`prefColumnCount`	`IntegerProperty`	Specifies the preferred number of text columns.

TABLE 5-6. *Properties of the TextField Class*

Property	Type	Description
prefColumnCount	IntegerProperty	Defines the preferred number of text columns.
prefRowCount	IntegerProperty	Defines the preferred number of text rows.
scrollLeft	DoubleProperty	Defines the pixel count by which the text is horizontally scrolled.
scrollTop	DoubleProperty	Defines the pixel count by which the text is vertically scrolled.
wrapText	BooleanProperty	Defines whether the text will wrap to another line if it exceeds the width of the TextArea.

TABLE 5-7. *Properties of the TextArea Class*

The following application uses some of the features of text input controls. In the example, you can use a menu to change the caret position of the TextField.

```java
package com.guigarage.masteringcontrols;
import javafx.application.Application;
import javafx.geometry.Pos;
import javafx.scene.Scene;
import javafx.scene.control.Label;
import javafx.scene.control.TextArea;
import javafx.scene.layout.HBox;
import javafx.scene.layout.VBox;
import javafx.scene.paint.Color;
import javafx.scene.text.Font;
import javafx.stage.Stage;
public class TextInputDemo extends Application {
    @Override
    public void start(Stage primaryStage) throws Exception {
        TextArea textArea = new TextArea("You've never heard of the Millennium Falcon?
                                    ... It's the ship that made the Kessel
                                    run in less than 12 parsecs.");
        textArea.setPrefColumnCount(60);
        textArea.setWrapText(true);
        textArea.setFont(new Font(32));

        Label caretLeftLabel = new Label("<");
        caretLeftLabel.setFont(new Font(24));
        caretLeftLabel.setTextFill(Color.BLUE);
        caretLeftLabel.setOnMouseEntered((e) -> caretLeftLabel.
            setTextFill(Color.ORANGE));
        caretLeftLabel.setOnMouseExited((e) -> caretLeftLabel.setTextFill(Color.BLUE));
        caretLeftLabel.setOnMouseClicked((e) -> textArea.backward());

        Label caretRightLabel = new Label(">");
        caretRightLabel.setFont(new Font(24));
        caretRightLabel.setTextFill(Color.BLUE);
        caretRightLabel.setOnMouseEntered((e) -> caretRightLabel.
            setTextFill(Color.ORANGE));
```

```
        caretRightLabel.setOnMouseExited((e) -> caretRightLabel.
            setTextFill(Color.BLUE));
        caretRightLabel.setOnMouseClicked((e) -> textArea.forward());

        Label caretStartLabel = new Label("<<");
        caretStartLabel.setFont(new Font(24));
        caretStartLabel.setTextFill(Color.BLUE);
        caretStartLabel.setOnMouseEntered((e) -> caretStartLabel.
            setTextFill(Color.ORANGE));
        caretStartLabel.setOnMouseExited((e) -> caretStartLabel.
            setTextFill(Color.BLUE));
        caretStartLabel.setOnMouseClicked((e) -> textArea.home());

        Label caretEndLabel = new Label(">>");
        caretEndLabel.setFont(new Font(24));
        caretEndLabel.setTextFill(Color.BLUE);
        caretEndLabel.setOnMouseEntered((e) -> caretEndLabel.setTextFill(Color.ORANGE));
        caretEndLabel.setOnMouseExited((e) -> caretEndLabel.setTextFill(Color.BLUE));
        caretEndLabel.setOnMouseClicked((e) -> textArea.end());

        Label wrapLabel = new Label("w");
        wrapLabel.setFont(new Font(24));
        wrapLabel.setTextFill(Color.BLUE);
        wrapLabel.setOnMouseEntered((e) -> wrapLabel.setTextFill(Color.ORANGE));
        wrapLabel.setOnMouseExited((e) -> wrapLabel.setTextFill(Color.BLUE));
        wrapLabel.setOnMouseClicked((e) -> textArea.
            setWrapText(!textArea.isWrapText()));

        HBox menu = new HBox(caretStartLabel, caretLeftLabel, wrapLabel,
                            caretRightLabel, caretEndLabel);
        menu.setSpacing(12);
        menu.setAlignment(Pos.CENTER);
        VBox box = new VBox(menu, textArea);
        Scene myScene = new Scene(box);
        primaryStage.setScene(myScene);
        primaryStage.setTitle("App");
        primaryStage.setWidth(300);
        primaryStage.setHeight(200);
        primaryStage.show();
    }
    public static void main(String[] args) {
        launch(args);
    }
}
```

In the application, I define a `TextArea` with some sample text and create some labels. These labels have `EventHandler` instances that handle mouse events to interact with the `TextArea`. I'm not using buttons here because the click of a button will request the focus of the application. Once this happens, the button will be in focus, and the `TextArea` loses the focus. A `TextArea` that is not focused won't render the caret, so I use customized labels here for a user interaction since labels are not focusable by default. By clicking the labels, the caret position in the `TextArea` will change, and the text wrap can be activated or disabled. In addition, I have customized the style and behavior of the controls. All controls have a big font size to render their content, and the labels will change their text color whenever the mouse hovers over them. Figure 5-6 shows the example application.

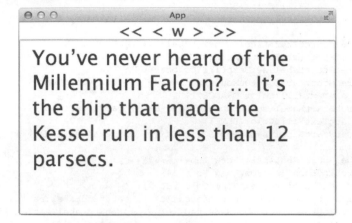

FIGURE 5-6. *Demo of a TextArea control*

The demo application can be created with buttons in the menu, too. To do so, you need a special type of button that doesn't request the focus when it is clicked. You do this by extending the `Button` class. In this case, the `requestFocus()` method should do nothing:

```
Button b = new Button() {
        @Override
        public void requestFocus() {}
    };
```

The button that is defined is rendered like a normal button. It can be clicked to fire an action event, but the button will never request the focus of the current window. The label instances in the previous sample can be changed to this special button to provide a more typical user experience.

Slider

The `Slider` class in JavaFX directly extends the `Control` class. The `Slider` control can be used to visualize a numeric value in a defined range and let the user define a value in the given range. To do so, a so-called thumb is displayed in the slider. This thumb defines the selected value; the user can drag it to change the value. The class contains a large set of properties that can be used to change the visual representation of the slider, the range, and its selectable steps in that range. The most fundamental properties of the `Slider` are `min`, `max`, and `value`. The `min` and `max` properties define the range. The `value` property is a number within this range. Table 5-8 describes all properties of the `Slider` class.

In addition to properties, the `Slider` class provides some methods to change the value programmatically, including `decrement()` and `increment()`. These methods behave as you would imagine, with `decrement()` reducing the value and `increment()` increasing the value by the counts defined by the `blockIncrement` property.

Property	Type	Description
blockIncrement	DoubleProperty	This defines the amount by which the value of the slider will change when the slider is used by keyboard or the snapToTicks property is true.
labelFormatter	ObjectProperty<StringConverter<Double>>	This defines how the labels of the major ticks should be formatted.
majorTickUnit	DoubleProperty	This defines the unit distance between major tick marks.
max	DoubleProperty	This defines the maximum value represented by this slider.
min	DoubleProperty	This defines the minimum value represented by this slider.
minorTickCount	IntegerProperty	This defines the number of minor ticks to place between two major ticks.
orientation	ObjectProperty<Orientation>	This defines the orientation of the Slider control.
showTickLabels	BooleanProperty	This defines whether labels for tick marks should be shown.
showTickMarks	BooleanProperty	This defines whether tick marks should be shown.
snapToTicks	BooleanProperty	If true, the value of the Slider will always be aligned with the defined tick marks.
value	DoubleProperty	This defines the current value represented by this Slider control.
valueChanging	BooleanProperty	When this is true, it indicates that the current value of this Slider control is changing.

TABLE 5-8.   *Properties of the Slider Class*

By using properties, you can customize instances of the Slider class in many ways. The following sample creates two Slider controls that are rendered differently and defines custom ranges to select a value, each customized using properties from the Slider class:

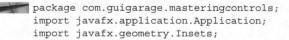

```
package com.guigarage.masteringcontrols;
import javafx.application.Application;
import javafx.geometry.Insets;
```

```java
import javafx.geometry.Orientation;
import javafx.geometry.Pos;
import javafx.scene.Scene;
import javafx.scene.control.Slider;
import javafx.scene.layout.HBox;
import javafx.scene.layout.Priority;
import javafx.stage.Stage;
import javafx.util.StringConverter;
public class SliderDemo  extends Application {
    @Override
    public void start(Stage primaryStage) throws Exception {
        Slider slider1 = new Slider(-200, 200, 23);
        slider1.setMajorTickUnit(25);
        slider1.setShowTickLabels(true);
        slider1.setShowTickMarks(true);
        slider1.setBlockIncrement(25);
        slider1.setSnapToTicks(true);
        slider1.setMinorTickCount(25);
        slider1.setOrientation(Orientation.VERTICAL);
        slider1.setLabelFormatter(new StringConverter<Double>(){
            @Override
            public String toString(Double object) {
                return object + " °C";
            }
            @Override
            public Double fromString(String string) {
                return new Double(string.substring(0, string.length() - 3));
            }
        });
        slider1.valueProperty().addListener((e) -> System.out.println(slider1.
          getValue() + " °C selected"));
        Slider slider2 = new Slider(-1.0, 1.0, 0.5);
        slider2.setMajorTickUnit(0.05);
        slider2.setShowTickLabels(false);
        slider2.setShowTickMarks(true);
        HBox box = new HBox(slider1, slider2);
        box.setAlignment(Pos.CENTER);
        box.setPadding(new Insets(12));
        HBox.setHgrow(slider2, Priority.ALWAYS);
        Scene myScene = new Scene(box);
        primaryStage.setScene(myScene);
        primaryStage.setTitle("Sliders");
        primaryStage.setWidth(300);
        primaryStage.setHeight(200);
        primaryStage.show();
    }
    public static void main(String[] args) {
        launch(args);
    }
}
```

As you can see in Figure 5-7, the two sliders look different: The orientation is varied, the tick marks are customized, and the slider ranges are completely different. The first slider has only a few tick marks that are labeled with custom text showing the values of the marks in degrees

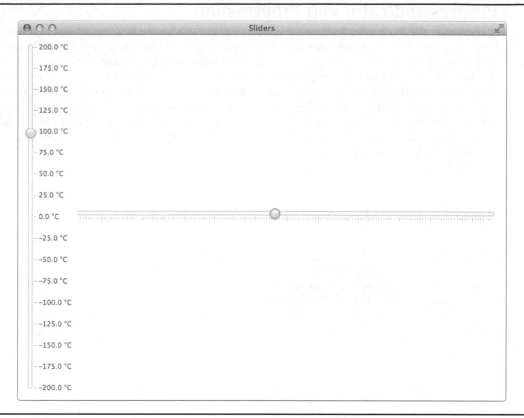

FIGURE 5-7. *Two visual representations of the Slider control*

Celsius. This was accomplished using a `StringConverter` instance. The second slider shows many unlabeled tick marks.

NOTE
As you saw in the previous example, JavaFX controls provide numerous properties that you can use to change the visual representation of the controls. Using these properties is the simplest way to change the view of a control. This is a great benefit compared to other UI toolkits such as Swing. The UI components in Swing provide attributes to change the visualization of controls but often lack the depth of manipulation possible in JavaFX. If the properties used so far aren't enough, you can also use a custom skin. I will discuss this more with custom controls in Chapter 10.

ProgressIndicator and ProgressBar

You can use the `ProgressIndicator` and `ProgressBar` controls to indicate an infinite or
finite progress. These controls are most often used to show the state of a task. If data is loaded
in the background, for example, a `ProgressBar` control can be used to show the progress of
this task. The `ProgressIndicator` class extends the `Control` class and is the superclass of the
`ProgressBar`. The `ProgressIndicator` contains two special properties to define the type and
the progress value of the control. The `indeterminate` property, a `ReadOnlyBoolean` property,
defines whether the `ProgressIndicator` shows indeterminate progress, while the `progress`
property, a `DoubleProperty`, is used to show the actual progress. If the value is negative, the
`ProgressIndicator` shows indeterminate progress.

The following application defines a background task by using the `javafx.concurrent` API
and uses a `ProgressIndicator` and a `ProgressBar` to visualize the state of the task:

```
package com.guigarage.masteringcontrols;
import javafx.application.Application;
import javafx.concurrent.Task;
import javafx.geometry.Insets;
import javafx.geometry.Pos;
import javafx.scene.Scene;
import javafx.scene.control.Button;
import javafx.scene.control.ProgressBar;
import javafx.scene.control.ProgressIndicator;
import javafx.scene.layout.VBox;
import javafx.stage.Stage;
import java.util.concurrent.Executors;
public class ProgressDemo extends Application {
    @Override
    public void start(Stage primaryStage) throws Exception {
        Task task = new Task<Void>() {
            @Override public Void call() {
                for (int i=1; i<=10000; i++) {
                    updateProgress(i, 10000);
                    try {
                        Thread.sleep(1);
                    } catch (InterruptedException e) {}
                }
                return null;
            }
        };
        ProgressIndicator progressIndicator = new ProgressIndicator();
        progressIndicator.progressProperty().bind(task.progressProperty());
        ProgressBar progressBar = new ProgressBar();
        progressBar.progressProperty().bind(task.progressProperty());
        Button button = new Button("Start");
        button.setOnAction((e) -> Executors.newSingleThreadExecutor().execute(task));
        VBox box = new VBox(progressIndicator, progressBar, button);
        box.setSpacing(12);
        box.setPadding(new Insets(12));
        box.setAlignment(Pos.CENTER);
        Scene myScene = new Scene(box);
        primaryStage.setScene(myScene);
```

```
        primaryStage.setTitle("Progress");
        primaryStage.setWidth(300);
        primaryStage.setHeight(200);
        primaryStage.show();
    }
    public static void main(String[] args) {
        launch(args);
    }
}
```

When the application starts, the two progress indicators are shown with infinite progress because the default value of progress property is –1. Once the button is clicked, the Task instance starts in a background thread. The Task class provides a progress property, which can be bound to the property of the ProgressIndicator and ProgressBar. Then, both controls will visualize the progress of the background task. Figure 5-8 shows the application in infinite and finite progress states.

NOTE
The Task class that is used in this application is part of the concurrency API of JavaFX. I won't cover concurrency in depth in this book, but all related classes can be found in the javafx .concurrency package, including properties for messaging and exceptions. Normally, the classes in this package can be used to create background tasks that can retrieve or upload data. A major benefit of the javafx.concurrency classes is the use of the property API. As shown in the example application, the Task class provides a progressProperty that can be easily bound to other properties.

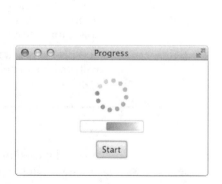

FIGURE 5-8. *States of the ProgressIndicator and ProgressBar*

Tooltip of a Control

Each control in JavaFX offers a `tooltip` property to show a tooltip whenever a mouse hovers over the control. A tooltip can be used to show the user helpful information about a control's usage. A tooltip in JavaFX is defined by the `Tooltip` class and is always shown as a pop-up over the control. Usually, a tooltip will contain plain text that describes the control and its use, but in JavaFX, a tooltip can also contain rich graphics or nodes by using the graphic property. You can use the `graphic` property like described for the `Labeled` control earlier. In addition to this property, the class contains some other properties to define the layout of the tooltip and the rendering of the text. Table 5-9 describes the defined properties.

Property	Type	Description
activated	ReadOnlyBooleanProperty	If the mouse enters the control of this tooltip, the `activated` property is true.
graphic	ObjectProperty<Node>	This specifies an optional node (maybe an icon) for the tooltip.
text	StringProperty	This specifies the text of the tooltip.
contentDisplay	ObjectProperty<ContentDisplay>	This specifies the positioning of the graphic relative to the text.
font	ObjectProperty<Font>	This specifies the font.
graphicTextGap	DoubleProperty	This specifies the space between the graphic and text.
textAlignment	ObjectProperty<TextAlignment>	This specifies the behavior for lines of multiline text.
textOverrun	ObjectProperty<OverrunStyle>	This defines the behavior to use if the text exceeds the available space for rendering.
wrapText	BooleanProperty	This defines whether the text will wrap to another line if it exceeds the width of the tooltip.

TABLE 5-9. *Methods of the Tooltip Class*

The following application demonstrates how the `Tooltip` class can be used in JavaFX to offer rich tooltips to the user. Here, I am adding a shape to the tooltip instead of simple plain text.

```
package com.guigarage.masteringcontrols;
import javafx.application.Application;
import javafx.geometry.Insets;
import javafx.geometry.Pos;
import javafx.scene.Scene;
import javafx.scene.control.Label;
```

```
import javafx.scene.control.Tooltip;
import javafx.scene.layout.VBox;
import javafx.scene.paint.Color;
import javafx.scene.shape.*;
import javafx.scene.shape.Rectangle;
import javafx.stage.Stage;

public class TooltipDemo extends Application {
    @Override
    public void start(Stage primaryStage) throws Exception {
        Label rectLabel = new Label("Rectangle");
        Tooltip rectTooltip = new Tooltip();
        rectTooltip.setGraphic(new Rectangle(50, 50, Color.ORANGE));
        rectLabel.setTooltip(rectTooltip);
        Label circleLabel = new Label("Circle");
        Tooltip circleTooltip = new Tooltip();
        circleTooltip.setGraphic(new Circle(20, 20, 40, Color.ORANGE));
        circleLabel.setTooltip(circleTooltip);
        VBox myPane = new VBox();
        myPane.setPadding(new Insets(12));
        myPane.setSpacing(12);
        myPane.setAlignment(Pos.CENTER);
        myPane.getChildren().addAll(rectLabel, circleLabel);
        Scene myScene = new Scene(myPane);
        primaryStage.setScene(myScene);
        primaryStage.setWidth(300);
        primaryStage.setHeight(200);
        primaryStage.show();
    }
    public static void main(String[] args) {
        launch(args);
    }
}
```

Figure 5-9 shows the result of this code. Here, the tooltip pop-up of the Circle label instance is shown. The size of the tooltip is calculated by the preferred size of its content. As you can see,

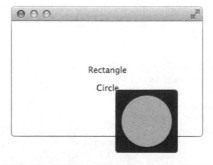

FIGURE 5-9. *A custom tooltip*

the tooltip contains a Circle shape instead of plain text. This is accomplished by setting a shape as the graphics object of the tooltip within the code. Although the tooltip currently contains no text, custom text can be added in addition to the shape.

NOTE
The graphic property of the Tooltip class can contain any node instance. Because panes and controls extend the Node class, a control or a complete layouted pane could be used in a tooltip. This might make sense if you develop a GUI editor, for example, but it doesn't make sense to add interaction to controls that are part of a tooltip. A tooltip will be closed whenever the mouse leaves the control that provides the tooltip, so the mouse can never enter the tooltip by default.

Using Menus in JavaFX

In addition to the Control classes reviewed so far, there are some special controls that can be used to create menus in JavaFX applications. There are several different ways a menu can be shown and used in an application, including the following:

- A MenuBar that is integrated in a window
- A ContextMenu that is shown as a pop-up for a control
- A system menu bar like in Mac OS

JavaFX provides two Control classes that can be used as containers for a menu: the MenuBar and the ContextMenu. This chapter will cover both types.

A ContextMenu can be used to show a pop-up on another Control instance. This pop-up can be used to provide specific actions or configurations that can be handled by the user. Some controls in JavaFX already use a ContextMenu by default. If you right-click in a TextArea, for example, a pop-up menu will appear that contains some basic operations, such as Copy and Paste. This functionality is implemented by a ContextMenu. As mentioned earlier in this chapter, the Control class contains a contextMenu property that can define a ContextMenu for a control. By simply setting a specific menu to this property, a pop-up with the content of the menu will be shown whenever the user right-clicks the control. On some operating systems, this behavior will change in the future, but by default, the right mouse button is the action trigger for this functionality.

A ContextMenu can contain different menu items, which I'll review in more detail after showing a basic sample. In the following application code, a simple ContextMenu is added to a Button instance:

```
package com.guigarage.masteringcontrols;
import javafx.application.Application;
import javafx.scene.Scene;
import javafx.scene.control.*;
import javafx.scene.layout.StackPane;
import javafx.stage.Stage;
public class ContextMenuDemo extends Application {
    @Override
    public void start(Stage primaryStage) throws Exception {
```

```
        Button button = new Button("Click me");
        ContextMenu menu = new ContextMenu();
        MenuItem rotateItem = new MenuItem("Rotate");
        rotateItem.setOnAction((e) -> button.setRotate(button.getRotate() + 45));
        CheckMenuItem underlineItem = new CheckMenuItem("Underline");
        button.underlineProperty().bindBidirectional(underlineItem.selectedProperty());
        menu.getItems().addAll(rotateItem, underlineItem);

        button.setContextMenu(menu);

        StackPane myPane = new StackPane();
        myPane.getChildren().add(button);
        Scene myScene = new Scene(myPane);
        primaryStage.setScene(myScene);
        primaryStage.setTitle("App");
        primaryStage.setWidth(300);
        primaryStage.setHeight(200);
        primaryStage.show();
    }
    public static void main(String[] args) {
        launch(args);
    }
}
```

As you can see in the code, I added two different items to the ContextMenu: a MenuItem and a CheckMenuItem. Only MenuItem instances or instances of classes that extend this superclass can be added to a ContextMenu. The MenuItem is a simple menu entry that can be clicked, and whenever an item is clicked, an action event will be handled. As shown in many samples, an event handler can be set to the onAction property of the control. This is done in this example application, too. The CheckMenuItem behaves like a CheckBox. It contains a selected property that will change with each click on the item. In the sample, the underline property of the Button instance is bound to this property. Each time this menu item is activated, the text of the Button instance will appear underlined. Figure 5-10 shows an example of this behavior.

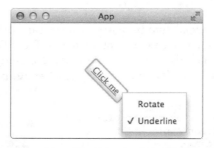

FIGURE 5-10. *A context menu*

Method	Description
`ObservableList<MenuItem> getItems()`	Contains the menu items on the context menu
`public void hide()`	Hides the `ContextMenu` and any visible submenus
`void show(Node anchor, double screenX, double screenY)`	Shows the `ContextMenu` at the specified screen coordinates
`void show(Node anchor, Side side, double dx, double dy)`	Shows the `ContextMenu` relative to the given anchor node

TABLE 5-10. *Methods of the ContextMenu*

As already shown in the example application, the `ContextMenu` class contains an `onAction` property. Like in all other classes that support action events, this property is defined as `ObjectProperty<EventHandler<ActionEvent>>` and will handle all action events. This will happen for each action that occurs on a menu item in the `ContextMenu`. So, whenever the Rotate menu item in the previous example is clicked, the event handler of the item itself and of the `ContextMenu` will be triggered. In addition, the `ContextMenu` provides some helpful methods, described in Table 5-10.

JavaFX contains the following item types that can be added to a menu:

- `MenuItem`
- `RadioMenuItem`
- `TabMenuItem`
- `CheckMenuItem`
- `CustomMenuItem`
- `SeparatorMenuItem`
- `Menu`

The `Menu` class is a special item because instances can contain additional menu items. By using the `Menu` class, you can create a menu hierarchy. The following application shows how to achieve this in code. As already mentioned, besides a `ContextMenu`, a `MenuBar` can be used to display menus onscreen. In the following example, a `MenuBar` with several menu items is added to the screen:

```
package com.guigarage.masteringcontrols;
import javafx.application.Application;
import javafx.scene.Scene;
import javafx.scene.control.*;
import javafx.scene.layout.BorderPane;
import javafx.stage.Stage;
public class MenuBarDemo extends Application {
```

```
    @Override
    public void start(Stage primaryStage) throws Exception {
        MenuBar menuBar = new MenuBar();
        Menu mainMenu = new Menu("Main");
        MenuItem rotateItem = new MenuItem("Load");
        CheckMenuItem underlineItem = new CheckMenuItem("Underline");
        mainMenu.getItems().addAll(rotateItem, underlineItem);
        Menu editMenu = new Menu("Edit");
        Menu convertMenu = new Menu("Convert");
        convertMenu.getItems().addAll(new MenuItem("PDF"), new MenuItem("PNG"));
        editMenu.getItems().addAll(convertMenu, new MenuItem("Rotate"));
        menuBar.getMenus().addAll(mainMenu, editMenu);
        BorderPane pane = new BorderPane();
        pane.setTop(menuBar);
        Scene myScene = new Scene(pane);
        primaryStage.setScene(myScene);
        primaryStage.setTitle("App");
        primaryStage.setWidth(300);
        primaryStage.setHeight(200);
        primaryStage.show();
    }

    public static void main(String[] args) {
        launch(args);
    }
}
```

When running the application, the window will contain a menu bar that holds all the defined menu items.

NOTE
Some operating systems such as Mac OS define a global menu bar, and not each application has its own bar that is wrapped in the application window. Instead, the OS contains a bar that is usually displayed at the top of the screen, and its content changes whenever another application receives the focus. You can use this kind of menu bar in JavaFX, too. To do so, the MenuBar *class contains the* useSystemMenuBar *property. By setting the* Boolean *value of this property to true, the content of the* MenuBar *won't be displayed in the window. Instead, all items of the* MenuBar *are displayed in the global one of the operating system.*

Using Separators

The Separator control defines a horizontal or vertical line that can be used as a visual separation in a view or a menu. The following sample adds a separator to a list of CheckBox instances. By doing so, a division of the elements is shown onscreen. Figure 5-11 shows the result.

```
package com.guigarage.masteringcontrols;
import javafx.application.Application;
import javafx.geometry.Insets;
import javafx.scene.Scene;
```

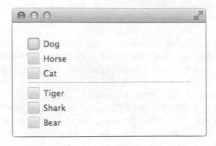

FIGURE 5-11. *Using a separator*

```
import javafx.scene.control.CheckBox;
import javafx.scene.control.Separator;
import javafx.scene.layout.Background;
import javafx.scene.layout.VBox;
import javafx.stage.Stage;
public class SeperatorDemo extends Application {
    @Override
    public void start(Stage primaryStage) throws Exception {
        String[] names = new String[]{"Dog", "Horse", "Cat",
                "Tiger", "Shark", "Bear"};
        CheckBox[] cbs - new CheckBox[names.];
        for (int i = 0; i < names.length; i++) {
            cbs[i] = new CheckBox(names[i]);
        }
        VBox vbox = new VBox(cbs);
        vbox.setSpacing(5);
        vbox.setPadding(new Insets(24));
        vbox.setBackground(Background.EMPTY);
        Separator separator = new Separator();
        vbox.getChildren().add(3, separator);
        Scene myScene = new Scene(vbox);
        primaryStage.setScene(myScene);
        primaryStage.setWidth(300);
        primaryStage.setHeight(200);
        primaryStage.show();
    }
    public static void main(String[] args) {
        launch(args);
    }
}
```

The Separator control in the previous example is displayed as a horizontal line, but a separator can be vertical, too, by using the orientation property. In some special cases, like in a toolbar, the separator will automatically appear vertically based on internal CSS definitions. In the following example, the Separator instance is created like before and no properties are set:

```java
package com.guigarage.masteringcontrols;
import javafx.application.Application;
import javafx.scene.Scene;
import javafx.scene.control.Button;
import javafx.scene.control.Separator;
import javafx.scene.control.TextArea;
import javafx.scene.control.ToolBar;
import javafx.scene.layout.BorderPane;
import javafx.stage.Stage;
public class SeperatorInToolbarDemo extends Application {
    @Override
    public void start(Stage primaryStage) {
        ToolBar toolBar = new ToolBar(
                new Button("New"),
                new Button("Open"),
                new Button("Save"),
                new Separator(),
                new Button("Run"),
                new Button("Debug"),
                new Separator(),
                new Button("Help")
        );
        BorderPane pane = new BorderPane();
        pane.setTop(toolBar);
        pane.setCenter(new TextArea());
        Scene myScene = new Scene(pane);
        primaryStage.setScene(myScene);
        primaryStage.setTitle("My little IDE");
        primaryStage.setWidth(300);
        primaryStage.setHeight(200);
        primaryStage.show();
    }
    public static void main(String[] args) {
        launch(args);
    }
}
```

Creating an Application with Basic Controls

Now that I have covered most of the basic controls in JavaFX, I'll show how to create a more complex application that utilizes the features discussed, as well as introducing new features, like FXML.

As you recall, it is best practice to define the views of a more complex application in FXML. By using Scene Builder, I created the following application in only a few minutes. Scene Builder is a WYSIWYG editor for FXML, and because an FXML file contains all the information about the alignment and layout of nodes in a view, it can become quite huge. In fact, the FXML for the application shown here is too large to print in full. I will rely on code snippets here, but you can access the complete code by following the instructions in the Introduction of this book. Thanks to Scene Builder, it's not necessary that developers know how an FXML file has to be defined, but you should know how to read an FXML file and understand its syntax and content. This will be helpful for finding bugs or tracking down layout issues in an application. The following code shows a basic FXML file. It defines the content of the FXML file that creates the login dialog that was shown at the beginning of the chapter.

```xml
<?xml version="1.0" encoding="UTF-8"?>
<?import java.lang.*?>
<?import java.util.*?>
<?import javafx.geometry.*?>
<?import javafx.scene.control.*?>
<?import javafx.scene.layout.*?>
<?import javafx.scene.paint.*?>
<GridPane hgap="6.0" vgap="6.0" xmlns:fx="http://javafx.com/fxml/1" xmlns="http://
javafx.com/javafx/2.2">
  <children>
    <Label text="User:" GridPane.columnIndex="0" GridPane.rowIndex="0" />
    <Label text="Password:" GridPane.columnIndex="0" GridPane.rowIndex="1" />
    <TextField prefWidth="200.0" promptText="username" GridPane.columnIndex="1"
        GridPane.rowIndex="0" />
    <PasswordField prefWidth="200.0" promptText="password" GridPane.columnIndex="1"
        GridPane.rowIndex="1" />
    <Button mnemonicParsing="false" text="Login" GridPane.columnIndex="0" GridPane.
        columnSpan="2" GridPane.halignment="CENTER" GridPane.rowIndex="2" />
  </children>
  <columnConstraints>
    <ColumnConstraints hgrow="NEVER" minWidth="10.0" prefWidth="100.0" />
    <ColumnConstraints hgrow="ALWAYS" minWidth="10.0" prefWidth="100.0" />
  </columnConstraints>
  <padding>
    <Insets bottom="6.0" left="6.0" right="6.0" top="6.0" />
  </padding>
  <rowConstraints>
    <RowConstraints minHeight="10.0" prefHeight="30.0" vgrow="SOMETIMES" />
    <RowConstraints minHeight="10.0" prefHeight="30.0" vgrow="SOMETIMES" />
    <RowConstraints minHeight="10.0" prefHeight="30.0" vgrow="SOMETIMES" />
  </rowConstraints>
</GridPane>
```

As you can see in the XML, all nodes of the view and its hierarchy are defined as XML tags. In addition, the initial values of properties are defined as XML attributes in these tags.

Figure 5-12 shows the application that was completely designed with Scene Builder. It is a demo application that can be used to change the visual nature of a simple shape. With the use of the controls discussed in this chapter, the user can customize the shape and some of its properties.

When creating a JavaFX application with the help of Scene Builder and FXML, it is best to use the Model-View-Control (MVC) pattern. This pattern separates the model, the controller, and the

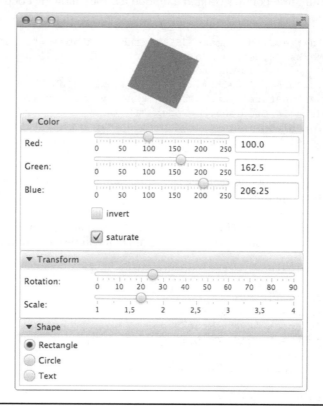

FIGURE 5-12. *An application created with basic controls*

view of an application. In JavaFX, the view will usually be created in FXML. This is done for the demo application, too. In the FXML file, all needed properties of the shown controls are defined with initial values. As an example, the definitions of the three labels that name the color sliders are shown here:

```
<Label text="Red:" GridPane.columnIndex="0" GridPane.rowIndex="0" />
<Label text="Green:" GridPane.columnIndex="0" GridPane.rowIndex="1" />
<Label text="Blue:" GridPane.columnIndex="0" GridPane.rowIndex="2" />
```

For each of the three labels, an initial value for the text property is set in FXML. In addition, some layout properties are defined to position the labels in its parent pane. In the application, the labels and sliders are wrapped in a GridPane. The three labels are just static content of the application view. Some other controls, like Slider, need to define some interaction with the user. This interaction will be added in Java code later. To create a link between the FXML file and the Java code, all these controls contain a unique ID. The following code snippet shows the FXML definition of the sliders:

```
<Slider fx:id="redSlider" max="255.0" showTickLabels="true"
    showTickMarks="true" snapToTicks="true" value="100.0" GridPane.
    columnIndex="1" GridPane.rowIndex="0" />
<Slider fx:id="greenSlider" max="255.0" showTickLabels="true"
    showTickMarks="true" snapToTicks="true" value="100.0" GridPane.
    columnIndex="1" GridPane.rowIndex="1" />
<Slider fx:id="blueSlider" blockIncrement="10.0" max="255.0"
    showTickLabels="true" showTickMarks="true" snapToTicks="true" value="100.0"
    GridPane.columnIndex="1" GridPane.rowIndex="2" />
```

The FXML tags that define the three sliders contain one new attribute. In addition to the initial values for all the properties and the layout information, the `fx:id` attribute defines a unique ID. You can use any text as the ID, and by doing so, you can create a link from the Java code to the FXML code by injecting the FXML-defined `Node` instance in your Java code. The following code defines a simplified version of the controller class that will be used for the FXML file:

```
package com.guigarage.masteringcontrols;

import javafx.fxml.FXML;
import javafx.scene.control.*;
import javafx.scene.layout.StackPane;
import javafx.scene.paint.Color;
import javafx.scene.shape.Circle;
import javafx.scene.shape.Rectangle;
import javafx.scene.shape.Shape;
import javafx.scene.text.Text;

public class ViewController {

    @FXML
    private Slider redSlider;

    @FXML
    private Slider greenSlider;

    @FXML
    private Slider blueSlider;

    ...
}
```

The `Java` class contains all three sliders as private fields. These fields are annotated with the `@FXML` annotation, which is used to create the link between Java and FXML. When the `ViewController` is instantiated by an `FXMLLoader`, all fields that are marked by the `@FXML` annotation will be injected with the created nodes that are defined in the FXML. It is important to know that the name of the fields must be the same as the previously defined `fx:id` value.

In JavaFX and FXML, the view defines its specific controller class. This is done in the FXML file as an attribute of the topmost node. In the example, a `BorderPane` is used as the `rootNode`, and the `ViewController` class is defined in its `fx:controller` attribute:

```xml
<?xml version="1.0" encoding="UTF-8"?>
<?import java.lang.*?>
<?import java.util.*?>
<?import javafx.geometry.*?>
<?import javafx.scene.control.*?>
<?import javafx.scene.layout.*?>
<?import javafx.scene.paint.*?>
<BorderPane fx:controller="com.guigarage.masteringcontrols.ViewController">
// content of the view
</BorderPane>
```

Once this is done, JavaFX can easily load the combination of view and controller. You just need to create a main class for the application that loads the FXML with an `FXMLLoader` instance and adds its root node to the scene, as shown here:

```java
package com.guigarage.masteringcontrols;
import javafx.application.Application;
import javafx.fxml.FXMLLoader;
import javafx.scene.Scene;
import javafx.stage.Stage;
public class FirstBigApp extends Application {
    @Override
    public void start(Stage primaryStage) throws Exception {
        FXMLLoader loader = new FXMLLoader(getClass().getResource("bigApp.fxml"));
        Scene myScene = new Scene(loader.load());
        primaryStage.setScene(myScene);
        primaryStage.show();
    }
    public static void main(String[] args) {
        launch(args);
    }
}
```

Because the controller class is currently named in the FXML file, you don't need to define the controller in the Java code. If you place the `bigApp.fxml` file in the same package as the `FirstBigApp` class, you can use the `getClass().getResource(...)` method to receive the URL of the FXML file.

NOTE
The `FXMLLoader` class provides more functionality than discussed here. The controller instance can be accessed by the class or can define a resource bundle, for example. Here, FXML should be used to exclude the layout of an application from the Java code. In a bigger application, it would be useful to create links between controllers in order to switch between different views. For additional information, review the FXML API and the flow API of DataFX (www.javafxdata .org). The flow API provides functionality to switch between different views and share data models between them.

The complete logic and interaction of the application is defined in the controller. The following shows the complete code of the `ViewController` class:

```java
package com.guigarage.masteringcontrols;
import javafx.fxml.FXML;
import javafx.scene.control.*;
import javafx.scene.layout.StackPane;
import javafx.scene.paint.Color;
import javafx.scene.shape.Circle;
import javafx.scene.shape.Rectangle;
import javafx.scene.shape.Shape;
import javafx.scene.text.Text;
public class ViewController {
    @FXML
    private Slider redSlider;
    @FXML
    private Slider greenSlider;
    @FXML
    private Slider blueSlider;
    @FXML
    private TextField redField;
    @FXML
    private TextField greenField;
    @FXML
    private TextField blueField;
    @FXML
    private CheckBox invertCheckbox;
    @FXML
    private CheckBox saturateCheckbox;
    @FXML
    private Slider rotationSlider;
    @FXML
    private Slider scaleSlider;
    @FXML
    private RadioButton rectangleToggle;
    @FXML
    private RadioButton circleToggle;
    @FXML
    private RadioButton textToggle;
    @FXML
    private StackPane canvas;

    private ToggleGroup group;

    public void initialize() {

        rectangleToggle.setUserData(new Rectangle(50, 50));
        circleToggle.setUserData(new Circle(50));
        textToggle.setUserData(new Text("TEXT"));
        group = new ToggleGroup();
        rectangleToggle.setToggleGroup(group);
        circleToggle.setToggleGroup(group);
        textToggle.setToggleGroup(group);
        group.selectToggle(rectangleToggle);

        group.selectedToggleProperty().addListener(event -> updateShape());
```

```
        redField.textProperty().bind(redSlider.valueProperty().asString());
        greenField.textProperty().bind(greenSlider.valueProperty().asString());
        blueField.textProperty().bind(blueSlider.valueProperty().asString());

        canvas.rotateProperty().bind(rotationSlider.valueProperty());
        canvas.scaleXProperty().bindBidirectional(scaleSlider.valueProperty());
        canvas.scaleYProperty().bindBidirectional(scaleSlider.valueProperty());
        redSlider.valueProperty().addListener(event -> updateShape());
        greenSlider.valueProperty().addListener(event -> updateShape());
        blueSlider.valueProperty().addListener(event -> updateShape());
        invertCheckbox.selectedProperty().addListener(event -> updateShape());
        saturateCheckbox.selectedProperty().addListener(event -> updateShape());

        updateShape();
    }

    private void updateShape() {
        canvas.getChildren().clear();
        Shape shape = (Shape) group.getSelectedToggle().getUserData();
        Color color = Color.rgb((int) redSlider.getValue(),
          (int) greenSlider.getValue(), (int) blueSlider.getValue());
        if(invertCheckbox.isSelected()) {
            color = color.invert();
        }
        if(saturateCheckbox.isSelected()) {
            color = color.saturate();
        }
        shape.setFill(color);
        canvas.getChildren().add(shape);
    }
}
```

When the application starts, you can use the controls in the menus to change the look of the shape that is shown in the top part of the application. Let's take a look at how this is done in the controller class. The first thing that is new is the `initialize()` method. This method is defined in the FXML API and will be called whenever a controller is created by an `FXMLLoader`. Because all fields that are annotated with @FXML will be injected after the constructor of the controller is called, this method needs to be used to access the injected fields.

The user can change the shape shown in the top of the application. To do this, I added three `RadioButton` instances to the application. When talking about `RadioButton` controls, I introduced the `ToggleGroup` class. This is the class used in this application to group the `RadioButton` controls. Each of the radio buttons defines a custom shape as its `userData`: One holds a `Rectangle` instance, one holds a `Circle` instance, and one holds a `Text` instance. All three radio buttons are part of the same `ToggleGroup`. Whenever the selection of the group changes, the `updateShape()` method will be called. This is done with a `ChangeListener` that is added to the `selectedToggle` property of the group. In this method, the shape that is defined as the user data of the selected radio button will be added to the screen.

The next lines of the `initialize()` method define some binding between properties of controls. I placed a `TextField` next to each of the slides in order to define the RGB value of the shape's fill color. The text of these fields is bound to the current value of the slider. Whenever a user changes the slider, the text value of the text field will update automatically. In addition, the shape can be transformed by wrapping it in a pane that is defined by the private `StackPane` `canvas` field. The `rotate` and `scale` properties of this pane are bound to the values of sliders. The user can change these sliders to change the transform of the shape.

In addition, I added `ChangeListener` instances to the `value` property of each slider in order to change the color of the shape. I did this for the two `CheckBox` instances (invert color and saturation) too. The listeners are defined as lambda expressions and call the `updateShape()` method whenever the value of the property is changed. This method creates the displayed shape and sets its fill to the defined color.

Even if this example contains only two Java classes and an FXML file, it is the most complex application I have shown until now. In the code, you can see how easily you can separate the view and controller in Java. The application is created with only panes and a set of basic controls. For the interaction of the application, you define bindings and listeners. In other UI toolkits, coding the same application would have presented a number of problems, including workarounds or special APIs to define bindings; in addition, the complete layout of the application would need to be done in Java code. Using functional interfaces in JavaFX allows you to drastically reduce the amount of boilerplate code.

Summary

This chapter showed you how to use basic controls in JavaFX. I covered the elementary concepts of the `Control` class and general controls and showed sample illustrations for all the basic JavaFX controls and their features. I explained the most important properties and methods of each control so you have insight into the endless possibilities these controls offer. As a more complex example, you saw an application that uses a lot of these features internally. JavaFX offers a huge set of additional nodes and controls beyond these basics that can be used to create modern applications that handle and visualize huge sets of data. You will look at these additional controls in the following chapter.

CHAPTER
6

Additional JavaFX Controls

I n the previous chapter, you looked at the basic controls available for JavaFX. JavaFX also contains more complex controls that are usually used to display data in an application. These controls, such as tables and lists, are especially useful when you have a huge amount of data. In addition, JavaFX contains some control types that have specific uses. For example, a `ColorPicker` provides a user interface that lets the user choose a color. In this chapter, I'll cover all the advanced controls and the possibilities they offer.

Controls with a Data Model

In many applications, developers will need to display lists of data and custom data models so the user can understand the data. JavaFX contains a number of controls that can be used to render lists of data or hierarchical data onscreen. By default, JavaFX provides the following controls in this category:

- `ComboBox<T>`
- `ListView<T>`
- `TableView<T>`
- `TreeView<T>`
- `TreeTableView<T>`

These controls are subclasses of the `Control` class, but the APIs and alternatives of how these controls can be used in an application are more flexible than what you saw in the previous chapter with the basic controls.

ComboBox

The `ComboBox<T>` control is the most common control that can be used to display a data selection from a list of data. If a list contains only five or six elements, this could be easily done with the use of a `RadioButton` and a `ToggleGroup`. But what if the list has 100 or more elements? What if the list is dynamic? In these cases, `RadioButtons` are not much help. Furthermore, sometimes it's not clear during development how many entries a data list will have at run time. These situations require a flexible selection, which is exactly what a `ComboBox` offers. The `ComboBox` provides a way to create a selection interface for any kind of data list. In addition, it provides much more useful features, such as custom cells that can be used to render the data of the list.

The easiest use case for a `ComboBox` is for a selection from a list of `String` instances. The following application shows how a `ComboBox` control can be created that uses a list with `String` instances as a data model:

```
package com.guigarage.masteringcontrols;
import javafx.application.Application;
import javafx.collections.FXCollections;
import javafx.collections.ObservableList;
import javafx.scene.Scene;
import javafx.scene.control.ComboBox;
import javafx.scene.layout.StackPane;
```

```
import javafx.stage.Stage;
public class SimpleComboboxDemo  extends Application {
    @Override
    public void start(Stage primaryStage) throws Exception {
        ComboBox<String> comboBox = new ComboBox<>();
        ObservableList<String> data = FXCollections.observableArrayList();
        data.addAll("Darth Vader", "Luke Skywalker", "Yoda");
        comboBox.itemsProperty().setValue(data);
        StackPane myPane = new StackPane();
        myPane.getChildren().add(comboBox);
        Scene myScene = new Scene(myPane);
        primaryStage.setScene(myScene);
        primaryStage.show();
    }
    public static void main(String[] args) {
        launch(args);
    }
}
```

As you can see in the code, the data model of the ComboBox is created as an ObservableList<String>. The list can hold any number of different Strings. In the sample, only three Strings were added to the list, but you could easily add thousands of items to the list. Once the given list of data is too large to be rendered directly in the selection pop-up, the ComboBox will offer a scroll bar so the user can scroll through the list and select a value. (While you could add thousands of elements to a ComboBox, this control wouldn't be the most appropriate selection method in that case. As I will show later, a ListView will match this use case much better.)

The ComboBox provides the item property, which defines the data model of the ComboBox. You simply set the defined list as the item property of the given ComboBox. Figure 6-1 shows how this example will look.

The data list of the ComboBox is defined as an ObservableList<String>, so it can be easily extended at run time. Once the list is set as the item property of the ComboBox, the ComboBox API internally registers a ChangeListener to the list. After that, the ComboBox will be notified of each change in the list. Thanks to this feature, the ComboBox can dynamically react to selection changes by adding new items to or removing items from the onscreen list. All the JavaFX control

FIGURE 6-1. *A ComboBox*

classes that can display any data type use `Generics` to define this data type. The next example shows how you can test this with the help of a `TextField` instance:

```
package com.guigarage.masteringcontrols;
import javafx.application.Application;
import javafx.collections.FXCollections;
import javafx.collections.ObservableList;
import javafx.geometry.Pos;
import javafx.scene.Scene;
import javafx.scene.control.ComboBox;
import javafx.scene.control.TextField;
import javafx.scene.layout.HBox;
import javafx.scene.layout.StackPane;
import javafx.scene.layout.VBox;
import javafx.stage.Stage;
public class SimpleComboboxDemo  extends Application {
    @Override
    public void start(Stage primaryStage) throws Exception {
        ComboBox<String> comboBox = new ComboBox<>();
        ObservableList<String> data = FXCollections.observableArrayList();
        data.addAll("Darth Vader", "Luke Skywalker", "Yoda");
        comboBox.itemsProperty().setValue(data);
        TextField inputField = new TextField();
        inputField.setPromptText("insert new data type");
        inputField.setOnAction(e -> data.add(inputField.getText()));
        VBox box = new VBox(6, inputField, comboBox);
        box.setAlignment(Pos.CENTER);
        Scene myScene = new Scene(box);
        primaryStage.setScene(myScene);
        primaryStage.show();
    }
    public static void main(String[] args) {
        launch(args);
    }
}
```

In this code, I've added a `TextField` to the application and defined an event handler for it. Whenever ENTER is pressed in the `TextField`, the event handler will add the current text content of the `TextField` to the `ObservableList`. Because this list is used as the data model of the `ComboBox`, the new value will appear in the selection pop-up, as shown in Figure 6-2.

NOTE
As you can see in the sample applications, it is easy to define a dynamic model for a ComboBox. Later, you will see that the same functionality is implemented in all other controls discussed in this chapter. This workflow will be new to developers who have used Swing as a UI toolkit where a special data model was needed to provide these features. Thanks to observable collections and the property API, this is no longer necessary in JavaFX.

FIGURE 6-2. *Adding values to a ComboBox*

The `ComboBox` class extends the `ComboBoxBase` class, which is a subclass of `Control`. This is done because other special controls such as `DatePicker` and `ColorPicker` share a lot of functionality and extend the `ComboBoxBase` too. The `ComboBoxBase` class provides a basic set of properties that can be used to define the behavior of a `ComboBox` or define interaction. Internally, the `ComboBoxBase` class is used as a superclass for all controls that provide a pop-up to select a value. Table 6-1 describes the properties of the `ComboBoxBase` class.

NOTE
In most cases, a subclass of `ComboBoxBase` will show a pop-up to select a value, but this isn't mandatory. Developers can create a subclass that uses, for example, a separate pane to show the selection. In addition, the `item` property is not specified in the `ComboBoxBase`. Some implementations of this abstract class don't have a list of values defined. The `DatePicker`, for example, has no defined list of values that could be selected. Here, any data can be set by a user. To provide for all these possibilities, the `ComboBoxBase` class provides only the value property to define the selected value and event handlers. These handlers can be used to implement the life cycle of a selection pop-up, as done for the `ComboBox` control.

The `ComboBox` class provides the properties described in Table 6-2. Some of them won't be discussed in this chapter. Properties such as the `cellFactory` property are also defined for other controls such as the `ListView` or `TableView` and will be handled in the following chapters. How custom cells can be created will be described when talking about the `ListView`, for example.

Beyond the example use case, the `ComboBox` provides the functionality to define a custom selection. Here a user can select a value from the selection pop-up or type any value directly in the `ComboBox`. Most users will know this behavior from the URL field of most web browsers,

Property	Type	Description
armed	BooleanProperty	This indicates that the ComboBox has been "armed." This defines the same behavior as the ButtonBase class.
editable	BooleanProperty	This defines whether the control allows user input.
onAction	ObjectProperty<EventHandler<ActionEvent>>	This defines the event handler for action events that are fired when the value property value is changed, such as when a user selects an item.
onHidden	ObjectProperty<EventHandler<Event>>	The handler will be invoked after the pop-up has been hidden.
onHiding	ObjectProperty<EventHandler<Event>>	The handler will be invoked before the pop-up is hidden.
onShowing	ObjectProperty<EventHandler<Event>>	The handler will be invoked before the pop-up is shown.
onShown	ObjectProperty<EventHandler<Event>>	The handler will be invoked after the pop-up has been shown.
promptText	StringProperty	This specifies the prompt text to display.
showing	ReadOnlyBooleanProperty	This defines whether the ComboBox pop-up is visible.
value	ObjectProperty<T>	This is the selected value.

TABLE 6-1. *Properties of the ComboBoxBase*

where you can type any URL by hand or open a selection pop-up that contains your last-visited sites or your favorites. You can create this behavior with the JavaFX ComboBox, too. In addition, you can use a ComboBox to provide a selection for any data type. In the previous examples, only a list with Strings was shown, but it is easy to create a ComboBox that can be used for a list of numbers or images. The ComboBox class uses a generic type parameter to define the type of data that should be used. To show the data as plain text in the selection, you can use a StringConverter. This is, in most cases, easier than writing a custom cell type to render the data onscreen. The

Property	Type	Description
`buttonCell`	`ObjectProperty<ListCell<T>>`	The defined cell is used to render the content of the `ComboBox`. To render the content of the selection pop-up, the `cellFactory` property is used.
`cellFactory`	`ObjectProperty<Callback<ListView<T>, ListCell<T>>>`	This defines a cell factory to provide custom cells for the selection pop-up.
`converter`	`ObjectProperty<StringConverter<T>>`	This converts the user-typed input of an editable `ComboBox` to an instance of `T`.
`editor`	`ReadOnlyObjectProperty<TextField>`	This is the editor for the `ComboBox`.
`items`	`ObjectProperty<ObservableList<T>>`	This is the list of items of the `ComboBox`.
`selectionModel`	`ObjectProperty<SingleSelectionModel<T>>`	This is the selection model for the `ComboBox`.
`visibleRowCount`	`IntegerProperty`	This is the maximum number of rows that are visible in the pop-up. All other rows can be accessed via scroll bars.

TABLE 6-2. *Properties of the ComboBox*

following example defines a `ComboBox` that can be used to select an `Integer`. Since this `ComboBox` is editable, the user can enter a custom number.

```
ComboBox<Integer> comboBox = new ComboBox<>();
comboBox.itemsProperty().setValue(data);
comboBox.setEditable(true);
comboBox.converterProperty().setValue(new StringConverter<Integer>() {
    @Override
    public String toString(Integer date) {
        if(date == null) {
            return null;
        }
```

```
                return date.toString();
        }
        @Override
        public Integer fromString(String string) {
            try {
                return new Integer(string);
            } catch (NumberFormatException e) {
                //TODO:
            }
        }
    });
    comboBox.valueProperty().addListener(e -> System.out.
        println("New Value: " + comboBox.getValue()));
```

Figure 6-3 shows how an editable ComboBox in the previous code will be shown onscreen. By using a generic type parameter, you define the ComboBox as ComboBox<Integer>, so only an ObservableList<Integer> can be used for the item property. To define an editable ComboBox, you set the editable property to true. Once this is done, a user could type values in the ComboBox, but these values need to be converted to String values. To do that, you need a StringConverter. In the previous code, you can see how a simple converter can look. In the sample, the exception handling is left out, but in a real application, you would add logic here to handle any String that can't convert to an Integer. The previous code can be easily converted to any value type.

ListView

You can also use the ListView<T> to render a list of data onscreen. In fact, the previous application already showed the ListView control; the ComboBox uses the ListView internally to render the content of the selection pop-up. I won't discuss how this is done internally in the

FIGURE 6-3. *An editable ComboBox*

JavaFX APIs, but the next example will show how many parallels appear between the ListView and the ComboBox. The following application defines a ListView and a ComboBox that will share a list as the data model:

```
package com.guigarage.masteringcontrols;
import javafx.application.Application;
import javafx.collections.FXCollections;
import javafx.collections.ObservableList;
import javafx.geometry.Pos;
import javafx.scene.Scene;
import javafx.scene.control.ComboBox;
import javafx.scene.control.ListView;
import javafx.scene.control.TextField;
import javafx.scene.layout.VBox;
import javafx.stage.Stage;
public class SimpleListDataDemo extends Application {
    @Override
    public void start(Stage primaryStage) throws Exception {
        ObservableList<String> data = FXCollections.observableArrayList();
        ComboBox<String> comboBox = new ComboBox<>();
        comboBox.itemsProperty().setValue(data);

        ListView<String> listView = new ListView<>();
        listView.itemsProperty().setValue(data);
        TextField inputField = new TextField();
        inputField.setPromptText("insert new data type");
        inputField.setOnAction(e -> data.add(inputField.getText()));
        VBox box = new VBox(6, inputField, comboBox, listView);
        box.setAlignment(Pos.CENTER);
        Scene myScene = new Scene(box);
        primaryStage.setScene(myScene);
        primaryStage.show();
    }
    public static void main(String[] args) {
        launch(args);
    }
}
```

This application looks a lot like the previous one, but it adds a ListView to the scene graph. The ListView control uses the defined ObservableList as its data model by setting it to the item property. As a result, the list will be used as the data model for the ComboBox and the ListView. In addition, you can use the TextField control to add items to the list. Figure 6-4 shows how the sample might look after some items are added to the list. As you can see, the ListView behaves like the select list of the ComboBox. For the ComboBox, though, a customized version of the ListView is used, and the ListView provides a lot of properties and methods to change its behavior or view. As you can see in Figure 6-4, the ListView will use a striped effect to show its content, and a user can simply select a value in the ListView.

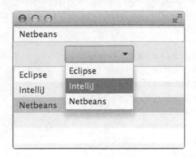

FIGURE 6-4. *A ComboBox and ListView with shared data model*

As with the `ComboBox`, the `ListView` can contain a list of data that is defined by its Generic type. This is defined by the `item` property too, but the `ListView` provides a lot of additional properties, as described in Table 6-3. In the next samples, you will see how to provide custom cells and look at the editing functionality of the `ListView`. An additional feature of the `ListView` is the ability to define a selection of multiple items. By default, the `ListView` provides a `SelectionModel` that allows only a single selection, but you can change this. How a multiple selection can be defined will be discussed later in this chapter when I talk about the `TableView`.

Custom Cells

In each of the previous applications, strings were rendered to show the content of the `ListView` or `ComboBox`. Sometimes, a completely different visualization is needed. JavaFX provides this functionality with the `Cell` class. The samples and functionality that are shown here for the `ListView` can easily be transferred to a `ComboBox`, `TableView`, or `TreeView`. All these controls provide a `cellFactory` property that can be used to create custom cell instances that are used to render the data of the given controls.

In JavaFX, a cell factory is defined as a callback. As a Java class, a cell factory must be an instance of `Callback<ListView<T>, ListCell<T>>`. This callback provides `ListCell` instances for a `ListView` to render data of type `T`. In most cases, where a `ListView` will contain one type of data and one custom `Cell` class, the definition of the factory will look like the following code snippet:

```
listView.setCellFactory(c -> new CustomListCell());
```

As you can see, the `Callback` instance provides a new instance of the `CustomListCell` class any time it is called. The `CustomListCell` class is the special cell implementation that will render the data onscreen. The cell API in JavaFX contains a lot of defined cell types. The superclass for all cells is the class `Cell`, and Figure 6-5 shows the inheritance hierarchy for the `ListCell` class that is the basic class for all cells that can be used in a `ListView`.

Property	Type	Description
cellFactory	ObjectProperty<Callback<ListView<T>, ListCell<T>>>	Defines a cell factory to provide custom cells.
editable	BooleanProperty	Defines whether the ListView is editable.
editingIndex	ReadOnlyIntegerProperty	Defines the index of the currently edited item or –1 if no item is being edited.
fixedCellSize	DoubleProperty	Defines whether all cells have a defined height. If set to a value less than or equal to zero, all cells will define its individual height.
focusModel	ObjectProperty<FocusModel<T>>	Defines the FocusModel to get or set the focus on a single item in the ListView.
items	ObjectProperty<ObservableList<T>>	Defines the items that are rendered in the ListView. This is the data model.
onEditCancel	ObjectProperty<EventHandler <ListView.EditEvent<T>>>	Defines an event handler that handles all events when the editing of an item in a cell is canceled.
onEditCommit	ObjectProperty<EventHandler <ListView.EditEvent<T>>>	Defines an event handler that handles all events when the editing of an item in a cell is commited.
onEditStart	ObjectProperty<EventHandler <ListView.EditEvent<T>>>	Defines an event handler that handles all events when the editing of an item in a cell starts.
onScrollTo	ObjectProperty<EventHandler <ScrollToEvent<Integer>>>	Defines an event handler that will be fired when the ListView should be scrolled to show a specific index.
orientation	ObjectProperty<Orientation>	Defines the orientation of the ListView.
placeholder	ObjectProperty<Node>	Defines a placeholder that is used when the ListView has no content to show.
selectionModel	ObjectProperty <MultipleSelectionModel<T>>	Defines the SelectionModel of the ListView.

TABLE 6-3. *Properties of the ListView*

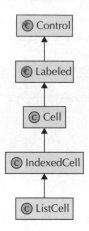

FIGURE 6-5. *Class hierarchy of cells*

Since, in most cases, a `Cell` class will be used to render plain text, it extends the abstract `Labeled` class that was described earlier in this book. The `Cell` class provides basic functionality and workflows to render an item. Each control that contains an indexed list of data that should be rendered in a specific order should use `IndexedCell` internally. This class maps the index of the defined item to its position in the data list. By doing so, instances of `IndexedCell` can handle information about the index of its internal value. The `ListCell` class also adds some special functionality that is needed when working with the `ListView`.

As a next step, a custom `ListCell` class should be created to handle and render lists of colors. The following code snippet shows a `ListView` that contains a list of colors:

```
ObservableList<Color> data = FXCollections.observableArrayList();
data.addAll(Color.ALICEBLUE, Color.ORANGE, Color.YELLOW, Color.INDIGO, Color.KHAKI);

ListView<Color> listView = new ListView<>();
listView.setItems(data);
```

But when this code is used in an application, the `ListView` will contain some cryptic text onscreen because it can't render the `Color` class. In this situation, a `Cell` class will call the `toString()` method and show its return value onscreen. Figure 6-6 shows how this may look onscreen.

To create a better output, you need a custom cell, and to create a custom cell, you must extend the `ListCell` class. Here is the code of a custom cell class that can render defined colors:

```
package com.guigarage.masteringcontrols;
import javafx.scene.control.ListCell;
import javafx.scene.paint.Color;
```

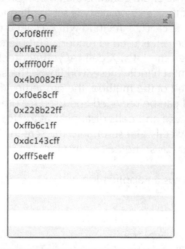

FIGURE 6-6. *Bad rendering of data in a ListView*

```
import javafx.scene.shape.Circle;
public class ColorListCell extends ListCell<Color> {
    @Override
    protected void updateItem(Color item, boolean empty) {
        super.updateItem(item, empty);
        setGraphic(null);
        setText(null);
        if (item != null) {
            setGraphic(new Circle(10, 10, 20, item));
            setText("Red: " + (int)(item.getRed() * 255.0) + ", Green: " +
                    (int)(item.getGreen() * 255.0) + ", Blue: " +
                    (int)(item.getBlue() * 255.0));
        }
    }
}
```

As you can see in the code, you use generic type parameters to specify the type of data that should be shown by this cell. The code shows the simplest way to create a custom cell. Here only the updateItem(...) method needs to be overridden. The method offers the item that should be shown by this cell. In addition, the `boolean empty` parameter is defined, which is necessary to define a difference between empty and null items. Let's suppose the list that is used as a data model of a ListView contains null as a value. In this case, null and false are passed as parameters to the method. Whenever the empty parameter is true, the cell is used to render a truly empty cell that doesn't represent an item of the data model.

Because the Cell class extends the Labeled class, you can use the graphic property here. As mentioned earlier, this property can add any node to a labeled control. In this sample, a circle shape is added to the cell. The circle contains the color represented by the cell as its fill color. Additionally, the content of the `text` property is set to plain text with some RGB information about the color. The `updateItem(...)` method will be called in different situations. Suppose the color has changed or the cell is used to render a completely different color out of the data list. This is allowed through the JavaFX cell recycling mechanism. Because of this, the `updateItem(...)` method must handle these workflows. The easiest way to do this is shown in the example: With every call of the method, the properties that are used will be reset to default values. As a result, the cell can be recycled and used for other renderings. Whenever a user scrolls in a very big `ListView` and cells disappear at the top or bottom of the list, recycling can be used to provide the new cells that scroll into the screen. Once the given `Cell` implementation is used by a `ListView` that has some `Color` instances in its data model, the result onscreen might look like Figure 6-7.

The following code shows an application with a `ListView` instance that uses the defined `Cell` class:

```
package com.guigarage.masteringcontrols;
import javafx.application.Application;
import javafx.collections.FXCollections;
import javafx.collections.ObservableList;
import javafx.scene.Scene;
import javafx.scene.control.Button;
import javafx.scene.control.ListView;
import javafx.scene.layout.StackPane;
```

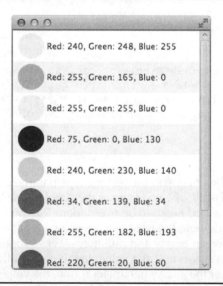

FIGURE 6-7. *A ListView with a custom Cell class*

```
import javafx.scene.paint.Color;
import javafx.stage.Stage;
public class ColorListCellDemo extends Application {
    @Override
    public void start(Stage primaryStage) throws Exception {
        ObservableList<Color> data = FXCollections.observableArrayList();
        data.addAll(Color.ALICEBLUE, Color.ORANGE, Color.YELLOW, Color.INDIGO,
                    Color.KHAKI, Color.FORESTGREEN, Color.LIGHTPINK, Color.CRIMSON,
                    Color.SEASHELL);

        ListView<Color> listView = new ListView<>();
        listView.setItems(data);
        listView.setCellFactory(c -> new ColorListCell());

        StackPane myPane = new StackPane();
        myPane.getChildren().add(listView);
        Scene myScene = new Scene(myPane);
        primaryStage.setScene(myScene);
        primaryStage.setWidth(300);
        primaryStage.setHeight(200);
        primaryStage.show();
    }
    public static void main(String[] args) {
        launch(args);
    }
}
```

As shown earlier, here you define a cell factory to use the `ColorListCell` class for the given `ListView`.

Note that JavaFX uses a completely different functionality to create a custom cell than Swing, and any developer who used custom cell rendering in Swing will find the process much improved in JavaFX. In Swing, a list or table contains only one instance of a renderer, and this renderer was used to paint all cells. In JavaFX, each `Cell` instance is a node and part of the scene graph. Internally, controls such as `ListView` or `TableView` use complex mechanisms to create new cells, add them to the scene graph, and remove them once they are no longer needed. As a result, only the cells that are visible on the screen are part of the scene graph. If a `ListView` contains a data model with 10,000 items but only 10 cells are shown in parallel on the screen, for instance, the scene graph will contain only 10 cells. As mentioned earlier, the cells could be recycled, in which case Java doesn't need to create new instances for each cell and the controls can handle a big data model without a loss of performance. Later in the chapter, I'll cover the improvements to editing the content of a cell.

Before describing how the content of a `ListView` can be edited by the user, let's look at an overview of the properties and methods of the cell classes. Some of these methods are needed to allow a user to edit a value. Table 6-4 describes all the necessary methods of the `Cell` class, and Table 6-5 describes all the properties that are defined by the class.

In addition to these properties, the `IndexedCell` class contains the `index` property, which can be used to receive the index of the defined item. The property is defined as `ReadOnlyIntegerProperty`. Finally, the `ListCell` contains the `listView` property. This property is defined as `ReadOnlyObjectProperty<ListView<T>>` and can be used to receive the `ListView` instance in which the cell is used.

Method	Description
`void updateItem(T item, boolean empty)`	This method will be called whenever the item of the cell has changed. You will normally not call this method but you will need it when implementing custom cell types. In this case you can override the method to handle the new data and visualize it.
`void startEdit()`	When this method is called, the cell will go into the editing state.
`void commitEdit(T newValue)`	When this method is called, the cell will leave the editing state, and the new value will be committed.
`void cancelEdit()`	When this method is called, the cell will leave the editing state. All changes will be canceled.

TABLE 6-4.   *Methods of the Cell Class*

Editing the Content of a ListView

The `ListView` provides the functionality to edit items of the data model through the cells in the `ListView`. To set a `ListView` to editable, only the value of the `editable` property needs to be set to true:

```
listView.setEditable(true);
```

Now the `ListView` will handle user input, such as a mouse double-click, to start editing mode. The default cell implementation that is used by the `ListView` doesn't support editing, but you can check the editing support of a `Cell` instance by looking at its `editable` property. So, if a `ListView` is needed so that a value of the data model can be changed by the user, the `ListView` and the `Cell` instance that renders the item need to be editable. JavaFX provides some basic `Cell` implementations that can be used directly to support editing. The simplest

Property	Type	Description
`editing`	`ReadOnlyBooleanProperty`	This defines whether the cell is in editing mode.
`editable`	`BooleanProperty`	This defines whether the cell is editable.
`empty`	`ReadOnlyBooleanProperty`	If this property is true, the cell has no content.
`item`	`ObjectProperty<T>`	This defines the data that should be rendered by the cell.
`selected`	`ReadOnlyBooleanProperty`	This defines whether the cell is selected.

TABLE 6-5.   *Properties of the Cell Class*

way is to use the TextFieldListCell, which provides a TextField in editing mode. This TextField will be shown in the cell whenever editing is starts. Once editing stops, the cell will return to the default representation shown earlier. Here is a simple example that uses the TextFieldListCell class to provide editing:

```java
package com.guigarage.masteringcontrols;
import javafx.application.Application;
import javafx.collections.FXCollections;
import javafx.collections.ObservableList;
import javafx.scene.Scene;
import javafx.scene.control.ListView;
import javafx.scene.control.cell.TextFieldListCell;
import javafx.scene.layout.StackPane;
import javafx.stage.Stage;
public class EditableListDemo extends Application {
    public static void main(String[] args) {
        launch(args);
    }
    @Override
    public void start(Stage primaryStage) throws Exception {
        ObservableList<String> data = FXCollections.observableArrayList();
        data.addAll("Franky", "Private", "Steve", "Murphy", "Junior");
        ListView<String> listView = new ListView<>();
        listView.setItems(data);
        listView.setCellFactory(TextFieldListCell.forListView());
        listView.setEditable(true);
        StackPane myPane = new StackPane();
        myPane.getChildren().add(listView);
        Scene myScene = new Scene(myPane);
        primaryStage.setScene(myScene);
        primaryStage.setWidth(300);
        primaryStage.setHeight(200);
        primaryStage.show();
    }
}
```

Whenever a user double-clicks a cell in the ListView, a TextField appears, and the user can change the String item. This is shown in Figure 6-8. As you can see in the code, most of the Cell implementations that are part of JavaFX provide static methods that can be used to define a cell factory. These methods return a Callback instance. A TextFieldListCell can also be used for any other data type in addition to String instances. In this case, you need the definition of a StringConverter, which I discussed in the earlier review of the ComboBox.

Besides the TextFieldListCell, JavaFX provides three additional cell types that can be used to edit the content of a cell, shown here:

- ChoiceBoxListCell
- CheckBoxListCell
- ComboBoxListCell

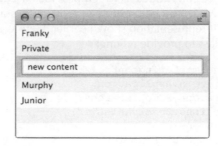

FIGURE 6-8. *Editing a value in a ListView*

I'll use the `CheckBoxListCell` in an example. The `ChoiceBoxListCell` and `ComboBoxListCell` behave similarly. These different types of cells are also provided for the `TreeView` and `TableView` in JavaFX and won't be discussed in detail in this book; just remember that you can use them in the same way as shown here for a `ListView`. The following source code shows how to use a `CheckBoxListCell`:

```
package com.guigarage.masteringcontrols;
import javafx.application.Application;
import javafx.beans.property.SimpleBooleanProperty;
import javafx.beans.value.ObservableValue;
import javafx.collections.FXCollections;
import javafx.collections.ObservableList;
import javafx.scene.Scene;
import javafx.scene.control.ListView;
import javafx.scene.control.cell.CheckBoxListCell;
import javafx.scene.layout.StackPane;
import javafx.stage.Stage;
import javafx.util.Callback;
public class EditableListDemo extends Application {
    public static void main(String[] args) {
        launch(args);
    }
    @Override
    public void start(Stage primaryStage) throws Exception {
        ObservableList<String> data = FXCollections.observableArrayList();
        data.addAll("Boot", "Bootie", "Kitten Heel", "Mary Jane", "Peep toe", "Pump",
                "Stiletto");
        ListView<String> listView = new ListView<>();
        listView.setItems(data);
        listView.setCellFactory(c -> new CheckBoxListCell<>
                            (createSelectionCallback()));
        listView.setEditable(true);
        StackPane myPane = new StackPane();
        myPane.getChildren().add(listView);
        Scene myScene = new Scene(myPane);
        primaryStage.setScene(myScene);
```

```
            primaryStage.setWidth(300);
            primaryStage.setHeight(200);
            primaryStage.setTitle("Silkes shoe list");
            primaryStage.show();
    }
    private Callback<String, ObservableValue<Boolean>> createSelectionCallback() {
        SimpleBooleanProperty selectionProperty = new SimpleBooleanProperty(false);
        return (param) -> {
            selectionProperty.addListener((e) -> {
                if (selectionProperty.get()) {
                    System.out.println("Shoe " + param + " is added to selection");
                } else {
                    System.out.println("Shoe " + param + "is removed from selection");
                }
            });
            return selectionProperty;
        };
    }
}
```

Figure 6-9 shows the output of this source code. The `CheckBoxListCell` needs an additional `Callback` instance to bind the items of the cell to `Boolean` values. The callback is defined by the `selectedStateCallback` property. This callback is needed to bind `Boolean` properties to the item that is rendered in the cell. The cell renders a `CheckBox` for each item, and whenever the selection of the `CheckBox` is changed, the `ObservableValue<Boolean>` that is created by the callback will change its value. In the sample, the callback is created by the `createSelectionCallback()` method. The callback implementation registers a `ChangeListener` to the `ObservableValue`, and each change will be printed to the console.

The item that is represented by the cell won't change here. Only the bound `Boolean` value will change. So, the `CheckBoxListCell` doesn't use the default editing mode of the `Cell` class. Table 6-6 describes the properties that are defined by the `CheckBoxListCell` class.

FIGURE 6-9. *Usage of CheckBoxListCell*

Property	Type	Description
converter	ObjectProperty<StringConverter<T>>	Defines a StringConverter to convert any object to a String that can be rendered in the cell
selectedStateCallback	ObjectProperty<Callback<T, ObservableValue<Boolean>>>	Defines the callback that is used to handle the Boolean selection state of the CheckBox

TABLE 6-6. *Properties of the CheckBoxListCell*

In addition to all the default implementations that are part of JavaFX, it is possible to create custom editable cells. To see how cell editing is done internally, you must extend the custom ColorListCell to provide for editing colors. The following code shows how an editable cell might look:

```
package com.guigarage.masteringcontrols;
import javafx.scene.control.Button;
import javafx.scene.control.Label;
import javafx.scene.control.ListCell;
import javafx.scene.control.TextField;
import javafx.scene.layout.VBox;
import javafx.scene.paint.Color;
import javafx.scene.shape.Circle;
public class ColorListCell extends ListCell<Color> {
    @Override
    protected void updateItem(Color item, boolean empty) {
        super.updateItem(item, empty);
        updateViewMode();
    }
    private void updateViewMode() {
        setGraphic(null);
        setText(null);
        if (isEditing()) {
            VBox box = new VBox();
            Label redLabel = new Label("Red:");
            Label greenLabel = new Label("Green:");
            Label blueLabel = new Label("Blue:");
            TextField redTextField = new TextField();
            TextField greenTextField = new TextField();
            TextField blueTextField = new TextField();
            if (getItem() != null) {
                redTextField.setText((int) (getItem().getRed() * 255) + "");
```

```
                greenTextField.setText((int) (getItem().getGreen() * 255) + "");
                blueTextField.setText((int) (getItem().getBlue() * 255) + "");
            }
            Button setColorButton = new Button("SET");
            setColorButton.setOnAction((e) -> commitEdit(Color.rgb(new
                Integer(redTextField.getText()),
                    new Integer(greenTextField.getText()),
                    new Integer(blueTextField.getText()))));
            box.getChildren().addAll(redLabel, redTextField, greenLabel,
                greenTextField, blueLabel, blueTextField, setColorButton);
            setGraphic(box);
        } else {
            if (getItem() != null) {
                setGraphic(new Circle(10, 10, 20, getItem()));
                setText("Red: " + (int) (getItem().getRed() * 255.0) + ", Green: "
                    + (int) (getItem().getGreen() * 255.0) + ", Blue: " + (int)
                    (getItem().getBlue() * 255.0));
            }
        }
    }
    @Override
    public void startEdit() {
        super.startEdit();
        updateViewMode();
    }
}
```

The code of the class is now much bigger; it adds the new method `updateViewMode()`. The `ColorListCell` as described in this code defines two different views: One view shows a color item as it was defined earlier, and whenever the cell is in editing mode, the user is presented with a completely different view. Figure 6-10 shows how the cell will look in editing and nonediting modes.

The `updateViewMode()` method checks whether the cell is currently in editing mode and adds the needed nodes to the cell. In editing mode, three `TextFields` are used. A user can change the RGB information of the color items with the help of these three `TextFields`. In addition, a `Button` control is added. Whenever a user clicks this button, the changes that are made in the `TextFields` will be committed, and a new color is set as the item of the cell. When doing this, the underlying data model that is an `ObservableList<Color>` instance in this case will contain the edited item. To commit the changes that are made while editing, the `commitEdit(T newValue)` method needs to be called. If all changes should be canceled, the `cancelEdit()` method should be called. In the given demo, only the `commitEdit(...)` method is used. In addition to the Set button, a Cancel button should be used that calls `cancelEdit()` on an action event. To make the demo more user-friendly, you could add an event handler to the `TextFields` too. Here is a code snippet that defines an additional handler:

```
blueTextField.setOnAction((e) -> commitEdit(Color.rgb(new
Integer(redTextField.getText()),
                    new Integer(greenTextField.getText()),
                    new Integer(blueTextField.getText()))));
```

One last change that is made in the `ColorListCell` class is the special implementation of the `startEdit()` method. As mentioned earlier, this method will be called whenever the editing

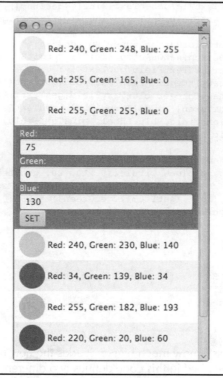

FIGURE 6-10. *Editing values in a custom Cell implementation*

mode of the cell starts. This method simply calls the new `updateViewMode()` method to show the editing view of the cell. The `commitEdit(T newValue)` and `cancelEdit()` methods do not need to be overridden because they result in a call of `updateItem(Color item, boolean empty)`, and all changes will be handled by this method.

As you can see, JavaFX and the cell API provide all the functionality that is needed to create custom and editable cells. As a benefit, all the workflows and functionalities that are used here can be reused for the `TableView`, `TreeView`, and `TreeTableView`, so I won't show additional examples in those respective sections.

Using the Selection Model of a ListView

A selection model is used to handle the selection of a `ListView`. A selection model for a `ListView` is defined by the `MultipleSelectionModel<T>` class and can be accessed by the `selectionModel` property of the `ListView`. A `MultipleSelectionModel` contains the selected indexes of a `ListView`. By default, only one entry can be selected in a `ListView`. The index of the selected cell and the data that is defined for the selected entry can be accessed by the selection model. Here, the `selectedIndex` property of type `ReadOnlyIntegerProperty` and the `selectedItem` property of type `ReadOnlyObjectProperty<T>` are defined. By using these properties, you can bind the selection of a `ListView` to the content of a `TextField`, for example. The following code defines a `ListView` and a `TextField` and creates a binding:

```
ObservableList<String> data = FXCollections.observableArrayList();
    data.addAll("The Bones", "Emil Bulls", "Story of the Year", "Trust Company",
    "The Used");

ListView<String> list = new ListView<>(data);

TextField textField = new TextField();
textField.setEditable(false);

textField.textProperty().bind(list.getSelectionModel().selectedItemProperty());
```

Whenever the user changes the selection in the `ListView`, the text in the `TextField` will automatically be updated to the selected entry.

NOTE
Both of the properties that are described here are part of the abstract SelectionModel<T> class. All selection models that are used in the JavaFX controls APIs extend this class. As mentioned, the ListView uses MultipleSelectionModel<T>, which extends the abstract class too.

As shown, the `ListView` supports the selection of only one entry by default. This can be changed by setting the `selectionMode` property of the `MultipleSelectionModel` instance. To define the different selection types, you use the `SelectionMode` enum. A `ListView` can handle single or multiple selections. You can activate multiple selections in a `TableView` by using the following code:

```
listView.getSelectionModel().setSelectionMode(SelectionMode.MULTIPLE);
```

Once you define multiple selection, a user can select more than one entry in the `ListView`. The selection is stored in the `MultipleSelectionModel` instance. The class provides two `ObservableList` instances that can be accessed to the selected indices and the corresponding values of the underlying data model, as shown here:

```
ObservableList<String> data = FXCollections.observableArrayList();
data.addAll("Wood", "Iron", "Water", "Fire");

ListView<String> list = new ListView<>(data);
list.getSelectionModel().setSelectionMode(SelectionMode.MULTIPLE);

ListView<String> boundedList = new ListView<>(list.getSelectionModel().
    getSelectedItems());
```

In the code snippet, the `ObservableList` that contains the selected entries of a `ListView` is used as the data model of a second `ListView`. When trying this code at run time, the content of the second list will change whenever the selection in the first list changes.

Because the selection model of a `ListView` is defined as an instance of the `MultipleSelectionModel` in the `ListView` instance and it can be accessed and set by the `selectionModel` property, it can be shared between different `Control` instances. The following sample defines two `ListView` controls that internally use the same selection model. A selection in one of the lists will automatically update the selection in the second list.

```
package com.guigarage.masteringcontrols;
import javafx.application.Application;
import javafx.collections.FXCollections;
import javafx.collections.ObservableList;
import javafx.geometry.Insets;
import javafx.geometry.Pos;
import javafx.scene.Scene;
import javafx.scene.control.ListView;
import javafx.scene.layout.VBox;
import javafx.stage.Stage;

public class ListSelectionDemo extends Application {

    @Override
    public void start(Stage primaryStage) throws Exception {
        ObservableList<String> data = FXCollections.observableArrayList();
        data.addAll("Wood", "Iron", "Water", "Fire");
        ListView<String> list = new ListView<>(data);
        ListView<String> secondList = new ListView<>(data);
        secondList.setSelectionModel(list.getSelectionModel());
        VBox myPane = new VBox();
        myPane.setAlignment(Pos.CENTER);
        myPane.setPadding(new Insets(12));
        myPane.setSpacing(12);
        myPane.getChildren().addAll(list, secondList);
        Scene myScene = new Scene(myPane);
        primaryStage.setScene(myScene);
        primaryStage.show();
    }
    public static void main(String[] args) {
        launch(args);
    }
}
```

TableView

Like `ListView`, the `TableView<T>` control can represent lists of data. To understand the workflow of a `TableView`, refer to the previous `ListView` description; most of the basic workflows are the same in both controls and not described here again.

Defining Columns

The `TableView` provides columns that can show the underlying data in more detail. You define columns using the `TableColumn` class and add them to a `TableView`, as shown here:

```
TableView table = new TableView();


TableColumn firstNameCol = new TableColumn("First Name");
TableColumn lastNameCol = new TableColumn("Last Name");
TableColumn jobColumn = new TableColumn("Job");


table.getColumns().addAll(firstNameCol, lastNameCol, jobColumn);
```

The `TableColumn` class extends the `TableColumnBase` class that contains basic methods that are shared between the `TableView` and the `TreeTableView`.

In addition, JavaFX supports nested columns, which can be useful to group related data. Therefore, a `TableColumn` instance can hold internal columns. This is shown in the following code snippet:

```
TableColumn firstNameColumn = new TableColumn("First Name");
TableColumn lastNameColumn = new TableColumn("Last Name");

TableColumn nameColumn = new TableColumn("Name");
nameColumn.getColumns().addAll(firstNameColumn, lastNameColumn);

TableColumn jobColumn = new TableColumn("Job");

table.getColumns().addAll(nameColumn, jobColumn);
```

In this example, the Name column contains two subcolumns. Figure 6-11 shows how a `TableView` that is created with these columns will look.

Filling a TableView with Custom Data

Like the `ListView`, the `TableView` defines an `items` property of type `ObjectProperty<Obser vableList<S>>`. This property will hold the data that is shown in the table. The next example shows a Java class that is created to define the data model:

```
public class Person {
    private String firstName;
    private String lastName;
    private String job;

    public Person(String firstName, String lastName, String job) {
        this.firstName = firstName;
        this.lastName = lastName;
        this.job = job;
    }
```

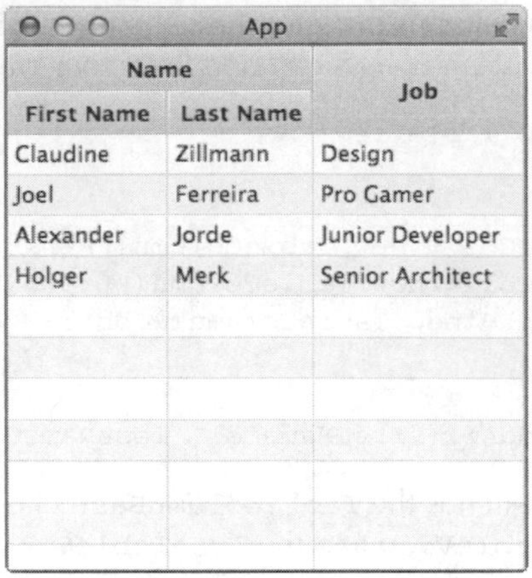

FIGURE 6-11. *A TableView*

```
    public String getFirstName() {
        return firstName;
    }
    public void setFirstName(String firstName) {
        this.firstName = firstName;
    }
    public String getLastName() {
        return lastName;
    }
    public void setLastName(String lastName) {
        this.lastName = lastName;
    }
    public String getJob() {
        return job;
    }
    public void setJob(String job) {
        this.job = job;
    }
}
```

As you can see in the code, the `Person` class defines fields that map to the columns of the `TableView`. As a next step, these bean properties of the class need to link to the columns of the table. The `TableColumn` class provides the `cellValueFactory` property. This property is defined as `ObjectProperty<Callback<CellDataFeatures<S,T>, ObservableValue<T>>>` and must be used to create a mapping between the column and the data. JavaFX contains the `PropertyValueFactory` class that can be used here. The following code shows how the `firstName` bean property of the `Person` class can link to a column of a table:

```
firstNameColumn.setCellValueFactory(
            new PropertyValueFactory<Person,String>("firstName")
    );
```

Internally, the Java reflection API is used to show the underlying data onscreen. You create the `PropertyValueFactory` by passing the `firstName` String to the constructor, and this String defines a bean property in the class of the data model, which is `Person` in this case. The class must provide a getter method for the bean property to access the data that should be shown in the cell.

NOTE
The cell value factory uses the `CellDataFeatures` internally. This class is a helper class that wraps all information that is needed for the callback. A `CellDataFeatures` instance contains the `TableView` instance, the `TableColumn` instance, and the data that is represented by the current row.

You can create a simple application that uses all the described functionalities with just a few lines of code. The next code uses the features I just covered and creates a simple table with tree columns and some lines of data:

```java
import javafx.application.Application;
import javafx.collections.FXCollections;
import javafx.collections.ObservableList;
import javafx.scene.Scene;
import javafx.scene.control.TableColumn;
import javafx.scene.control.TableView;
import javafx.scene.control.cell.PropertyValueFactory;
import javafx.scene.layout.StackPane;
import javafx.stage.Stage;

public class TableDemo extends Application {
    @Override
    public void start(Stage primaryStage) throws Exception {
        ObservableList<Person> data = FXCollections.observableArrayList(
                new Person("Claudine", "Zillmann", "Design"),
                new Person("Joel", "Ferreira", "Pro Gamer"),
                new Person("Alexander", "Jorde", "Junior Developer"),
                new Person("Holger", "Merk", "Senior Architect")
        );
        TableView<Person> table = new TableView<>();
        table.itemsProperty().setValue(data);
        TableColumn<Person, String> firstNameColumn = new TableColumn<>("First Name");
        TableColumn<Person, String> lastNameColumn = new TableColumn<>("Last Name");
        TableColumn<Person, String> jobColumn = new TableColumn<>("Job");
        firstNameColumn.setCellValueFactory(
                new PropertyValueFactory<Person,String>("firstName")
        );
        lastNameColumn.setCellValueFactory(
                new PropertyValueFactory<Person,String>("lastName")
        );
        jobColumn.setCellValueFactory(
                new PropertyValueFactory<Person,String>("job")
        );
        table.getColumns().addAll(firstNameColumn, lastNameColumn, jobColumn);
        StackPane myPane = new StackPane();
        myPane.getChildren().add(table);
        Scene myScene = new Scene(myPane);
```

```
        primaryStage.setScene(myScene);
        primaryStage.setTitle("App");
        primaryStage.setWidth(300);
        primaryStage.setHeight(200);
        primaryStage.show();
    }
    public static void main(String[] args) {
        launch(args);
    }
}
```

The `PropertyValueFactory` class is the fastest way to show specific data in a `TableColumn`. But internally the class uses reflection, and the name of a bean property has to be defined as a String. This creates code that can't be refactored by an IDE. Once the field in the `Person` class is renamed, the `firstName` has to be changed manually. In addition, using reflection will result in a loss of performance. Thanks to the JavaFX property API and lambda support, you can create the binding in a better way. The following code snippet shows how a `cellValueFactory` property can be defined without using reflection:

```
firstNameColumn.setCellValueFactory((e) -> new SimpleStringProperty(e.
    getValue().getFirstName()));
```

Here, you create a `SimpleStringProperty` that acts as a wrapper for the current `firstName` value of the underlying data. If you use this approach, you do not need reflection. Sadly, this code has another problem. Whenever the underlying `firstName` bean property is changed, the `TableColumn` won't be updated. Therefore, it is best to use the JavaFX property API directly in the data model. So, the `Person` class needs to be refactored, as shown here:

```
public class Person {
    private SimpleStringProperty firstName;
    private SimpleStringProperty lastName;
    private SimpleStringProperty job;
    public Person(String firstName, String lastName, String job) {
        this.firstName = new SimpleStringProperty(firstName);
        this.lastName = new SimpleStringProperty(lastName);
        this.job = new SimpleStringProperty(job);

        this.firstName.addListener((e) -> System.out.println("First Name
            changed to " + this.firstName.get()));
        this.lastName.addListener((e) -> System.out.println("Last Name changed
            to " + this.lastName.get()));
        this.job.addListener((e) -> System.out.println("Job changed to " +
            this.job.get()));
    }
    public StringProperty firstNameProperty() {
        return firstName;
    }
    public StringProperty lastNameProperty() {
        return lastName;
    }
    public StringProperty jobProperty() {
        return job;
    }
```

```java
    public String getFirstName() {
        return firstName.get();
    }
    public void setFirstName(String firstName) {
        this.firstName.set(firstName);
    }
    public String getJob() {
        return job.get();
    }
    public void setJob(String job) {
        this.job.set(job);
    }
    public String getLastName() {
        return lastName.get();
    }
    public void setLastName(String lastName) {
        this.lastName.set(lastName);
    }
}
```

NOTE

In the constructor of the class, some listeners are registered to the internal properties. This is done for debugging reasons. When running the following demos, the editing of the content in a TableView will be shown. Here the data in the Person instances will be changed. To check this behavior, some logging output will be printed to the console by these listeners.

Now the cellValueFactory property of the firstNameColumn can be defined, as shown in the following code snippet:

```java
firstNameColumn.setCellValueFactory((e) -> e.getValue().firstNameProperty());
```

By creating a data model of this and using the properties of the data model directly for the cellValueFactory, the properties are bound to the TableColumn, and changes will be shown directly onscreen.

Adding Different Cell Types to a TableView

The content of a TableColumn is rendered by a cell, as was described for the ListView. When using a TableView, all cell instances need to extend the TableCell class. Instead of defining a cell factory for the complete control, each TableColumn can reference its own factory. To see this functionality, you add a new property to the Person class:

```java
public class Person {

    ...


    private SimpleBooleanProperty employeeOfTheMonth;
```

```
        public Person(String firstName, String lastName, String job, boolean
                   employeeOfTheMonth) {
           this.firstName = new SimpleStringProperty(firstName);
           this.lastName = new SimpleStringProperty(lastName);
           this.job = new SimpleStringProperty(job);
           this.employeeOfTheMonth = new SimpleBooleanProperty(employeeOfTheMonth);}
        public SimpleBooleanProperty employeeOfTheMonthProperty() {
           return employeeOfTheMonth;
    }
}
```

In the sample, a `TableColumn` is added to the `TableView` too. The following code snippet contains the needed new lines in the class:

```
TableColumn<ExtendedPerson, Boolean> employeeOfTheMonthColumn = new
TableColumn<>("Employee of the month");
employeeOfTheMonthColumn.setCellValueFactory((e) -> e.getValue().
   employeeOfTheMonthProperty());

table.getColumns().add(employeeOfTheMonthColumn);
```

Once the application is running, "true" and "false" are shown as data in the new column. To represent these data entries in a better way, though, you need another cell type. Specifically, JavaFX contains a `CheckBox`-based cell for the `TableView`: the `CheckBoxTableCell` class. The class provides some static methods that can be used to create the needed instance. The following code snippet defines a `CheckBoxTableCell` instance for the new cell:

```
employeeOfTheMonthColumn.setCellFactory(CheckBoxTableCell.forTableColumn((i)
   -> data.get(i).employeeOfTheMonthProperty()));
```

Because the `CheckBoxTableCell` class is designed in a general way and can be used in different ways, a custom callback is needed that returns the `BooleanProperty` that should be shown in the cell.

NOTE
In addition to the `TableColumn` class, the `TableView` uses the `TableRow` class internally. A `TableRow` instance defines a row in the table and can be created by the `Callback` instance that is defined by the `rowFactory` property of the `TableView` class. Usually, you don't need to work with this class because often a `TableView` can be customized by using the `TableColumn` class and custom cells. Only experts should work with the `TableRow` class.

Editing the Content of a Cell

Like the `ListView`, a `TableView` can be used to edit data; you just need to define the `TableView` as editable, and the used columns and cells must support the editing of its values. For the example, you need a different cell type for all columns that show String data because the default cell type doesn't support editing.

To support editing, the following properties must define a true `Boolean` value:

- `editable` property of the `TableView`
- `editable` property of the `TableColumn`
- `editable` property of the `TableCell`

The `TableColumn` instance is editable by default. So, you need to set only the `TableView` property. But, as mentioned, you need another `Cell` class too. JavaFX provides editing with the `TextFieldTableCell` class. This can be used to edit String content in a table. Here are the additional lines of code that must be added to the example to provide edit functionality for the `TableView`:

```
firstNameColumn.setCellFactory(TextFieldTableCell.forTableColumn());
lastNameColumn.setCellFactory(TextFieldTableCell.forTableColumn());
jobColumn.setCellFactory(TextFieldTableCell.forTableColumn());


table.setEditable(true);
```

The cell factory that is used for the `employeeOfTheMonthColumn` already supports editing and doesn't need to change. Once this is done, all data in the `TableView` can be edited. Because all columns are bound to the properties of the `Person` instances, the data model will be changed. So, if you share the `ObservableList<Person>` data in this sample in different controls, you can see the changes on the fly.

To show the support of custom cells, I will add a column to the `TableView`. This column will be special because it won't render additional data. Instead, it will contain a `Button` control that can be clicked to delete the complete data entry. To do this, I need a custom cell class that extends the `TableCell` class, as shown here:

```
package com.guigarage.masteringcontrols;
import javafx.scene.control.Button;
import javafx.scene.control.TableCell;
import java.util.function.Consumer;

public class ActionTableCell<S> extends TableCell<S, Void> {

    private Button button;


    public ActionTableCell(String text, Consumer<Integer> action) {
        button = new Button(text);
        button.setOnAction((e) -> action.accept(getIndex()));
        setAlignment(Pos.CENTER);
    }

    @Override
    protected void updateItem(Void item, boolean empty) {
        setGraphic(null);
        if (!empty) {
```

```
            setGraphic(button);
        }
    }
}
```

Internally, the cell will contain a button that shows the text that is passed to the constructor of the `ActionTableCell` class. Whenever the button is clicked, a custom action will be handled. This action will call a custom `Consumer`, which needs to be defined in the constructor too. The current index of the table row will be passed as input value to the `Consumer`. With the help of this general class, a cell can be created that deletes a row of the data model by clicking the internal button. Here is the code snippet that adds the cell to the table:

```
TableColumn<Person, Void> deleteColumn = new TableColumn<>("Delete");
deleteColumn.setCellFactory((c) -> new ActionTableCell<ExtendedPerson>("X",
    (i) -> data.remove(i.intValue())));
table.getColumns().add(deleteColumn);
```

The new `TableColumn` doesn't need a `cellValueFactory` because no data is shown in the cells. The `Consumer` that is passed to the `ActionTableCell` removes the correct instance from the underlying data.

After some changes, the sample defines some columns with different cell types. In addition, the data in the table can be edited and rows can be deleted. The following code shows the complete application with all the features:

```
package com.guigarage.masteringcontrols;

import javafx.application.Application;
import javafx.collections.FXCollections;
import javafx.collections.ObservableList;
import javafx.scene.Scene;
import javafx.scene.control.TableColumn;
import javafx.scene.control.TableView;
import javafx.scene.control.cell.CheckBoxTableCell;
import javafx.scene.control.cell.TextFieldTableCell;
import javafx.scene.layout.StackPane;
import javafx.stage.Stage;

public class TableDemo2 extends Application {

    @Override
    public void start(Stage primaryStage) throws Exception {
        ObservableList<Person> data = FXCollections.observableArrayList(
                new Person("Claudine", "Zillmann", "Design", true),
                new Person("Joel", "Ferreira", "Pro Gamer", false),
                new Person("Alexander", "Jorde", "Junior Developer", false),
                new Person("Holger", "Merk", "Senior Architect", false)
        );
        TableView<Person> table = new TableView<>();
        table.itemsProperty().setValue(data);
```

```
TableColumn<Person, String> firstNameColumn = new TableColumn<>("First Name");
TableColumn<Person, String> lastNameColumn = new TableColumn<>("Last Name");
TableColumn<Person, String> jobColumn = new TableColumn<>("Job");
TableColumn<Person, Boolean> employeeOfTheMonthColumn = new
    TableColumn<>("Employee of the month");
TableColumn<Person, Void> deleteColumn = new TableColumn<>("Delete");

firstNameColumn.setCellValueFactory((e) -> e.getValue().firstNameProperty());
lastNameColumn.setCellValueFactory((e) -> e.getValue().lastNameProperty());
jobColumn.setCellValueFactory((e) -> e.getValue().jobProperty());
employeeOfTheMonthColumn.setCellValueFactory((e) -> e.getValue().
    employeeOfTheMonthProperty());

firstNameColumn.setCellFactory(TextFieldTableCell.forTableColumn());
lastNameColumn.setCellFactory(TextFieldTableCell.forTableColumn());
jobColumn.setCellFactory(TextFieldTableCell.forTableColumn());
employeeOfTheMonthColumn.setCellFactory(CheckBoxTableCell.forTableColumn((i)
    -> data.get(i).employeeOfTheMonthProperty()));
deleteColumn.setCellFactory((c) -> new ActionTableCell<Person>("X", (i) ->
    data.remove(i.intValue())));

table.setEditable(true);
table.getColumns().addAll(firstNameColumn, lastNameColumn, jobColumn,
    employeeOfTheMonthColumn, deleteColumn);

StackPane myPane = new StackPane();
myPane.getChildren().add(table);
Scene myScene = new Scene(myPane);
primaryStage.setScene(myScene);
primaryStage.show();
    }

    public static void main(String[] args) {
        launch(args);
    }
}
```

Figure 6-12 displays the application.

Sorting Data

The TableView provides the functionality to sort its underlying data. Usually, the data will be sorted when a user clicks a column header. In this case, the data of a TableView will be sorted by the functionality that is defined for the column. With a second click on the column header, the sorting order will be changed from ascending to descending. A third click will disable the sorting. By pressing the SHIFT key while clicking the headers, the user can sort the data of a TableView by multiple columns. Here the priority of each column in the sort operation will be specified by the order in which the columns are clicked. The TableColumnBase class provides the sortable property that can be used to deactivate the sorting functionality for a column.

You can use the basic sorting functionality of a TableView for all data that is comparable. This means the data class must implement the java.lang.Comparable interface. Sometimes you may have defined a custom data type in a table column and want to sort it too. In those

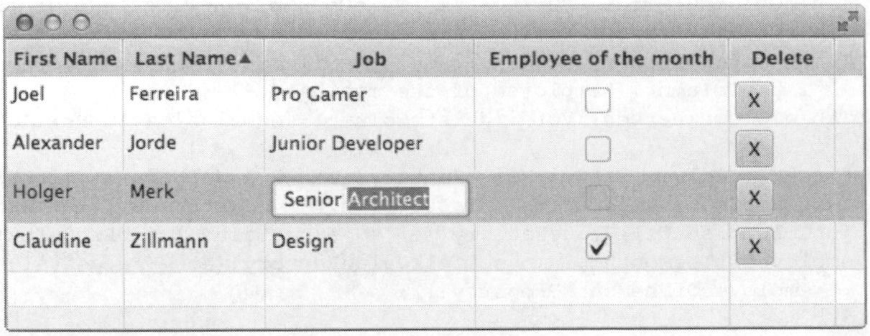

FIGURE 6-12. *The TableView as defined in the sample*

cases, you can use the `comparator` property of a column. Let's use the following enum in a table and sort it:

```
public enum Priority {
    MEDIUM, HIGH, LOW;
}
```

To do this, you must define a custom `Comparator`. You can set this `Comparator` to the `comparator` property of the table cell, as shown here:

```
TableColumn<Data, Priority> priorityColumn = new TableColumn<>("Priority");
priorityColumn.setComparator((Priority p1, Priority p2) -> {
    if(p1.equals(p2)) {return 0;}
    if(p1.equals(Priority.HIGH)) {return 1;}
    if(p1.equals(Priority.MEDIUM) && p2.equals(Priority.LOW)) {return 1;}
    return -1;
});
```

Whenever a user clicks the header of the Priority column, the defined `Comparator` instance will be used to sort the data of the table. To change the default sort order, you can use the `sortType` property of the `TableColumn` class. Therefore, JavaFX contains the `SortType` enum that defines the ascending and descending sort order:

```
priorityColumn.setSortType(TableColumn.SortType.DESCENDING);
```

Note that to change the complete sort behavior of a table, you can use the `sortPolicy` property of the `TableView`. The `sortPolicy` property defines a `Callback` that internally executes the sorting of a table. By default, a `Callback` is used here that just calls `FXCollections.sort(tableView.getItems())`. The priority order of the columns can be accessed by using the `getSortOrder()` method of the `TableView` too.

NOTE
The sorting of a table won't affect the underlying data model. The indices of the items in the `ObservableList` *that is defined as the model of the* `TableView` *won't change when a user sorts the content of a* `TableView`. *The sorting will affect only the visual representation of the content.*

How the Selection Model Works

The `TableViewSelectionModel<S>` class that is used to define the selection model of a `TableView` extends the `MultipleSelectionModel<T>` class that was discussed when talking about the selection in a `ListView` and adds some features. The basic features can be used like it was shown for the `ListView`. A single row or multiple rows can be selected in a table by the user. In addition, the `TableViewSelectionModel` provides the selection of single cells. To do this, you must set the `cellSelectionEnabled` property to true. Once this is done, a user can select a single cell or multiple cells. Furthermore, the selection model of the `TableView` contains some useful methods that can be used to select ranges of cells or to move the selection to the top, bottom, left, or right cell of the currently selected one.

To access the selected data when cell selection is active, the `TableViewSelectionModel` provides the `getSelectedCells()` method that returns a `ObservableList<TablePosition>`. The `TablePosition` class defines the row and column of the selected cell. It is important to know that the indices that are used here define the row indices as shown onscreen. When a table is sorted, these values don't match the indices of the underlying data model. Instead, an index is always defined as it is shown onscreen. Converter methods such as those provided in Swing to convert a view index to a model index are currently not part of JavaFX. There is a workaround for this topic that I will show later in this chapter when I discuss the `SortedList` class.

NOTE
The `TableViewSelectionModel` *class extends the* `TableSelectionModel` *class that contains basic functionality. This class extends the* `MultipleSelectionModelBase` *class. The* `MultipleSelectionModel` *that is used as the selection model in the* `ListView` *is the superclass of the* `MultipleSelectionModelBase` *class. As you can see, there is a complex class hierarchy defined for the selection models of different control types. You can see the benefit of this when developing custom controls that need a selection model. You use the base class that matches the needed functionality.*

Additional Table API Properties

The classes of the `TableView` API that are used in the samples provide properties that have not been covered in this chapter, so the following tables contain an overview of these properties. Table 6-7 describes all properties of the `TableView` class, and Table 6-8 and Table 6-9 describe the properties of the abstract `TableColumnBase` and `TableColumn` classes. In addition, Table 6-10 contains the properties of the `TableCell`.

Property	Type	Description
columnResizePolicy	ObjectProperty<Callback <ResizeFeatures, Boolean>>	The Callback is called when the user completes a column resize.
comparator	ReadOnlyObjectProperty <Comparator<S>>	This property represents the current state of the sort order list.
editable	BooleanProperty	This defines whether the TableView is editable.
editingCell	ReadOnlyObjectProperty <TablePosition<S,?>>	This defines the cell that is currently being edited.
fixedCellSize	DoubleProperty	This defines the height of all cells. If this value is less than or equal to zero, all cells are individually sized.
focusModel	ObjectProperty <TableViewFocusModel<S>>	This defines the TableViewFocusModel for the TableView.
items	ObjectProperty<ObservableList<S>>	This defines the data model for the TableView.
onScrollTo	ObjectProperty<EventHandler <ScrollToEvent<Integer>>>	The event handler is called for each request to scroll the viewport of the TableView to a specific row.
onScrollToColumnProperty	ObjectProperty<EventHandler <ScrollToEvent<TableColumn<S, ?>>>>	The event handler is called for each request to scroll the viewport of the TableView to a specific column.
onSortProperty	ObjectProperty<EventHandler <SortEvent<TableView<S>>>>	This is called when there's a request to sort the control.
placeholderProperty	ObjectProperty<Node>	This defines a node that is shown when the TableView has no content to show.
rowFactoryProperty	ObjectProperty<Callback <TableView<S>, TableRow<S>>>	This defines a Callback that creates the TableRow instances. This should be used only by experts.

TABLE 6-7. *Properties of TableView Class*

Property	Type	Description
selectionModel	ObjectProperty<TableViewSelection Model<S>>	This defines the SelectionModel of the TableView.
sortPolicy	ObjectProperty<Callback <TableView<S>, Boolean>>	This defines how sorting in this TableView should be performed.
tableMenuButtonVisible	BooleanProperty	This defines a menu button that shows and hides all TableColumns of the TableView.

TABLE 6-7.   *Properties of TableView Class* (continued)

Property	Type	Description
comparator	ObjectProperty<Comparator<T>>	This defines the Comparator that is used when sorting this table column.
contextMenu	ObjectProperty<ContextMenu>	This defines the menu that will be shown when a user right-clicks within the header of the column.
editable	BooleanProperty	This defines whether the column is editable.
graphic	ObjectProperty<Node>	This defines a graphic that is shown in the column header.
id	StringProperty	This defines the ID of this column.
maxWidth	DoubleProperty	This defines the maximum width of the column.
minWidth	DoubleProperty	This defines the minimum width of the column.
parentColumn	ReadOnlyObjectProperty <TableColumnBase<S,?>>	This contains the parent of this column if nested columns are being used.
prefWidth	DoubleProperty	This defines the preferred width of the column.
resizable	BooleanProperty	This defines whether the width of this column can be changed.
sortable	BooleanProperty	This defines whether the column is sortable.

(continued)

TABLE 6-8.   *Properties of the TableColumnBase Class*

Property	Type	Description
sortNode	ObjectProperty<Node>	This defines the node that is used as the "sort arrow" in the column header.
style	StringProperty	This defines a string representation of the CSS style associated with the column.
text	StringProperty	This defines the text that is shown in the header.
visible	BooleanProperty	This defines whether the column is visible.
width	ReadOnlyDoubleProperty	This defines the current width of this column.

TABLE 6-8. *Properties of the TableColumnBase Class* (continued)

Property	Type	Description
cellFactory	ObjectProperty<Callback<TableColumn<S,T>, TableCell<S,T>>>	This defines the cell factory for all cells in this column.
cellValueFactory	ObjectProperty<Callback<CellDataFeatures<S,T>, ObservableValue<T>>>	The cell value factory defines a Callback that produces the values that are used internally in the cells of the column as the cell data.
onEditCancel	ObjectProperty<EventHandler<CellEditEvent<S,T>>>	The defined event handler will be fired when the user cancels editing.
onEditCommit	ObjectProperty<EventHandler<CellEditEvent<S,T>>>	The defined event handler will be fired when the user commits editing.
onEditStart	ObjectProperty<EventHandler<CellEditEvent<S,T>>>	This defined event handler will be fired when the user initiates editing.

TABLE 6-9. *Properties of the TableColumn Class*

Property	Type	Description
sortType	ObjectProperty<SortType>	This defines whether the column should be sorted in ascending or descending order.
tableView	ReadOnlyObjectProperty<TableView<S>>	This defines the TableView that this TableColumn belongs to.

TABLE 6-9. *Properties of the TableColumn Class* (continued)

TreeView

You can use the TreeView<T> control to display data that has a hierarchical structure. Most people will know this visualization from file explorers. File systems can contain directories that hold files or other directories, and this structure can be represented by a tree.

To create a tree structure, you use the TreeItem<T> class. This class provides the functionality to create a data model that contains a hierarchy of values, and each TreeItem instance can have other TreeItem instances as children. In addition, a TreeItem can hold a value that represents the data of the item. Here is a short sample that creates a tree of TreeItems:

```
TreeItem<Person> cto = new TreeItem<>(new Person("S. Gocha"));
TreeItem<Person> manager1 = new TreeItem<>(new Person("S. Trockel"));
TreeItem<Person> manager2 = new TreeItem<>(new Person("M. Kirschner"));
TreeItem<Person> employee1 = new TreeItem<>(new Person("J. Schmale"));
TreeItem<Person> employee2 = new TreeItem<>(new Person("M. Eil"));
TreeItem<Person> employee3 = new TreeItem<>(new Person("M. Bennemann"));
TreeItem<Person> employee4 = new TreeItem<>(new Person("H. Barth"));
TreeItem<Person> employee5 = new TreeItem<>(new Person("T. Reker"));

cto.getChildren().addAll(manager1, manager2);
manager1.getChildren().addAll(employee1, employee2, employee3);
manager2.getChildren().addAll(employee4, employee5);
```

Property	Type	Description
tableColumn	ReadOnlyObjectProperty<TableColumn<S,T>>	This defines the TableColumn instance that backs this TableCell.
tableRow	ReadOnlyObjectProperty<TableRow>	This defines the TableRow that this TableCell currently finds itself placed within.
tableView	ReadOnlyObjectProperty<TableView<S>>	This defines the TableView associated with this TableCell.

TABLE 6-10. *Properties of TableCell Class*

The code creates a tree of people that reflects the employment of the defined people. Each `TreeItem` instance can be expanded or collapsed. In the `TreeView`, all the children of an expanded `TreeItem` will be shown. If the item is collapsed, no children will be shown. All items that are rendered in a `TreeView` can be expanded by the user with a mouse click. In addition, the state can be changed by using the `expanded` property in code. In addition to this property, the `TreeItem` class provides some additional ones, as described in Table 6-11.

To set a hierarchy of `TreeItem` instances to a `TreeView`, you must set the root of the hierarchy, and the `TreeView` provides the `root` property. The following example creates a `TreeView` with some data and shows it onscreen:

```
package com.guigarage.masteringcontrols;
import javafx.application.Application;
import javafx.scene.Scene;
import javafx.scene.control.TreeItem;
import javafx.scene.control.TreeView;
import javafx.scene.layout.StackPane;
import javafx.stage.Stage;

public class TreeViewDemo extends Application {
    @Override
    public void start(Stage primaryStage) throws Exception {
        TreeView<String> treeView = new TreeView<>();
        TreeItem<String> item = new TreeItem<>("javafx");
```

Property	Type	Description
expanded	BooleanProperty	This defines whether the item is expanded or collapsed.
graphic	ObjectProperty<Node>	This defines a node that is normally shown in the visual representation of the item in the `TreeView`.
leaf	ReadOnlyBooleanProperty	This defines whether the `TreeItem` is a leaf, which is true if the item has no children.
parent	ReadOnlyObjectProperty<TreeItem<T>>	This defines the parent in the tree hierarchy. This will be null for the root of a tree.
value	ObjectProperty<T>	This property can be used to hold application-specific data.

TABLE 6-11. *Properties of the TreeItem Class*

```
        TreeItem<String> item2 = new TreeItem<>("scene");
        item.getChildren().add(item2);
        TreeItem<String> item3 = new TreeItem<>("control");
        item2.getChildren().add(item3);
        item3.getChildren().add(new TreeItem<>("Button"));
        item3.getChildren().add(new TreeItem<>("TreeView"));
        item2.getChildren().add(new TreeItem<>("Scene"));
        TreeItem<String> item4 = new TreeItem<>("stage");
        item.getChildren().add(item4);
        item4.getChildren().add(new TreeItem<>("Stage"));
        treeView.setRoot(item);
        StackPane myPane = new StackPane();
        myPane.getChildren().add(treeView);
        Scene myScene = new Scene(myPane);
        primaryStage.setScene(myScene);
        primaryStage.show();
    }
    public static void main(String[] args) {
        launch(args);
    }
}
```

In this example, only the `root` property of the `TreeView` is used. The class provides some additional properties to change the behavior and visualization of the rendered tree. Table 6-12 describes all the properties of the `TreeView` class.

As you can see in Table 6-12, a lot of properties are the same as the ones defined in the `ListView` or `TableView`. That is a great benefit of JavaFX. Once you understand the concept of the `ListView`, you can transform most of the functionalities to the `TableView` and `TreeView` classes. Because of that, I won't show here how editing is working or how the selection model can be used. You can deduce all the functionality from the `ListView` or `TableView` sections.

The following example contains a more complex data model and uses custom cells. Specifically, you'll create a tree of the file system, so as a first step, you create a hierarchy of `TreeItem` instances. The following method creates the needed structure for a given folder in the local file system:

```
private TreeItem<File> createTree(File file) {
        TreeItem<File> item = new TreeItem<>(file);
        File[] childs = file.listFiles();
        if (childs != null) {
            for (File child : childs) {
                item.getChildren().add(createTree(child));
            }
            item.setGraphic(new ImageView(getClass().getResource("folder.png").
                toExternalForm()));
        } else {
            item.setGraphic(new ImageView(getClass().getResource("text-x-generic.png").
                toExternalForm()));
        }
        return item;
    }
```

Property	Type	Description
editable	BooleanProperty	This defines whether the TreeView is editable.
editingItem	ReadOnlyObjectProperty <TreeItem<T>>	This defines the item that is currently being edited or null if no item will be edited.
expandedItemCount	ReadOnlyIntegerProperty	This defines the count of all expanded tree items and their children.
fixedCellSize	DoubleProperty	This defines a fixed height that will be used for all cells. If the value is less than or equal to zero, each cell can have its individual height.
focusModel	ObjectProperty<FocusModel <TreeItem<T>>>	This defines the FocusModel of the TreeView.
onEditCancel	ObjectProperty<EventHandler <EditEvent<T>>>	The EventHandler instance will be fired when the user cancels editing a cell.
onEditCommit	ObjectProperty<EventHandler <EditEvent<T>>>	The EventHandler instance will be fired when the user commits an edit.
onEditStart	ObjectProperty<EventHandler <EditEvent<T>>>	The EventHandler instance will be fired when the user begins an edit.
onScrollTo	ObjectProperty<EventHandler <ScrollToEvent<Integer>>>	The EventHandler instance will be fired when there's a request to scroll an index into the view.
root	ObjectProperty<TreeItem<T>>	This defines the root item of the underlying TreeItem hierarchy.
selectionModel	ObjectProperty<MultipleSelectionModel <TreeItem<T>>>	This defines the SelectionModel of the TreeView.
showRoot	BooleanProperty	This defines whether the root TreeItem should be shown in the TreeView.

TABLE 6-12. *Properties of the TreeView*

For each file or directory, you create a `TreeItem` that holds the file as its data value. In addition, in this code you set an image for each `TreeItem`. If the file is a directory, a folder icon should be rendered for the item. Otherwise, a file icon should be shown. The class creates the hierarchy of all files in the given directory by using recursion.

NOTE

The code snippet uses the `ImageView` class. That is a special node type in JavaFX that can be used to render images onscreen. I'll discuss this class in Chapter 7 in more detail.

Once you've done this, you create a `TreeView` that uses the given data structure and renders the file system as a tree on the screen. The default cell type that is used in the `TreeView` would call the `toString()` method on each file instance to receive the text that should be shown onscreen for each item in the tree. Because you want a better output here, you need a custom cell. The following code defines a JavaFX application that renders the tree to the screen:

```java
package com.guigarage.masteringcontrols;
import javafx.application.Application;
import javafx.scene.Scene;
import javafx.scene.control.TreeCell;
import javafx.scene.control.TreeItem;
import javafx.scene.control.TreeView;
import javafx.scene.image.ImageView;
import javafx.scene.layout.StackPane;
import javafx.stage.Stage;
import java.io.File;

public class FileTree extends Application {
    public static void main(String[] args) {
        launch(args);
    }
    @Override
    public void start(Stage primaryStage) throws Exception {
        TreeView<File> tree = new TreeView<>();
        tree.setRoot(createTree(new File(".")));
        tree.setCellFactory((e) -> new TreeCell<File>(){
            @Override
            protected void updateItem(File item, boolean empty) {
                super.updateItem(item, empty);
                if(item != null) {
                    setText(item.getName());
                    setGraphic(getTreeItem().getGraphic());
                } else {
                    setText("");
                    setGraphic(null);
                }
            }
        });
        StackPane myPane = new StackPane();
        myPane.getChildren().add(tree);
        Scene myScene = new Scene(myPane);
        primaryStage.setScene(myScene);
        primaryStage.setTitle("File Tree");
        primaryStage.show();
    }
```

```
private TreeItem<File> createTree(File file) {
    TreeItem<File> item = new TreeItem<>(file);
    File[] childs = file.listFiles();
    if (childs != null) {
        for (File child : childs) {
            item.getChildren().add(createTree(child));
        }
        item.setGraphic(new ImageView(getClass().getResource("folder.png").
            toExternalForm()));
    } else {
        item.setGraphic(new ImageView(getClass().getResource("text-x-generic.png").
            toExternalForm()));
    }
    return item;
}
}
```

Figure 6-13 shows the view of the application. Here you can see that the rendered tree looks like the file explorer that comes with most operating systems. The custom cell that is used here is

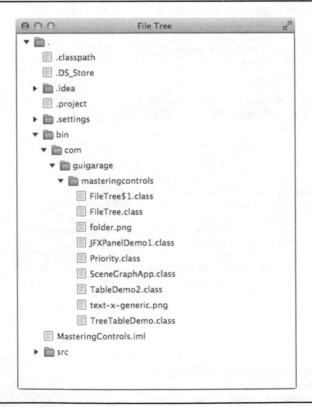

FIGURE 6-13. *A TreeView that shows the structure of a directory*

quite simple: The text of the cell is set to the name of the given file that is wrapped in the
`TreeItem`. In addition, the graphic node that is defined in the `TreeItem` is set to the `graphic`
property of the cell.

NOTE
*The content of the `graphic` property that is defined for a `TreeItem`
will automatically be used for the `graphic` property of the `TreeCell`
instance that displays the item. In addition, the result of the `toString()`
method of the value that is defined in the `TreeItem` instance will be
used for the text of the cell.*

The `TreeCell` class extends the `IndexedCell` class and adds some `TreeView`-specific
properties, as described in Table 6-13.

TreeTableView

The `TreeTableView<T>` control has the same benefits of a `TableView` and a `TreeView`. By
using this control, you can display hierarchical data that is defined by the `TreeItem` class like
you do in a `TreeView`. In addition, table columns are shown for each `TreeItem` instance to
provide additional information on the data object.

The following example extends the simple file explorer example that was created as a sample
for the `TreeView` and shows additional information for the files that are part of the data model:

```
package com.guigarage.masteringcontrols;
import javafx.application.Application;
import javafx.beans.property.SimpleObjectProperty;
import javafx.beans.property.SimpleStringProperty;
import javafx.scene.Scene;
import javafx.scene.control.TreeItem;
import javafx.scene.control.TreeTableColumn;
import javafx.scene.control.TreeTableView;
import javafx.scene.image.ImageView;
import javafx.scene.layout.VBox;
import javafx.stage.Stage;
```

Property	Type	Description
disclosureNode	ObjectProperty<Node>	Defines the visual representation of the `TreeItem` state. By default, this is a triangle that indicates whether the `TreeItem` is expanded or collapsed.
treeItem	ReadOnlyObjectProperty <TreeItem<T>>	Defines the `TreeItem` instance that is represented by the `TreeCell`.
treeView	ReadOnlyObjectProperty <TreeView<T>>	Defines the `TreeView` in which the `TreeCell` is shown.

TABLE 6-13.   *Properties of the TreeCell Class*

```
import java.io.File;
import java.util.Date;
public class TreeTableDemo extends Application {
    @Override

    public void start(Stage primaryStage) throws Exception {
        TreeTableView<File> treeTable = new TreeTableView<>();

        TreeTableColumn<File, String> nameColumn = new TreeTableColumn<>("Name");
        TreeTableColumn<File, Long> sizeColumn = new TreeTableColumn<>("Size");
        TreeTableColumn<File, Date> modifiedColumn = new TreeTableColumn<>("Last
            Modified");

        nameColumn.setCellValueFactory((f) -> new SimpleStringProperty(f.getValue().
            getValue().getName()));
        sizeColumn.setCellValueFactory((f) -> new SimpleObjectProperty<>(f.getValue().
            getValue().length()));
        modifiedColumn.setCellValueFactory((f) -> new SimpleObjectProperty<>(new
            Date(f.getValue().getValue().lastModified())));
        treeTable.setRoot(createTree(new File(".")));
        treeTable.getColumns().addAll(nameColumn, sizeColumn, modifiedColumn);
        VBox vbox = new VBox();
        vbox.getChildren().addAll(treeTable);
        primaryStage.setScene(new Scene(vbox));
        primaryStage.show();
    }

    private TreeItem<File> createTree(File file) {
        TreeItem<File> item = new TreeItem<>(file);
        File[] childs = file.listFiles();
        if (childs != null) {
            for (File child : childs) {
                item.getChildren().add(createTree(child));
            }
            item.setGraphic(new ImageView(getClass().getResource("folder.png").
                toExternalForm()));
        } else {
            item.setGraphic(new ImageView(getClass().getResource("text-x-generic.png").
                toExternalForm()));
        }
        return item;
    }

    public static void main(String[] args) {
        launch(args);
    }
}
```

As you can see in the code, the `TreeItem` structure is created as in the previous sample. But instead of adding the root item to a `TreeView`, you add it to a `TreeTableView`. For this `TreeTableView`, columns are defined as with a normal `TableView`. For each column, a cell value factory is defined to extract the information that should be shown in the column. Figure 6-14 shows the running application. As you can see, the first column of the control is rendered as a tree.

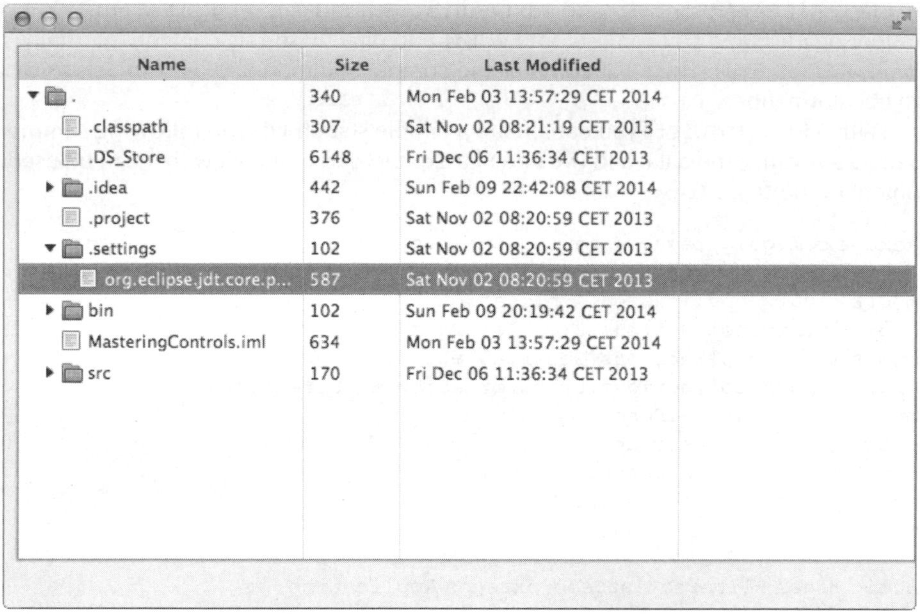

FIGURE 6-14. *The TreeTableView control*

With the `TreeTableColumn` and `TreeTableCell`, there are special column and cell classes that are part of JavaFX. These classes must be used when working with the `TreeTableView`; they contain most of the properties as described for the `TreeView` and `TableView`, so I won't discuss them again here. Developers who have worked with the `TableView` and the `TreeView` will find that they will become familiar with the API of the `TreeTableView` in a short amount of time.

The `TreeTableView` class contains one additional property that is not part of the `TreeView` or `TableView`: The `treeColumn` property that is of type `ObjectProperty<TreeTableColumn<S, ?>>` defines which of the given columns will be rendered as a tree and provides the functionality to collapse or expand items. By default, the first column will be used as this column (this was shown in Figure 6-14 for the demo application). You can simply define another column by setting it to the `treeColumn` property of the `TreeTableView`.

Sorting and Filtering Data

Most of the controls that are shown in this chapter use lists of objects for the data model. As you know now, you must use an `ObservableList<E>` for this. In addition to the default implementations of this interface, JavaFX contains some more collection types that extend the collections that are known from the Java collections API. JavaFX contains the `TransformationList<E>` class. This abstract class is a base class for all lists that wraps other lists and can be used to change the content or order of a list. The class implements the

ObservableList<E> interface, and JavaFX contains two concrete implementations of the class: FilteredList<E> and SortedList<E>. You can use FilteredList to filter the content of a list, and you can use SortedList to directly sort its content. Internally, another ObservableList is used that contains the complete unmodified list and acts as a base for all the transformations.

With FilteredList, you can create a simple search UI. The following sample defines a ListView with some data, and I've added a TextField to the view that can be used to filter the content of the ListView:

```java
package com.guigarage.masteringcontrols;

import javafx.application.Application;
import javafx.collections.FXCollections;
import javafx.collections.ObservableList;
import javafx.collections.transformation.FilteredList;
import javafx.scene.Scene;
import javafx.scene.control.ListView;
import javafx.scene.control.TextField;
import javafx.scene.layout.VBox;
import javafx.stage.Stage;

public class FilteredListDemo extends Application {

    @Override
    public void start(Stage primaryStage) throws Exception {
        ObservableList<String> list = FXCollections.
            observableArrayList("Angelo", "Steffi", "Jan", "Silke");
        FilteredList<String> filteredList = new FilteredList<String>(list);
        filteredList.setPredicate((e) -> true);
        ListView<String> listView = new ListView<>(filteredList);
        TextField textField = new TextField();
        textField.textProperty().addListener((e) -> filteredList.
            setPredicate((v) -> (textField.getText() == null || textField.
            getText().length() == 0 || v.startsWith(textField.getText()))));
        VBox myPane = new VBox(textField, listView);
        Scene myScene = new Scene(myPane);
        primaryStage.setScene(myScene);
        primaryStage.show();
    }

    public static void main(String[] args) {
        launch(args);
    }
}
```

As you can see in the code, a Predicate is defined for the FilteredList<E> instance. This Predicate defines whether an item of the underlying ObservableList should be part of the FilteredList. By default, the Predicate will always return true, and therefore each element of the ObservableList is part of the FilteredList. But when a user enters text in the TextField, a custom Predicate will be set to the FilteredList. In this case, only items of the list that match the Predicate, and therefore the entered text, will be shown in the ListView.

The next example uses a `SortedList<E>` in a `TableView`. As mentioned when discussing how to sort the `TableView` control, the underlying `ObservableList` that defines the data model of the table won't be sorted. If you use a `SortedList` as the data model of a `TableView`, though, you can change this default behavior.

```java
package com.guigarage.masteringcontrols;

import javafx.application.Application;
import javafx.beans.property.SimpleStringProperty;
import javafx.collections.FXCollections;
import javafx.collections.ObservableList;
import javafx.collections.transformation.SortedList;
import javafx.geometry.Insets;
import javafx.geometry.Pos;
import javafx.scene.Scene;
import javafx.scene.control.TableColumn;
import javafx.scene.control.TableView;
import javafx.scene.layout.VBox;
import javafx.stage.Stage;

public class SelectionModelDemo extends Application {

    @Override
    public void start(Stage primaryStage) throws Exception {
        ObservableList<String> data = FXCollections.observableArrayList(
                "Z", "B", "A", "X", "W", "C", "F"
        );
        SortedList sortedList = new SortedList(data);
        TableView<String> table = new TableView<>();
        table.itemsProperty().setValue(sortedList);
        sortedList.comparatorProperty().bind(table.comparatorProperty());
        TableColumn<String, String> column = new TableColumn<>("Data");
        column.setCellValueFactory((e) -> new SimpleStringProperty(e.
            getValue()));
        table.getColumns().add(column);
        VBox myPane = new VBox();
        myPane.setAlignment(Pos.CENTER);
        myPane.setPadding(new Insets(12));
        myPane.setSpacing(12);
        myPane.getChildren().add(table);
        Scene myScene = new Scene(myPane);
        primaryStage.setScene(myScene);
        primaryStage.show();
    }

    public static void main(String[] args) {
        launch(args);
    }
}
```

The `SortedList<E>` class defines a `comparator` property that is used to sort the content of the underlying `ObservableList` instance. In the sample, the property of the `SortedList` is bound to the `comparator` property of the table. Whenever a user changes the sorting of the `TableView`, the `Comparator` that is used to sort the data onscreen will be used to sort the underlying data. Therefore, the order of the items onscreen and in the data model is in sync.

As you can see, you can use `TransformationList` and its concrete implementations to easily extend the functionality of JavaFX controls.

Controls That Act as Containers

JavaFX contains some control types that can be used as containers to wrap other node instances. The following node types will be shown here:

- `Pagination`
- `SplitPane`
- `Accordion`
- `TabPane`
- `TitledPane`

All these nodes can contain other nodes. Normally, these types are used to switch between different views. You should know most of these controls from other UI toolkits, and they are used often in applications. For example, all modern browsers use a `TabPane` to show several web sites in different tabs. Figure 6-15 contains an overview of all the controls and how they will appear onscreen.

You'll see each of the different control types in the following examples. These short examples are meant to demonstrate the basics of each control and are not comprehensive of all their features. Reference the JavaDoc of the `Control` class for additional use and customization scenarios.

Let's first look at the `SplitPane` class, which can be used to split a view into several subviews by using dividers. In other UI toolkits such as Swing, a `SplitPane` can contain only one divider and hold two different views. In JavaFX, a `SplitPane` can hold any number of subviews. A subview is defined as a node here, so each node can be added to a `SplitPane`. The following sample adds three buttons to a `SplitPane`, as shown in Figure 6-15:

```
package com.guigarage.masteringcontrols;
import javafx.application.Application;
import javafx.scene.Scene;
import javafx.scene.control.Button;
import javafx.scene.control.SplitPane;
import javafx.scene.layout.StackPane;
import javafx.stage.Stage;
public class SplitPaneDemo extends Application {
    @Override
    public void start(Stage primaryStage) throws Exception {
        SplitPane splitPane = new SplitPane();
        splitPane.getItems().add(new StackPane(new Button("Button 1")));
```

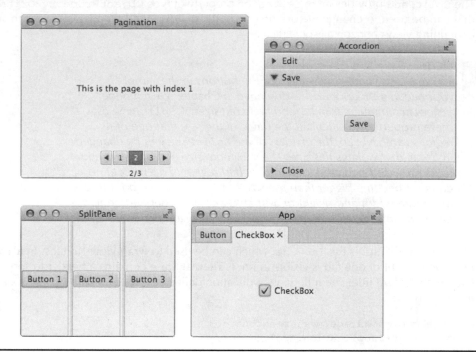

FIGURE 6-15.   *Visualization of Pagination, SplitPane, Accordion, TitledPane, and TabPane*

```
        splitPane.getItems().add(new StackPane(new Button("Button 2")));
        splitPane.getItems().add(new StackPane(new Button("Button 3")));
        StackPane myPane = new StackPane();
        myPane.getChildren().add(splitPane);
        Scene myScene = new Scene(myPane);
        primaryStage.setScene(myScene);
        primaryStage.setTitle("SplitPane");
        primaryStage.setWidth(300);
        primaryStage.setHeight(200);
        primaryStage.show();
    }
    public static void main(String[] args) {
        launch(args);
    }
}
```

As you can see in the code, the SplitPane provides an item list. This ObservableList<Node> and custom nodes can easily be added to the list. Each node in the list is a subview of the SplitPane. The width of the views can be changed by moving the dividers with the mouse.

The SplitPane provides an orientation property of type ObjectProperty<Orientation> that can be used to change the orientation of the dividers, and the SplitPane can split the containing views horizontally or vertically.

NOTE
You may ask yourself why each of the buttons in the sample is wrapped in a StackPane. As described in Chapter 3, each node defines minimum, maximum, and preferred sizes. A SplitPane uses these properties to calculate the range of the size that one of its regions can have. So, the dividers of the SplitPane can be changed in a way that violates this size. The maximum size of a button is equal to its preferred one, and therefore a child region in a SplitPane couldn't become bigger than the size of the internal button. But the maximum width and height of a StackPane don't depend on its children, and therefore a StackPane can be bigger than its children.

The next control is the TabPane, which can be used to wrap views in tabs. In a TabPane, only the content of one tab is visible at once. The TabPane contains a header to show all tabs, each with its own title. The following application defines a TabPane with two tabs, as shown in Figure 6-15:

```java
package com.guigarage.masteringcontrols;
import javafx.application.Application;
import javafx.scene.Scene;
import javafx.scene.control.Button;
import javafx.scene.control.CheckBox;
import javafx.scene.control.Tab;
import javafx.scene.control.TabPane;
import javafx.scene.layout.StackPane;
import javafx.stage.Stage;

public class TabPaneDemo extends Application {

    @Override
    public void start(Stage primaryStage) throws Exception {
        TabPane tabPane = new TabPane();
        Tab tab1 = new Tab("Button");
        tab1.setContent(new StackPane(new Button("Button")));
        Tab tab2 = new Tab("CheckBox");
        tab2.setContent(new StackPane(new CheckBox("CheckBox")));
        tabPane.getTabs().addAll(tab1, tab2);
        StackPane myPane = new StackPane();
        myPane.getChildren().add(tabPane);
        Scene myScene = new Scene(myPane);
        primaryStage.setScene(myScene);
        primaryStage.setTitle("App");
        primaryStage.setWidth(300);
        primaryStage.setHeight(200);
        primaryStage.show();
```

```
        }
        public static void main(String[] args) {
            launch(args);
        }
    }
```

Each tab in a `TabPane` is defined by the `Tab` class. Only `Tab` instances can be added to a `TabPane`, as shown in the example. The content of a tab is defined in its content property. Any node can be used as the content of a tab. In addition, each tab can define text that is used as its name or header. In the sample, the `Tab` instances are created by using a constructor that defines the name of the tab. Internally, the `Tab` class provides a `text` property that holds the header of the tab. The `TabPane` will render the text onscreen, as you can see in Figure 6-15. In addition to the text property, the `Tab` class provides a lot more properties. By using the `closeable` property that is defined as `BooleanProperty`, the tab can be defined as closeable or not. If a tab can be closed, an *X* is shown in its header as a link. When the user clicks the link, the `Tab` instance will be removed. In addition to properties that can be used to change the view and behavior of the tab, the class provides some event handler properties. These can be used to react to specific events, as shown in earlier samples. One example for these properties is the `onCloseRequest` property. The event handler that is defined by this property will be called whenever an external request to close the tab occurs. This can be used to prevent the closing of the tab by consuming the received event, for example.

NOTE
At first glance, the control types that are shown here may look like more than pane types, but are defined as controls by JavaFX. This is because of the following reasons: A pane normally doesn't define a custom-rendered view with visual elements. The controls such as the `SplitPane` have a visual representation. For the `SplitPane`, the dividers need to be rendered, and how a divider looks is defined in its visual skin. Each control in JavaFX has a defined skin that specifies how an instance will be rendered onscreen, but the skin of a control can change to create a custom rendering. I will discuss this when talking about themes and CSS. In addition, all the control types shown here define a behavior for interaction. In the `TabPane`, the selected tab can be changed, for example. All pane types in JavaFX don't have a skin that is needed to render the pane in a special way, and they don't have any behavior.

The `Accordion` control can hold a list of nodes. All these nodes can be expanded or collapsed. This is useful if you need a complex menu structure in an application, for example. The different menu entries can be grouped in logical groups, and the user can open or close the individual groups to see only the wanted menus onscreen. The following code shows the `Accordion` control and defines an application, as shown in Figure 6-15:

```
import javafx.application.Application;
import javafx.scene.Scene;
import javafx.scene.control.Accordion;
import javafx.scene.control.Button;
```

```
import javafx.scene.control.TitledPane;
import javafx.scene.layout.StackPane;
import javafx.stage.Stage;
public class AccordionDemo extends Application {
    @Override
    public void start(Stage primaryStage) throws Exception {
        Accordion accordion = new Accordion();
        TitledPane pane1 = new TitledPane("Edit", new Button("Edit"));
        TitledPane pane2 = new TitledPane("Save", new Button("Save"));
        TitledPane pane3 = new TitledPane("Close", new Button("Close"));
        accordion.getPanes().addAll(pane1, pane2, pane3);
        StackPane myPane = new StackPane();
        myPane.getChildren().add(accordion);
        Scene myScene = new Scene(myPane);
        primaryStage.setScene(myScene);
        primaryStage.setTitle("Accordion");
        primaryStage.show();
    }
    public static void main(String[] args) {
        launch(args);
    }
}
```

Each node that can be added to an Accordion must be wrapped in a TitledPane instance. The name of this class may be misleading because the TitledPane doesn't extend the Pane class. Instead, it extends the Labeled class. As a result, the class contains all properties that are needed to render the text onscreen. This text is shown in the header of the TitledPane. As mentioned, a TitledPane wraps a custom node. This node is internally stored in the content property that is defined as ObjectProperty<Node>. The node is shown in the main area of the TitledPane whenever it is expanded in the Accordion.

The last control type that is shown in Figure 6-15 is the Pagination control, which can be used to create navigation between pages of content. This type of control is often used in applications or web sites to create a so-called carousel that navigates between a list of images. Let's take a look at the code of a sample that uses the Pagination control:

```
package com.guigarage.masteringcontrols;
import javafx.application.Application;
import javafx.scene.Scene;
import javafx.scene.control.Label;
import javafx.scene.control.Pagination;
import javafx.scene.layout.StackPane;
import javafx.stage.Stage;
public class PaginationDemo extends Application {
    @Override
    public void start(Stage primaryStage) throws Exception {
        Pagination pagination = new Pagination();
        pagination.setPageCount(3);
        pagination.setPageFactory((i) -> new Label("This is the page with index " + i));
        StackPane myPane = new StackPane();
        myPane.getChildren().add(pagination);
        Scene myScene = new Scene(myPane);
```

```
        primaryStage.setScene(myScene);
        primaryStage.setTitle("Pagination");
        primaryStage.setWidth(300);
        primaryStage.setHeight(200);
        primaryStage.show();
    }
    public static void main(String[] args) {
        launch(args);
    }
}
```

To provide the content of a `Pagination` control, you need a factory. This so-called page factory is defined by the `pageFactory` property of type `ObjectProperty<Callback<Integer, Node>>`. The callback that is used here creates the content of a single page in the `Pagination` control. The input parameter of the callback method is an integer that defines the current page index for which the callback should provide the page content. The content can be any node. In the example, a `Label` is returned that contains the page index in its text. The page count is defined by the `pageCount` property of type `IntegerProperty`. If `Pagination.INDETERMINATE` is used here, the `Pagination` instance will use an indeterminate page count. The control provides items to navigate between the pages, as shown in Figure 6-15.

Additional Controls

JavaFX contains some useful control classes that do not align neatly with the categories discussed so far. These additional controls include an `HTMLEditor`, `DatePicker`, and `ColorPicker`. These three controls allow the developer to provide user interfaces for these specific use cases:

- Working with rich text
- Selecting data
- Selecting a color

These functionalities are often needed in applications; in fact, the `DatePicker` is especially useful when developing forms. Instead of using just plain `TextField` instances, a user can pick a date with the mouse.

HTMLEditor

With the use of the `HTMLEditor` control, you can show and edit HTML text. The control contains a toolbar with several functions such as changing the font or the alignment of the text. Figure 6-16 shows the `HTMLEditor`. The control can be used like a What You See Is What You Get (WYSIWYG) editor, and the styled text is created in HTML syntax. In addition, HTML syntax can be shown in the `HTMLEditor`. The control can be used in applications such as a rich editor for text input and rendering.

The following sample shows how the `HTMLEditor` control can be used in code:

```
package com.guigarage.masteringcontrols;
import javafx.application.Application;
import javafx.scene.Scene;
```

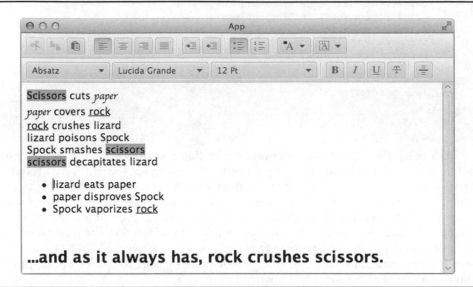

FIGURE 6-16. *The HTMLEditor control*

```
import javafx.scene.layout.StackPane;
import javafx.scene.web.HTMLEditor;
import javafx.stage.Stage;
public class HTMLEditorDemo extends Application {
    @Override
    public void start(Stage primaryStage) throws Exception {
        HTMLEditor htmlEditor = new HTMLEditor();
        StackPane myPane = new StackPane();
        myPane.getChildren().add(htmlEditor);
        Scene myScene = new Scene(myPane);
        primaryStage.setScene(myScene);
        primaryStage.setTitle("App");
        primaryStage.setWidth(300);
        primaryStage.setHeight(200);
        primaryStage.show();
    }
    public static void main(String[] args) {
        launch(args);
    }
}
```

The `HTMLEditor` class defines some methods, as described in Table 6-14.

Method	Description
`String getHtmlText()`	Returns the HTML content of the editor
`void setHtmlText(String htmlText)`	Sets the HTML content of the editor
`void print(PrinterJob job)`	Prints the content

TABLE 6-14. *Methods of the HTMLEditor*

DatePicker

The DatePicker control is one of the new controls in JavaFX 8. It lets the user select or enter a date. The class extends the ComboBoxBase class and provides a pop-up that can be used to select a date. The following example shows how a DatePicker can be used:

```
package com.guigarage.masteringcontrols;
import javafx.application.Application;
import javafx.scene.Scene;
import javafx.scene.control.DatePicker;
import javafx.scene.layout.StackPane;
import javafx.stage.Stage;
public class DatePickerDemo extends Application {
    @Override
    public void start(Stage primaryStage) throws Exception {
        DatePicker datePicker = new DatePicker();
        StackPane myPane = new StackPane();
        myPane.getChildren().add(datePicker);
        Scene myScene = new Scene(myPane);
        primaryStage.setScene(myScene);
        primaryStage.setTitle("App");
        primaryStage.setWidth(300);
        primaryStage.setHeight(200);
        primaryStage.show();
    }
    public static void main(String[] args) {
        launch(args);
    }
}
```

Figure 6-17 shows how the DatePicker control is rendered onscreen. The figure shows the pop-up of the control where the user can select a date. The year and month can be selected in the top of the pop-up, and all days of the selected month are shown in the main area of the pop-up.

The DatePicker class also contains some useful properties that can be used to define the view and behavior of the control, as shown in Table 6-15.

FIGURE 6-17. *The DatePicker control*

Property	Type	Description
chronology	ObjectProperty<Chronology>	Defines the internal calendar system that is used for parsing, displaying, and choosing dates
converter	ObjectProperty<StringConverter <LocalDate>>	Defines a converter to convert the input text to a LocalDate, and vice versa
dayCellFactory	ObjectProperty<Callback <DatePicker, DateCell>>	Defines a cell factory that provides the day cells in the DatePicker pop-up
editor	ReadOnlyObjectProperty <TextField>	Defines the input field for the DatePicker
showWeekNumbers	BooleanProperty	Defines whether the DatePicker pop-up displays week numbers

TABLE 6-15. *Properties of the DatePicker*

ColorPicker

The ColorPicker control extends the BaseComboBox class. It offers the functionality for the user to select a custom color via a pop-up palette. By default, this palette contains a set of basic colors. The user isn't limited to the palette and may utilize an additional dialog that contains controls to define or select a custom color. This dialog can be opened by clicking the Custom Color link on the pop-up. As with any other control, you can easily add the ColorPicker to an application. The following code shows a basic example:

```java
package com.guigarage.masteringcontrols;
import javafx.application.Application;
import javafx.geometry.Insets;
import javafx.geometry.Pos;
import javafx.scene.Scene;
import javafx.scene.control.ColorPicker;
import javafx.scene.control.Label;
import javafx.scene.layout.VBox;
import javafx.scene.text.Font;
import javafx.stage.Stage;
public class ColorPickerDemo extends Application {
    @Override
    public void start(Stage primaryStage) throws Exception {
        Label label = new Label("Demo Label");
        label.setFont(new Font(24));
        ColorPicker colorPicker = new ColorPicker();
        colorPicker.setOnAction((e) -> label.setTextFill(colorPicker.getValue()));
        VBox box = new VBox(label, colorPicker);
        box.setAlignment(Pos.CENTER);
        box.setPadding(new Insets(24));
        box.setSpacing(24);
        Scene myScene = new Scene(box);
        primaryStage.setScene(myScene);
        primaryStage.setWidth(300);
        primaryStage.setHeight(200);
        primaryStage.show();
    }
    public static void main(String[] args) {
        launch(args);
    }
}
```

In Figure 6-18 you can see a ColorPicker with a pop-up. In addition, the Custom Colors dialog is shown here. As you can see, a user can pick a color with a mouse click. The color also can be defined by using sliders. Here, HSB, RGB, and Web modes are supported. The ColorPicker class contains an ObservableList<Color> customColors that can be used to define the colors that are part of the color palette.

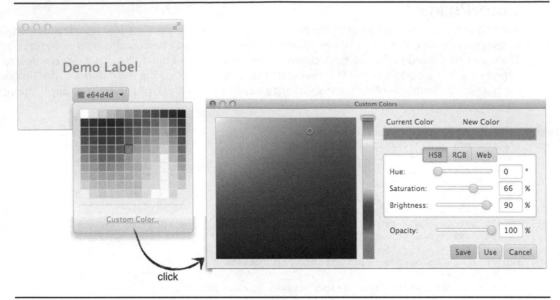

FIGURE 6-18. *A ColorPicker*

An Interview with Jonathan Giles, Engineer on the JavaFX Team, Oracle

Oracle engineer Jonathan Giles has implemented parts of the JavaFX control API. I had the chance to interview Jonathan in February 2014; he offers an inside perspective on these APIs and discusses the internal API design and the future of JavaFX controls.

Hi, Jonathan! Please introduce yourself and your role in regard to JavaFX controls.

Hi, Hendrik. My name is Jonathan Giles, and I'm an engineer on the JavaFX team at Oracle. Specifically, my focus is on the UI controls area of the toolkit, which means I care about their API and implementation and, to a lesser degree, their visuals and user interactions (but fortunately we also have others who are talented in user experience and design that help out).

I've been working on JavaFX UI controls since mid-2009, so it's coming up on five years this year, which is a long time! I've been involved with probably every control to varying degrees, but I spend a large bulk of my time focused on the virtualized controls such as `ListView`, `TreeView`, `TableView`, and, in JavaFX 8.0, `TreeTableView`.

Perfect. This means that you are an expert about the topics discussed in this chapter. When talking about the JavaFX controls, what do you think is the biggest benefit over other UI toolkits?

I think there are at least four benefits that JavaFX UI controls have:

- **Consistent and modern API design** We have spent a huge amount of time considering and designing the JavaFX UI controls API. This is based on a lot of research of previous UI toolkits such as Swing, as well as our contemporaries, such as what is available in the HTML world.

  Designing an API is really, really hard, and from an outsider's perspective, it can be difficult to appreciate this. Once an API is released, it is set in stone and cannot be changed without breaking end users, so it is important to get it right (or as close as can be) the first time around. I am really quite proud of our APIs, and, of course, whilst I wish we could fix a few mistakes, by and large, it is the best we could do considering we can't release a final product in one release, and often our crystal ball doesn't quite allow us to see what requirements are needed in the future. On top of this, we can, of course, leverage features of the Java 7 and 8 world, such as generics, enumerations, annotations, lambdas, and default methods, to make a far more powerful and succinct experience. This is a particular pain point that Swing has—it feels so antiquated now to pass in ints rather than enums, for example!

- **Integration with JavaFX binding and collections** A major selling point of JavaFX has always been its concept of binding and observable properties/collections. Our UI controls are designed from the ground up to support these and integrate with other aspects of the JavaFX toolkit. For example, it is trivial to bind the state of a progress bar to the progress of something else such as a `WebView` loading, or for a `ListView` to automatically update its display based on a change to the underlying `ObservableList`. Our goal has been to enable as much power and convenience by default, without ever resorting to magic or confusing API. Again, I'm incredibly pleased with how everything just plays together nicely.

- **Powerful CSS styling** Styling our user interfaces has never been as simple or powerful as it is in JavaFX. CSS allows you to reach every node in the user interface and to completely change the style of what is shown to the user. Already we have developed two separate looks for JavaFX (named Caspian and Modena), and the community has contributed additional looks that replicate Apple's Aqua, Microsoft's Metro, and web styles such as Bootstrap.

- **A great visual style (in JavaFX 8.0, it is on by default)** As mentioned, we have two UI styles in JavaFX. Modena is new in JavaFX 8.0, and it is incredibly well polished. The nice thing it does is that it has a lot of rules for when containers are placed inside containers to get rid of unsightly borders (which was a bane of my life when I used to do a lot of Swing!).

The last two topics that you mentioned will be shown in the following chapters, but the first two benefits are already discussed here. Let's take a deeper look at the API design that is, in my eyes, really great. The JavaFX controls API contains mainly no interfaces but a lot of abstract classes. Why have you chosen this structure, and what are the benefits of this approach?

(Continued)

When we were developing the JavaFX APIs, we were very conscious of a few things that were gaining in importance in the technical landscape:

- Embedded devices were on the rise. These devices often have limited memory and lower CPU performance. Every class or interface included in JavaFX is an additional static footprint and CPU time to class load, so we really wanted to keep classes (be they interfaces, abstract classes, or concrete classes) to a minimum.

- Lambdas were coming down the pipeline in Java 8, and we wanted to be able to make use of them because they help to cut down on the boilerplate noise that is often present in GUI code. The big design decision here is that we designed our APIs so that the callback methods (e.g., `Callback`, `EventHandler`, `ChangeListener`, `InvalidationListener`, etc.) were all functional interfaces. A functional interface is simply an interface with a single method defined in it and, therefore, can be directly used as a lambda in Java 8. In other words, rather than write code like this:

```
button.setOnAction(new EventHandler<ActionEvent>() {
@Override public void handle(ActionEvent e) {
System.out.println("Event: " + e);
}
});
```

we can now write the following:

```
button.setOnAction(e -> System.out.println("Event: " + e));
```

which is functionally equivalent, but without all the cruft. I think you'll agree it helps to cut down on the noise and makes the code far more readable.

In terms of how this impacted our API design, we had to switch forms from how API was designed back before functional interfaces were important. For example, in Swing, you would call `button.addMouseListener(...)` and pass in a `MouseListener` implementation. The `MouseListener` interface defines five methods (`clicked`, `entered`, `exited`, `pressed`, and `released`). There is no way this interface would work in the Java 8 lambda world, so we turned the API around in JavaFX, instead having multiple methods on the `Button` class (actually, it's `Node`, but that is unimportant) for `setOnMouseClicked`, `setOnMouseEntered`, and so on. Then, for each of these methods, we can pass in an event handler, which, as shown earlier, is a functional interface and therefore can be made into a lambda expression.

- With a few useful generic interfaces/abstract classes, there really is no need to create custom interfaces for everything. This links back to the point about embedded devices but stands on its own, too—there is actually little need to create custom interfaces for every case, and conceptually, it makes sense to reuse existing interfaces if they are applicable. In fact, during JavaFX 2.0 development, I even took this to the extreme and introduced RunnableX interfaces, which were just like the Runnable interface that Java has had forever, but the X counted from 1 to 9 and represented the number of arguments going into the `run()` method. Fortunately, this never shipped!

Going back to your question, the other part was why have we preferred abstract classes over interfaces. I'm not entirely sure that is true; my own gut feeling is that we are roughly 50/50 interfaces and abstract classes. In any case, the reason is simple: API design is really, really hard, and you never get it totally right the first time. In conjunction with this, up until Java 8 (with its support for "default methods" in interfaces), interfaces are far more rigid than abstract classes—you can't add new methods like you can in abstract classes. This, of course, is a lifesaver when you want to grow your API over time, and this is the primary reason for choosing abstract classes over interfaces. The other reason is simply that abstract classes allow for a default implementation, which can often prove useful.

In JavaFX 2.x, fluent builder APIs were provided for all control types. Why are these builder classes marked as deprecated in JavaFX 8?

We made a mistake in defining the API and depended on a bug in the Java 7 compiler that wasn't available in the Java 8 compiler. This meant that we could not ship the fluent builder APIs without breaking the API, so we decided to take the opportunity to simply deprecate them in Java 8 and to remove them in Java 9. You can read more at the following URL: http://mail.openjdk.java.net/pipermail/openjfx-dev/2013-March/006725.html.

Thanks for these detailed insights in the development of the JavaFX framework and the controls API. Let's talk about one last topic. Are there any functions or controls that you currently miss in the controls API?

Of course—there is always a long list of things to do to improve the framework, but fortunately, there are plenty of open source projects that can be far more agile than the JavaFX project can be, and they're doing a great job filling in the gaps in the meantime.

At the same time, whenever you add features, you risk introducing new bugs and performance regressions, and, of course, there is always a backlog of bugs and performance issues to deal with. Because of this, I actually spend a lot of my time (especially now with JavaFX 8.0 complete and my focus switched to Java 8u20) focused purely on my bug backlog and getting the most critical issues fixed. It takes a lot of discipline to not go off and implement new features, but as long as you can mentally reward yourself for bug fixes, it can be rewarding in its own right.

Off the top of my head, some areas that need more research and development in JavaFX include the following:

- A dialogs API
- A docking framework control
- Rich text editing
- Full accessibility support
- Improved focus traversal support
- Improved performance (especially on embedded devices)

I should note that this is primarily related to my specific area of JavaFX—UI controls—and not necessarily what the priorities are of the wider JavaFX team. Also, I should add that a number of these areas are covered in third-party projects such as JFXtras (http://jfxtras.org) and ControlsFX (www.controlsfx.org).

(Continued)

I think your statements will underline the great work that has been done by your team in the past few years. I think you all created a modern framework that will help developers build awesome applications. Is there any additional information or tips that you want to share with the readers of this book?

Sure, just briefly I better call out the excellent work being done by the community. I try my best to highlight this on a weekly basis on my web site at www.jonathangiles.net and www.fxexperience.com. The community is doing a great job testing, using, experimenting, and reporting bugs. If you are new to JavaFX and want to join the community but don't know where to begin, I highly recommend you just reach out to someone such as myself or Hendrik, and we'll happily give you guidance. I can be reached at jonathan.giles@oracle.com.

We're about to release JavaFX 8.0 in the coming weeks, and it is going to be an excellent release, but we never stand still, and already Java 8u20 is in the works, which will be even better. My point is—if at all possible, I highly encourage you to work with the bleeding edge of JavaFX to ensure you have the best experience and to help me and the rest of the JavaFX team squash bugs.

Thank you for the great interview.

Summary

This chapter discussed several advanced JavaFX controls. As you can see, the framework provides a huge set of special control types that can be used in custom applications. The `ListView`, `TableView`, and `TreeView` APIs especially provide a lot of functionality that I can't entirely cover here. The most important parts and functionalities of all controls were covered, and you can find more special use cases in the JavaDoc of the controls.

CHAPTER
7

Additional JavaFX Nodes

JavaFX contains a set of extra node classes that you can use to represent specific data and content onscreen. These nodes do not extend the `Control` class, so I will discuss them separately in this chapter because of their special functions and behavior. This chapter will introduce these special nodes and show how to use them by illustrating the following node types:

- `Charts`
- `WebView`
- `Canvas`
- `ImageView`
- `MediaView`

Most of these components provide a huge set of functionality, but I will focus on the core features and common use cases.

Charts

JavaFX contains an API to create modern charts. All chart types in JavaFX extend the `Chart` class, which extends `Node`. Here are the types of charts that JavaFX supports:

- `PieChart`
- `BubbleChart`
- `StackedAreaChart`
- `ScatterChart`
- `BarChart`
- `AreaChart`
- `LineChart`
- `StackedBarChart`

With the exception of the `PieChart`, all chart types are defined as x-y charts. This means that all values in these charts are shown in x-y coordinate systems, and often the x-axis defines different types or categories instead of a range of values. Except for the `PieChart` class, all charts extend the basic class `XYChart<X,Y>`. As you can see, the type of the x- and y-axis is defined by generics. Figure 7-1 shows an overview of all the chart types.

Let's first look at the `PieChart`. Like the other charts, the `PieChart` class extends the `Node` class and can be added to a scene graph like any other node. The following code snippet shows how to create a `PieChart`:

```
private PieChart getPieChart() {
    ObservableList<PieChart.Data> pieChartData =
        FXCollections.observableArrayList(
            new PieChart.Data("SWT", 13),
            new PieChart.Data("AWT", 10),
            new PieChart.Data("Swing", 22),
            new PieChart.Data("JavaFX", 30));
```

```
        final PieChart chart = new PieChart(pieChartData);
        chart.setTitle("Ui Toolkits");
        return chart;
    }
```

As you can see, the chart needs an `ObservableList<PieChart.Data>` as its data model. The `PieChart.Data` class defines a tuple where a value is mapped to a numeric value. From this list, the control renders the top-left chart in Figure 7-1. All chart types define properties that you can use to change the rendering and behavior of the chart. Although all the properties of the chart nodes won't be shown here, you can find a comprehensive list in the JavaDoc of the chart classes.

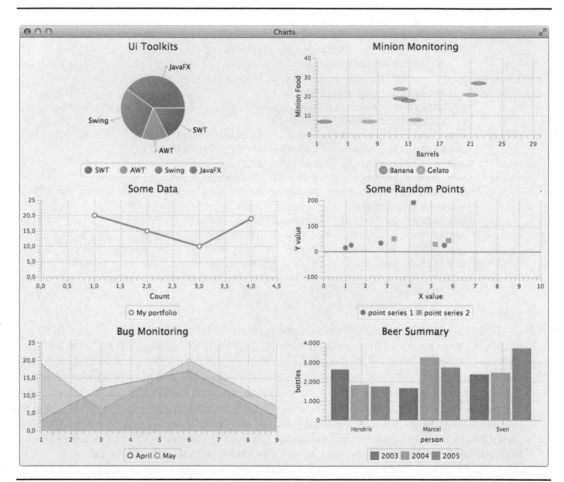

FIGURE 7-1. *Chart types in JavaFX*

NOTE
*For all chart types, the `ObservableList` is used to define the data
of the chart so the chart can observe its data and react dynamically
whenever the data changes. In other words, all charts will update
its view whenever the data changes via an animation. You use the
`animated` property of the `Chart` class to toggle this functionality. In
an `XYChart`, you can even access the axis and define animations for
both the axis and its range.*

As mentioned earlier, all other chart classes extend the `XYChart`. Given this similarity, I'll
show one example here. The following code snippet creates the `AreaChart` that is shown at the
bottom-left corner of Figure 7-1:

```
private AreaChart<Number,Number> getAreaChart() {
        final NumberAxis xAxis = new NumberAxis(1, 9, 1);
        final NumberAxis yAxis = new NumberAxis();
        final AreaChart<Number,Number> ac =
                new AreaChart<>(xAxis,yAxis);
        ac.setTitle("Bug Monitoring");
        XYChart.Series<Number,Number> seriesApril= new XYChart.Series<>();
        seriesApril.setName("April");
        seriesApril.getData().add(new XYChart.Data(1, 3));
        seriesApril.getData().add(new XYChart.Data(3, 12));
        seriesApril.getData().add(new XYChart.Data(6, 17));
        seriesApril.getData().add(new XYChart.Data(9, 4));
        XYChart.Series<Number,Number> seriesMay = new XYChart.Series<>();
        seriesMay.setName("May");
        seriesMay.getData().add(new XYChart.Data(1, 19));
        seriesMay.getData().add(new XYChart.Data(3, 6));
        seriesMay.getData().add(new XYChart.Data(6, 20));
        seriesMay.getData().add(new XYChart.Data(9, 7));
        ac.setData(FXCollections.observableArrayList(seriesApril, seriesMay));
        return ac;
    }
```

Data can be defined for all two-axis chart series, and these series are defined by the
`XYChart.Series<X,Y>` class. In the example, both axes are numeric, so the example uses
`XYChart.Series<Number,Number>`. Each series can be defined by a name, and each series
can contain data tuples that map an x-value to a y-value. These tuples are defined by the
`XYChart.Data<X,Y>` class. In the example code, you can see how to add data to a series.
The `Series` class contains a `name` property of type `StringProperty` that will hold the name of
the series. Also, as shown in the example, a chart can contain several series of data. The `XYChart`
class defines the `data` property of type `ObjectProperty<ObservableList<Series<X,Y>>>`
that will hold all the data series. You can use this workflow for all the chart types.

In addition to the data rendering, each chart contains a legend with an overview of the different
data series that are rendered in the chart. The visual appearance of the legend and the chart can be

configured by properties or by CSS. (Chapter 9 shows an example of how a chart can be styled by CSS.) Here are some examples of settings that can be changed in code or CSS:

- The label of the axis
- Minimum and maximum tick marks
- The gap between tick marks
- The position of the legend

NOTE
Like most of the other more complex node types in JavaFX, the charts internally are constructed by several nodes. In a BarChart, *each bar in the diagram is a node in the scene graph. You can access these nodes using the* node *property of the* XYChart.Data<X,Y> *class. In fact, more advanced developers can apply visual effects to these nodes or transform them whenever a mouse hovers over a bar in a* BarChart, *for example.*

WebView

JavaFX supports the rendering of HTML content with the help of the WebView. A WebView is a node that renders a web page into the scene graph. Unlike in older UI toolkits, WebView supports dynamic as well as static HTML pages. The node uses WebKit internally to render the defined page. WebKit is an HTML rendering engine that is used in browsers such as Apple Safari. Therefore, the WebView supports all the HTML, CSS, and JavaScript features that are supported by WebKit. Additionally, the WebView contains a WebEngine that can be used to interact with the defined page or to execute JavaScript, for example. The following application uses a WebView and loads any web page:

```
package com.guigarage.masteringcontrols;
import javafx.application.Application;
import javafx.scene.Scene;
import javafx.scene.control.ProgressBar;
import javafx.scene.control.TextField;
import javafx.scene.layout.HBox;
import javafx.scene.layout.Priority;
import javafx.scene.layout.StackPane;
import javafx.scene.layout.VBox;
import javafx.scene.web.WebView;
import javafx.stage.Stage;
public class WebViewApplication extends Application {
    @Override
    public void start(Stage primaryStage) throws Exception {
        WebView webView = new WebView();
        TextField urlField = new TextField();
        urlField.setOnAction(e -> webView.getEngine().load(urlField.getText()));
        ProgressBar progressBar = new ProgressBar();
        progressBar.setMaxWidth(Double.MAX_VALUE);
        progressBar.progressProperty().bind(webView.getEngine().getLoadWorker().
            progressProperty());
```

```
        VBox myPane = new VBox();
        myPane.getChildren().addAll(urlField, webView, progressBar);
        Scene myScene = new Scene(myPane);
        primaryStage.setScene(myScene);
        primaryStage.setTitle("Guigarage Viewer");
        primaryStage.show();
    }
    public static void main(String[] args) {
        launch(args);
    }
}
```

When starting the application, you can enter a custom URL in the text field. After pressing ENTER, the web page will be loaded and rendered in the `WebView`. Figure 7-2 shows an example of a loaded page. As you can see in the code, all interaction with the HTML content of the

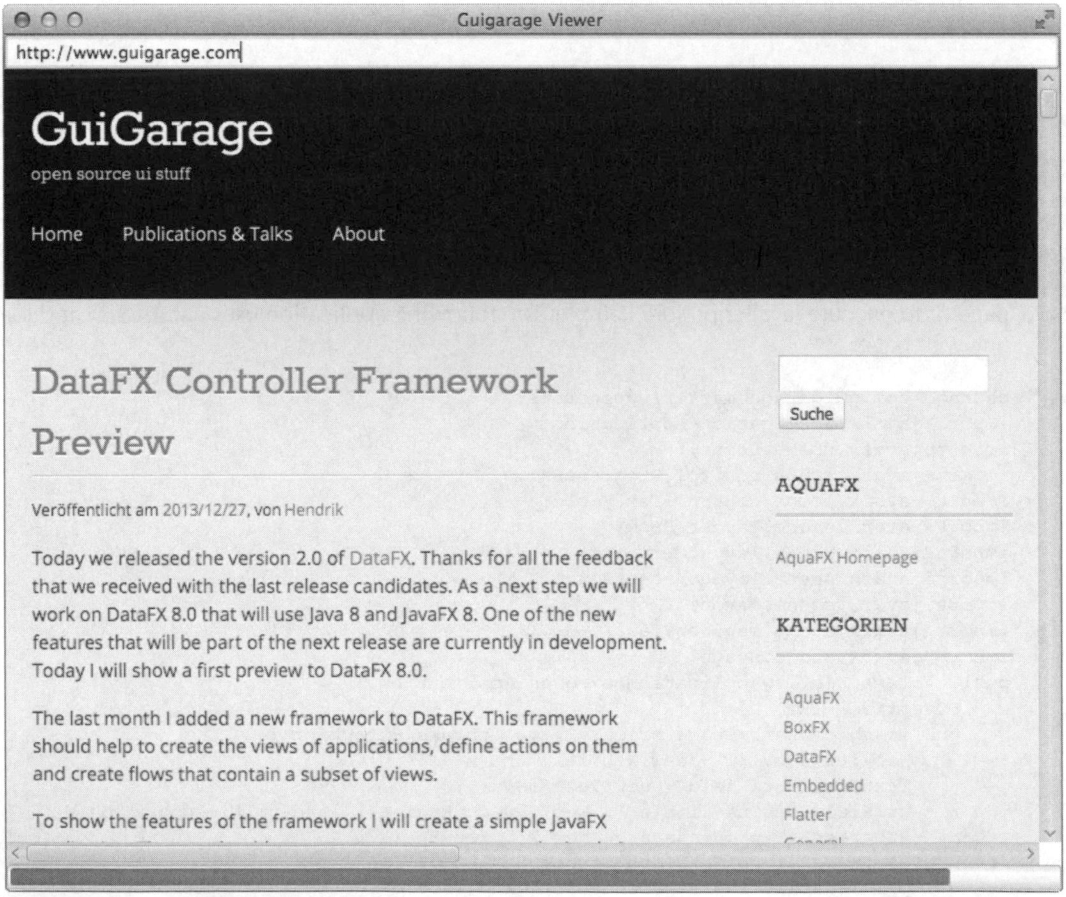

FIGURE 7-2. *WebView that renders a web page*

WebView is performed on the WebEngine. You access the engine by using the getEngine() method of the WebView. To load a custom page, the engine offers a load(...) method. In the sample, this method is invoked whenever the ENTER key is pressed in the text field. In addition to the TextField and the WebView, the example application uses a ProgressBar control, and the progress property of this progress bar is bound to the load progress of the current site. In Figure 7-2, most of the data of the defined web site has loaded, and like in all modern web browsers, the loaded parts of the page are shown on the screen. But as you can see in the figure, some content has not loaded because the progress bar is not completely filled.

The WebView node offers some properties that can be used to define the visual rendering of a web page. This can be done in a JavaFX application too. Table 7-1 contains the properties of the WebView class.

All interaction with the web page and the JavaScript support is wrapped in the WebEngine class, which offers a set of properties to define the behavior of the web page and the handling of

Property	Type	Description
contextMenuEnabled	BooleanProperty	Defines whether the context menu is enabled.
fontScale	DoubleProperty	Defines a scale factor that is applied to the font size in a rendered HTML content.
fontSmoothingType	ObjectProperty <FontSmoothingType>	Specifies a requested font-smoothing type.
Zoom	DoubleProperty	Defines the zoom factor applied to the whole HTML content.
Height	ReadOnlyDoubleProperty	Defines the height of the WebView.
Width	ReadOnlyDoubleProperty	Defines the width of the WebView.
maxHeight	ReadOnlyDoubleProperty	Defines the maximum height of the WebView.
maxWidth	ReadOnlyDoubleProperty	Defines the maximum width of the WebView.
minHeight	ReadOnlyDoubleProperty	Defines the minimum height of the WebView.
minWidth	ReadOnlyDoubleProperty	Defines the minimum width of the WebView.
prefHeight	ReadOnlyDoubleProperty	Defines the preferred height of the WebView.
prefWidth	ReadOnlyDoubleProperty	Defines the preferred width of the WebView.

TABLE 7-1. *Properties of the WebView*

JavaScript. To understand some of these properties, you need a basic knowledge of JavaScript and web development. I won't discuss these properties in depth here, but you can see an overview of them in Table 7-2.

In addition to these properties, the `WebEngine` class offers several useful methods, including the one that is shown in the demo application, which loads and renders new content in `WebView` by calling the `load(String url)` method of the engine. In addition to the `load(...)` method, the content of a `WebView` can be reloaded or a custom script can be executed in the context of the current web page. Table 7-3 shows the public methods of the `WebEngine` class.

The following example uses some of the properties that are part of the `WebView`. These properties will affect the rendering of the web page. In the example, the font scale and zoom are

Property	Type	Description
confirmHandler	ObjectProperty <Callback<String, Boolean>>	Defines the handler that is invoked when the JavaScript `confirm(...)` function is called internally.
createPopupHandler	ObjectProperty<Callback <PopupFeatures, WebEngine>>	Defines the handler that is invoked when a script on the web page creates a pop-up.
document	ReadOnlyObjectProperty <Document>	Defines the current document object for the current web page.
location	ReadOnlyStringProperty	Defines the URL of the current page.
onAlert	ObjectProperty<EventHandler <WebEvent<String>>>	Defines the handler that is invoked when the JavaScript `alert(...)` function is called internally.
onError	ObjectProperty<EventHandler <WebErrorEvent>>	Defines the event handler called when an error occurs.
onResized	ObjectProperty<EventHandler <WebEvent<Rectangle2D>>>	Defines the handler that is invoked when JavaScript wants to resize the window object of the page.
onStatusChanged	ObjectProperty<EventHandler <WebEvent<String>>>	Defines the handler that is invoked when the `window.status` is set by JavaScript.

TABLE 7-2.   *Properties of the WebEngine*

Property	Type	Description
onVisibilityChanged	ObjectProperty<EventHandler <WebEvent<Boolean>>>	Handler that is invoked when a JavaScript wants to change the visibility of the window object.
promptHandler	ObjectProperty<Callback <PromptData, String>>	Defines the handler that is invoked when the JavaScript prompt (...) function is called internally.
title	ReadOnlyStringProperty	Defines the title of the shown page.
userAgent	StringProperty	Defines the value of the User-Agent HTTP header.
userDataDirectory	ObjectProperty<File>	Defines a directory that is used by the engine to store user data.
userStyleSheetLocation	StringProperty	Defines the URL of the user style sheet.
javaScriptEnabled	BooleanProperty	Defines whether JavaScript is enabled.

TABLE 7-2.   *Properties of the WebEngine* (continued)

Method	Description
Object executeScript(String script)	Executes a script in the context of the current page and returns the result.
WebHistory getHistory()	Returns the history of the session.
Worker<Void> getLoadWorker()	Returns a worker that can be used to track the loading progress of a web site.
void load(String url)	Loads the web page that is defined by the URL.
void loadContent(String content)	Loads the given HTML content directly.
void print(PrinterJob job)	Prints the current web page using the given printer job.
reload()	Reloads the current content.

TABLE 7-3.   *Methods of the WebEngine*

FIGURE 7-3.   *A customized WebEngine*

defined. For both of these properties, 1.0 is the default value. By setting the two properties to 1.5, all fonts on the rendered page will appear in a bigger size and the page will be zoomed in. Figure 7-3 shows the same web site as before that is now rendered by a `WebView` with the changed properties.

```
package com.guigarage.masteringcontrols;
import javafx.application.Application;
import javafx.scene.Scene;
import javafx.scene.layout.StackPane;
import javafx.scene.web.WebView;
import javafx.stage.Stage;
public class WebViewApplication extends Application {
    @Override
    public void start(Stage primaryStage) throws Exception {
```

```
WebView webView = new WebView();
webView.setFontScale(1.5);
webView.setZoom(1.5);
webView.getEngine().load("http://www.guigarage.com");
StackPane myPane = new StackPane();
myPane.getChildren().add(webView);
Scene myScene = new Scene(myPane);
primaryStage.setScene(myScene);
primaryStage.setTitle("Guigarage Viewer");
primaryStage.show();
    }
    public static void main(String[] args) {
        launch(args);
    }
}
```

NOTE
Because the WebView *and all other components that are shown in this chapter are nodes in a scene graph, they can be easily transformed like any other node object. To do that, you define a rotation for the* WebView, *as shown in Chapter 3. The following code snippet shows how this can be done:*

```
webView.setRotate(45.0);
```

The zoom *property of the* WebView *is used by the WebKit internally, and the page is rendered in the defined zoom. If you scale the WebKit as described in Chapter 3, it can end in blurry pixels because JavaFX will scale the rendered result that is pixel based and not vector based.*

As mentioned, WebView and the WebKit-based engine support JavaScript. The following example shows how JavaScript can be used to create interaction between web content and JavaFX. The demo is a simple HTML page containing a small JavaScript section. In the script, the alert (…) function will be called. This function is a JavaScript default function that normally will create a pop-up that is shown onscreen. The script will be executed when a hyperlink on the page is clicked.

```
<html><head><title>Alert Demo</title>
</head><body>
<a href="javascript:alert('Alert message')">show alert</a>
</body></html>
```

The HTML file can be opened with a web browser like Chrome or Safari. Once the hyperlink is clicked, an alert dialog will be shown. The dialog contains the alert message. In JavaFX you can define a handler for the alert (…). The following application loads the HTML file in a WebView and defines a special handler for JavaScript alert (…) executions:

```
package com.guigarage.masteringcontrols;
import javafx.application.Application;
import javafx.scene.Scene;
```

```
import javafx.scene.layout.StackPane;
import javafx.scene.web.WebView;
import javafx.stage.Stage;
public class WebViewApplication extends Application {
    @Override
    public void start(Stage primaryStage) throws Exception {
        WebView webView = new WebView();
        webView.getEngine().setOnAlert(e -> System.out.println("JS Alert: " +
            e.getData()));
        webView.getEngine().load("file:///path/to/alertDemo.html");
        StackPane myPane = new StackPane();
        myPane.getChildren().addAll(webView);
        Scene myScene = new Scene(myPane);
        primaryStage.setScene(myScene);
        primaryStage.titleProperty().bind(webView.getEngine().titleProperty());
        primaryStage.show();
    }
    public static void main(String[] args) {
        launch(args);
    }
}
```

Whenever the hyperlink is clicked in the `WebView`, the alert handler will fire an event, and a message will be printed on the console. As shown in Table 7-2, the `WebEngine` class provides the ability to define different handlers for default JavaScript functions in addition to the alert one. The application uses an additional property of the engine too. The `title` property of the `WebEngine` is bound to the title of the JavaFX stage. As you can see in the HTML file, the title of the web page is defined as Alert Demo. Once the page is loaded in the application, the title of the window will change to the one defined in the web page.

Beyond this simple example, the `WebEngine` provides everything needed to create complete interaction between HTML content and JavaFX. Anyone familiar with JavaScript can integrate a web application in a JavaFX application and use the best features from both worlds.

Canvas

The `Canvas` node in JavaFX is comparable to the HTML5 canvas or the `Graphics2D` class from Java2D. The `Canvas` can be used to draw any figure, image, or collage onscreen. Like the `Canvas` objects in other programming languages, the `Canvas` node provides a graphics context that has all the needed methods to draw lines, splines, shapes, or images in the canvas. In JavaFX, the graphics context is defined by the `GraphicsContext` class, and you can retrieve the context by calling the `canvas.getGraphicsContext2D()` method. The class provides a set of graphics commands, and if you have used a canvas-based API before, you will be familiar with these methods. This book won't cover all of these methods, but a good overview is available in the JavaDoc of the `GraphicsContext` class.

The following example uses a `Canvas` node and draws some figures on it:

```
package com.guigarage.masteringcontrols;
import javafx.application.Application;
import javafx.scene.Scene;
import javafx.scene.canvas.Canvas;
import javafx.scene.canvas.GraphicsContext;
import javafx.scene.layout.StackPane;
```

```java
import javafx.scene.paint.Color;
import javafx.scene.shape.ArcType;
import javafx.stage.Stage;
public class CanvasDemo extends Application {
    @Override
    public void start(Stage primaryStage) throws Exception {
        Canvas canvas = new Canvas(220, 220);
        GraphicsContext gc = canvas.getGraphicsContext2D();
        gc.setFill(Color.AQUA);
        gc.setStroke(Color.MAGENTA);
        gc.setLineWidth(2);
        gc.strokeLine(10, 10, 100, 100);
        gc.fillRoundRect(10, 120, 80, 80, 10, 10);
        gc.strokeRoundRect(120, 10, 80, 80, 10, 10);
        gc.setStroke(Color.GREEN);
        gc.strokeArc(120, 120, 80, 80, 16, 290, ArcType.ROUND);
        StackPane myPane = new StackPane();
        myPane.getChildren().add(canvas);
        Scene myScene = new Scene(myPane);
        primaryStage.setScene(myScene);
        primaryStage.setTitle("Canvas Demo");
        primaryStage.show();
    }
    public static void main(String[] args) {
        launch(args);
    }
}
```

As you can see, the `Canvas` object isn't created with an empty constructor. Here, the width and height of the node are defined. Because a canvas can contain any drawing, it can't know its own size, so you need to specify the size of a canvas. In the example code, some figures are drawn by using the `GraphicsContext` of the `Canvas`. Figure 7-4 shows the result of this drawing.

The `Canvas` and the `GraphicsContext` won't clear the drawing in the canvas. Unlike in Swing where the internal API clears the complete canvas with each repaint, you need to do this by hand in JavaFX. As a result, the JavaFX Canvas API is more flexible. The following sample defines an interactive canvas. Rectangles can be drawn in the canvas by mouse clicks. In addition, the canvas can be cleared.

```java
package com.guigarage.masteringcontrols;
import javafx.application.Application;
import javafx.geometry.Insets;
import javafx.geometry.Pos;
import javafx.scene.Scene;
import javafx.scene.canvas.Canvas;
import javafx.scene.canvas.GraphicsContext;
import javafx.scene.control.Button;
import javafx.scene.layout.HBox;
import javafx.scene.layout.VBox;
import javafx.scene.paint.Color;
import javafx.stage.Stage;
import java.util.Random;
```

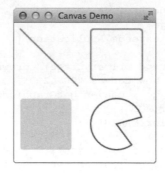

FIGURE 7-4. *The Canvas node*

```java
public class CanvasDemo extends Application {

    @Override
    public void start(Stage primaryStage) throws Exception {
        Canvas canvas = new Canvas(800, 600);
        GraphicsContext gc = canvas.getGraphicsContext2D();
        canvas.setOnMouseClicked(e -> stamp(gc, e.getX(), e.getY()));
        Button fillButton = new Button("fill");
        fillButton.setOnAction(e -> fill(gc));
        Button clearButton = new Button("clear");
        clearButton.setOnAction(e -> clear(gc));
        HBox box = new HBox(fillButton, clearButton);
        box.setSpacing(6);
        box.setAlignment(Pos.CENTER);
        box.setPadding(new Insets(6));
        VBox myPane = new VBox();
        myPane.getChildren().addAll(canvas, box);
        Scene myScene = new Scene(myPane);
        primaryStage.setScene(myScene);
        primaryStage.setTitle("Canvas Demo");
        primaryStage.show();
    }

    private void fill(GraphicsContext gc) {
        Random random = new Random(System.currentTimeMillis());
        Color color = Color.color(random.nextDouble(), random.nextDouble(),
            random.nextDouble());
        gc.setFill(color);
        gc.fillRect(0, 0, gc.getCanvas().getWidth(), gc.getCanvas().getHeight());
    }

    private void clear(GraphicsContext gc) {
        gc.clearRect(0, 0, gc.getCanvas().getWidth(), gc.getCanvas().getHeight());
    }

    private void stamp(GraphicsContext gc, double x, double y) {
        Random random = new Random(System.currentTimeMillis());
        Color color = Color.color(random.nextDouble(), random.nextDouble(),
            random.nextDouble());
```

```
        gc.setFill(color);
        double size = random.nextDouble() * 300;
        gc.fillRect(x - size / 2, y - size / 2, size, size);
    }
    public static void main(String[] args) {
        launch(args);
    }
}
```

The class defines three methods that will draw in the canvas: The `fill`(...) method will fill the complete canvas with a custom color, the `clear`(...) method will clear the canvas, and the `stamp`(...) method will add a rectangle to the canvas. By adding an event handler for mouse events to the `Canvas`, you can add rectangles to the `Canvas`, as shown in Figure 7-5.

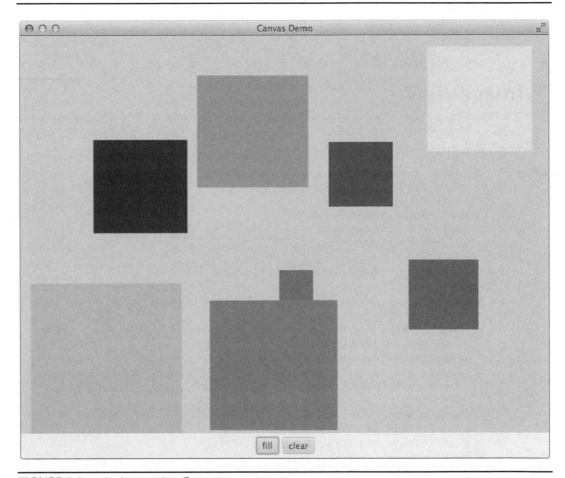

FIGURE 7-5. *An interactive Canvas*

Some drawing features of the `Canvas` are not shown in the demo applications. For example, the `GraphicsContext` provides a great path API that can be used to draw a path with Bézier curves on the screen. Furthermore, images can be drawn.

NOTE
JavaFX provides a lot of basic shapes, such as rectangles and lines, as nodes that can be used directly in the scene graph. Some developers may ask themselves why the `Canvas` node is needed in addition to these shapes. Each node in JavaFX contains basic functionalities such as CSS support, skinning, and a lot of properties. Sometimes, this is not needed, and when drawing in a `Canvas`, this "overhead" doesn't apply. All the nodes need to be added to the scene graph, and panes must provide the layout for them. In a `Canvas`, a developer can draw shapes by simply defining x-y coordinates. In addition, shapes that are drawn to a `Canvas` don't exist as object instances and can't be changed in the future. In some special cases, using the `Canvas` is much faster and provides more performance than defining all drawings in the scene graph.

ImageView

The `ImageView` is the default component to show any image in a defined size in a scene graph. To do so, you need an image as defined by the `Image` class in JavaFX. The following example shows how to use the `ImageView` node:

```java
package com.guigarage.masteringcontrols;
import javafx.application.Application;
import javafx.scene.Scene;
import javafx.scene.image.Image;
import javafx.scene.image.ImageView;
import javafx.scene.layout.StackPane;
import javafx.stage.Stage;
public class ImageViewDemo extends Application {
    @Override
    public void start(Stage primaryStage) throws Exception {
        StackPane myPane = new StackPane();
        Image image = new Image(getClass().getResource("pic.jpg").toString());
        ImageView imageView = new ImageView(image);
        imageView.setPreserveRatio(true);
        imageView.fitWidthProperty().bind(myPane.widthProperty());
        imageView.fitHeightProperty().bind(myPane.heightProperty());
        myPane.getChildren().add(imageView);
        Scene myScene = new Scene(myPane);
        primaryStage.setScene(myScene);
        primaryStage.setTitle("Image Viewer");
        primaryStage.setWidth(300);
        primaryStage.setHeight(200);
        primaryStage.show();
    }
```

```
public static void main(String[] args) {
    launch(args);
}
}
```

The code loads an image that is part of the `classpath` and is stored in the same package as the `Application` class. The loaded image will be shown in an `ImageView` and is defined by an instance of the `Image` class. Because the `ImageView` is always maximized in the sample application window and the image might be smaller or bigger than the `ImageView`, a binding is used in the example. The width and the height of the `StackPane` that is the parent of the `ImageView` are bound to the size of the image. By doing it this way, the window can be resized, and the image will always fit perfectly into it. Additionally, the `preserveRatio` property of the `ImageView` node is set. As a result, the `ImageView` will always preserve the aspect ratio of the image when resizing it. Figure 7-6 shows the application.

The `ImageView` class defines a set of properties that can be used to change the rendering of the defined image. Some of them, such as the `preserveRatio` property, are used in the example. Table 7-4 contains all properties of the `ImageView` class.

FIGURE 7-6. *An ImageView*

Property	Type	Description
fitHeight	DoubleProperty	Defines the height of a bounding box. The image will be scaled to fit in it.
fitWidth	DoubleProperty	Defines the width of a bounding box. The image will be scaled to fit in it.
image	ObjectProperty<Image>	Defines the image that is rendered in the ImageView.
viewport	ObjectProperty<Rectangle2D>	Defines the area of the image that is shown in the ImageView.
preserveRatio	BooleanProperty	Defines whether the aspect ratio of the image should be preserved when a fitHeight or fitWidth is defined.
smooth	BooleanProperty	Defines whether the image should be rendered by a better-quality filtering algorithm or a faster one.
x	DoubleProperty	Defines the x-coordinate of the ImageView origin.
y	DoubleProperty	Defines the y-coordinate of the ImageView origin.

TABLE 7-4.   *Properties of the ImageView Class*

The ImageView always needs an Image object to render anything onscreen. An Image object is always defined by the Image class, whose properties are shown in Table 7-5.

The Image class also provides some constructors that can be used to load an image. These constructors support different sources and options; Table 7-6 gives an overview of the parameters that can be found in the constructors of the Image class. As you can see, an image can be loaded by an URL or a stream. Currently, JavaFX supports JPEG, PNG, GIF, and BMP images. The API to add image types is still private in JDK 8. If a custom image is needed or if the visual content of an image needs to be changed, you should use the WriteableImage. This class extends the Image class and offers a PixelWriter to set the RGB value of specific pixels. You can access the writer by using the getPixelWriter() method. In addition, the Image class contains the getPixelReader() method that offers a PixelReader that provides access to the pixels of an image. With the help of these two methods, images can be easily changed. As a result, you can create custom filters that change the saturation or brightness of an image, for example.

Property	Type	Description
error	ReadOnlyBooleanProperty	Indicates whether an error was detected while loading an image
exception	ReadOnlyObjectProperty<Exception>	Defines the exception that caused image loading to fail
height	ReadOnlyDoubleProperty	Defines the image height
progress	ReadOnlyDoubleProperty	Defines the progress while the image is loaded
width	ReadOnlyDoubleProperty	Defines the image width

TABLE 7-5. *Properties of the Image Class*

NOTE
JavaFX supports animated images too. A GIF, for example, can be animated. This image can be loaded by the Image *class like any other image. You can use the* isAnimation() *method of the* Image *class to check whether an image is animated. If an image is animated, a* PixelReader *can't be used. In this case, the* pixelsReadable() *method of the image instance will return false.*

Parameter	Type	Description
url	String	Defines the URL of the image. To define an image, an URL or an InputStream is needed.
InputStream	InputStream	Defines the data of the image as a stream. To define an image, an URL or an InputStream is needed.
requestedWidth	double	Defines the width of a bounding box. The image will be scaled to fit in it.
requestedHeight	double	Defines the height of a bounding box. The image will be scaled to fit in it.
preserveRatio	boolean	Defines whether the aspect ratio of the image should be preserved when a requestedWidth or requestedHeight is defined.
Smooth	boolean	Defines whether the image should be resized by a better-quality filtering algorithm or a faster one.
backgroundLoading	boolean	Defines whether the image should be loaded in the background.

TABLE 7-6. *Constructor Parameters of the Image Class*

MediaView

The MediaView is a JavaFX control that can render video playback onscreen. The MediaView internally uses the JavaFX media API, and this API is defined in the javafx.scene.media package. The API can be used to play audio too. Because the MediaView is shown here, the following description is limited to video support.

The following video formats are currently supported by JavaFX:

- FLV containing VP6 video and MP3 audio
- MPEG-4 multimedia container with H.264/Advanced Video Coding (AVC) video compression

NOTE
On some older Windows versions and Linux systems, additional software packages may be needed to support specific video codecs. Information about these topics can be found in the JavaFX system requirements: http://docs.oracle.com/javafx/release-documentation.html.

The following example shows how to display a video in a JavaFX application:

```java
package com.guigarage.masteringcontrols;
import javafx.application.Application;
import javafx.scene.Scene;
import javafx.scene.layout.StackPane;
import javafx.scene.media.Media;
import javafx.scene.media.MediaPlayer;
import javafx.scene.media.MediaView;
import javafx.stage.Stage;
public class MediaViewDemo extends Application {
    @Override
    public void start(Stage primaryStage) throws Exception {
        Media media = new Media("http://download.oracle.com/otndocs/
                                products/javafx/oow2010-2.flv");
        MediaPlayer player = new MediaPlayer(media);
        MediaView mediaView = new MediaView(player);
        player.play();
        StackPane myPane = new StackPane();
        myPane.getChildren().add(mediaView);
        Scene myScene = new Scene(myPane);
        primaryStage.setScene(myScene);
        primaryStage.setWidth(300);
        primaryStage.setHeight(200);
        primaryStage.show();
    }
    public static void main(String[] args) {
        launch(args);
    }
}
```

As you can see in the code, the video is defined as a `Media` instance. Here, the path to the video data is assigned as a URL to the `Media` constructor. To play any media in JavaFX, you need a `MediaPlayer` instance. A player contains one `Media` instance that can be played, and the `MediaPlayer` defines different methods to handle the playback of the media. In the sample, the `play()` method is used. This method starts the playback. To render the video onscreen, you need a `MediaView`. When starting the sample, the video will be directly shown on the screen.

The `MediaPlayer` class provides a lot of useful methods and properties that can be used to handle the playback of the video, the audio volume, and other useful functionalities. By using these methods, the media playback can become interactive. It is easy to create "play" and "pause" buttons, for example. The following code shows how to define these methods:

```
Button playButton = new Button("play");
playButton.setOnAction((e) -> player.play());

Button pauseButton = new Button("pause");
pauseButton.setOnAction((e) -> player.pause());
```

Summary

All the node types covered in this chapter are great benefits of JavaFX because the nodes provide the ability to render different data types on the screen. Developers can add movies with the help of the `MediaView` to an application or render business data by using the chart API. Thanks to native dependencies such as WebKit and different video codecs, JavaFX provides state-of-the-art rendering for the mentioned data types. You won't find these visual components and their features in the basic APIs of older Java UI toolkits. With the use of the JavaFX APIs, it is easy to enrich an application, and I think that this will happen in a lot of desktop applications in the next years.

CHAPTER
8

Integrating JavaFX, Swing, and SWT

I n previous chapters, I used small JavaFX samples and applications to demonstrate JavaFX APIs and controls and showed how to create JavaFX applications by applying various functionalities and classes. Using these APIs, you'll master the basics necessary to create applications, and these APIs will enable larger-scale tasks for your work with JavaFX, such as creating business applications that use background tasks and that communicate with a server application or a database. In some cases, you may already have a desktop application that was created with Swing or SWT. If you want to migrate these applications to JavaFX or add some JavaFX features, you will find helpful classes and methods in JavaFX that enable interoperability between JavaFX and Swing/SWT. This chapter will show these parts of the JavaFX framework along with some best practices and use cases.

Combining JavaFX and Swing

JavaFX provides two classes that can be used to create an application that mixes JavaFX and Swing:

- `javafx.embed.swing.JFXPanel`
- `javafx.embed.swing.SwingNode`

The `JFXPanel` is a Swing JComponent that can be used to add a JavaFX scene graph to a Swing component hierarchy. The `SwingNode` is a JavaFX node that can be used to add Swing components to a JavaFX scene graph. These two classes allow integration between Swing and JavaFX in either direction: Swing can be integrated in JavaFX, and vice versa. Let's take a look at both uses.

Using the JFXPanel

With the help of the JFXPanel, you can enrich an existing Swing application with JavaFX. Therefore, the `JFXPanel` class provides the ability to add a JavaFX scene graph to a Swing application. The `JFXPanel` extends the `javax.swing.JComponent` class and is, therefore, a default Swing JComponent. Because of this, it can be added to any Swing component hierarchy, as shown in the following code snippet:

```
JFrame swingFrame = new JFrame("Integrate JavaFX in Swing");
swingFrame.getContentPane().setLayout(new BorderLayout());

swingFrame.getContentPane().add(BorderLayout.NORTH, new JButton("I'm a Swing button"));

JFXPanel jfxPanel = new JFXPanel();
swingFrame.getContentPane().add(BorderLayout.CENTER, jfxPanel);

swingFrame.setVisible(true);
```

This code defines a Swing `JFrame` that is shown on the screen. The frame contains a Swing-based button that is defined by the `JButton` class and an instance of the `JFXPanel` class. I won't discuss all the Swing internal mechanisms and how the Swing framework should be used; the important part is the JFXPanel instance that is added to the Swing frame. This instance is currently empty, and when running the sample, only the Swing button will be shown in the application window. For the next step, you can use the JFXPanel to add JavaFX controls to the Swing application, as shown here:

```
Button jfxButton = new Button("I'm a JavaFX button");
StackPane jfxPane = new StackPane(jfxButton);
Scene jfxScene = new Scene(jfxPane);
jfxPanel.setScene(jfxScene);
```

This code creates a JavaFX scene graph, which contains a JavaFX button that is wrapped in a StackPane. The last line of the snippet sets the scene graph to the JFXPanel. While this seems easy, there is a big problem: The code snippets shown cannot be mixed in a single thread. Swing operations need to be executed on the event dispatch thread (EDT), and all JavaFX operations need to be executed on the JavaFX application thread. Both Swing and JavaFX provide helpful methods to execute code on the needed thread. In Swing, you can use the SwingUtilites.invokeLater(Runnable doRun) method to execute a runnable on the EDT.

JavaFX's comparable method is Platform.runLater(Runnable doRun).

With the help of these methods, the code snippets shown can be wrapped in Runnable instances and executed on the right application threads. Let's start with the Swing part and create a simple sample application that uses the code snippet that was shown previously:

```
package com.guigarage.masteringcontrols;

import javafx.embed.swing.JFXPanel;

import javax.swing.*;
import java.awt.*;

public class JFXPanelDemo1 {
    public static void main(String[] args) {
        SwingUtilities.invokeLater(() -> {
            JFrame swingFrame = new JFrame("Integrate JavaFX in Swing");
            swingFrame.getContentPane().setLayout(new BorderLayout());
            swingFrame.getContentPane().add(BorderLayout.NORTH, new
                JButton("I'm a Swing button"));
            JFXPanel jfxPanel = new JFXPanel();
            swingFrame.getContentPane().add(BorderLayout.CENTER, jfxPanel);
            swingFrame.setVisible(true);
        }
        );
    }
}
```

In the sample, the complete code that is Swing specific is wrapped in a `Runnable` lambda expression and executed on the EDT. To add the JavaFX scene graph to the sample, the JavaFX code must be executed on a different thread. The following code demonstrates how to achieve this:

```java
package com.guigarage.masteringcontrols;

import javafx.application.Platform;
import javafx.embed.swing.JFXPanel;
import javafx.scene.Scene;
import javafx.scene.control.Button;
import javafx.scene.layout.StackPane;
import javax.swing.*;
import java.awt.*;

public class JFXPanelDemo1 {

    public static void main(String[] args) {
        SwingUtilities.invokeLater(() -> {
            JFrame swingFrame = new JFrame("Integrate JavaFX in Swing");
            swingFrame.getContentPane().setLayout(new BorderLayout());
            swingFrame.getContentPane().add(BorderLayout.NORTH, new
                JButton("I'm a Swing button"));
            JFXPanel jfxPanel = new JFXPanel();
            swingFrame.getContentPane().add(BorderLayout.CENTER, jfxPanel);
            Platform.runLater(() -> {
                Button jfxButton = new Button("I'm a JavaFX button");
                StackPane jfxPane = new StackPane(jfxButton);
                Scene jfxScene = new Scene(jfxPane);
                jfxPanel.setScene(jfxScene);
            });

            swingFrame.setVisible(true);
        }
        );
    }
}
```

The sample creates a Swing frame that contains a Swing-based button and a JavaFX button, as shown in Figure 8-1.

As you can see in the sample code, you now have a block that is wrapped in a `Runnable` and executed on the EDT. In this code block, the `Platform.runLater(...)` method is used to execute a `Runnable` on the JavaFX application thread. Here, the JavaFX button is defined. This approach greatly increases the complexity of the code but is necessary because both UI toolkits are defined as single-threaded toolkits, and therefore all the code that uses or modifies controls of the specific toolkit must be executed on the right thread. If you don't do this, an exception will be thrown at run time because the JavaFX scene wasn't initialized in the JavaFX application thread.

```
Exception in thread "AWT-EventQueue-0" java.lang.IllegalStateException: Not on
FX application thread; currentThread = AWT-EventQueue-0
```

FIGURE 8-1. *Mixing Swing and JavaFX*

Handling both UI threads will become even more complex when interaction between the two UI toolkits is needed. In the following example, an action listener is added to the Swing button that will influence the JavaFX button, and an action handler is defined for the JavaFX button that will modify the Swing one:

```
package com.guigarage.masteringcontrols;
import javafx.application.Platform;
import javafx.embed.swing.JFXPanel;
import javafx.scene.Scene;
import javafx.scene.control.Button;
import javafx.scene.layout.StackPane;
import javax.swing.*;
import java.awt.*;
public class JFXPanelDemo2 {

    private static JButton swingButton;
    private static Button jfxButton;

    public static void main(String[] args) {

        SwingUtilities.invokeLater(() -> {
            JFrame swingFrame = new JFrame("Integrate JavaFX in Swing");
            swingFrame.getContentPane().setLayout(new BorderLayout());
            swingButton =  new JButton("I'm a Swing button");
            swingFrame.getContentPane().add(BorderLayout.NORTH, swingButton);
            swingButton.addActionListener((e) ->{
                Platform.runLater(() -> {
                    jfxButton.setDisable(!jfxButton.isDisable());
                });
            });

            JFXPanel jfxPanel = new JFXPanel();
            swingFrame.getContentPane().add(BorderLayout.CENTER, jfxPanel);
            Platform.runLater(() -> {
```

```
        jfxButton = new Button("I'm a JavaFX button");
        StackPane jfxPane = new StackPane(jfxButton);
        Scene jfxScene = new Scene(jfxPane);
        jfxPanel.setScene(jfxScene);
        jfxButton.setOnAction((e) -> {
            SwingUtilities.invokeLater(() -> {
                swingButton.setEnabled(!swingButton.isEnabled());
            });
        });
    });

    swingFrame.setVisible(true);
}
);
}
}
```

The JavaFX and Swing toolkits both define that the code of a handler or listener will always be executed on the correct UI thread. Therefore, the lambda expression that is added as an `ActionListener` instance to the Swing button will be executed in the EDT, but the code will affect the JavaFX button and change its `disable` property. Therefore, the `Platform.runLater(…)` method must be used here again. Now the code block will be executed in the JavaFX application thread and change the `disable` property. A similar course of action is needed in the action handler of the JavaFX button. Here, `SwingUtilities.invokeLater(…)` is used to change the `enabled` bean property of the Swing button.

NOTE
In the previous sample, the button instances are defined as static fields of the class. This is normally not a good architecture, but it is used here to create a simple demo application in only a few lines of code. Normally, an instance of a custom class should be created, and this class can then contain the UI and the controller logic of the application.

As you can see, mixing both UI toolkits isn't trivial. So, why would you use this approach? You would do this if a given Swing application can't be migrated to JavaFX in only one step. By using the `JFXPanel`, individual parts of an application can be migrated one by one from Swing to JavaFX. This approach would also benefit you if you needed a special JavaFX control, such as the `WebView`, the graph API, or the `MediaView`, in a Swing application. Swing, for example, doesn't contain components such as the `WebView` or the `MediaView` that are defined as basic nodes in JavaFX. The graph API is another part of JavaFX that has no complement in the Swing basic components. Integrating JavaFX in a Swing application would allow you to add a `WebView` instance to a Swing application and show special HTML content onscreen. So, HTML5 and CSS3 can be rendered in an existing Swing app; only a few `Platform.runLater(…)` calls are needed, and it won't add to the complexity of the code too much.

NOTE

As you will see later, there is an experimental JavaFX feature that can be used to remove all the threading issues and make the EDT the same thread as the JavaFX application thread. Because this feature is still experimental and a developer should still know about handling the two threads, the first approach is discussed here.

The `JFXPanel` class extends the `JComponent` class, and therefore all the default methods that are known from Swing can be found and used here. In addition, the class provides only the two methods `getScene()` and `setScene(…)`, which can be used to define and access the internal scene graph of the component.

NOTE

In addition to the mentioned classes, JavaFX provides the `javafx .embed.swing.SwingFXUtils` class that contains a set of helpful methods when using Swing and JavaFX APIs in one application. Methods to convert `BufferedImage` instances to JavaFX Images, for example, can be found here.

Using the SwingNode

The `SwingNode` is a JavaFX node that can be used to integrate Swing components in a JavaFX application. As mentioned in the previous section, it is important to know about the different toolkit threads when working with the `SwingNode`. The following example defines a JavaFX sample and adds a Swing button to the application:

```
package com.guigarage.masteringcontrols;
import javafx.application.Application;
import javafx.application.Platform;
import javafx.embed.swing.SwingNode;
import javafx.geometry.Insets;
import javafx.geometry.Pos;
import javafx.scene.Scene;
import javafx.scene.control.Button;
import javafx.scene.layout.VBox;
import javafx.stage.Stage;
import javax.swing.*;
public class SwingNodeDemo extends Application {
    private Button jfxButton;

    private JButton swingButton;

    @Override
    public void start(Stage primaryStage) throws Exception {
        jfxButton = new Button("JavaFX Button");
        jfxButton.setOnAction((e) -> {
            SwingUtilities.invokeLater(() -> {
                swingButton.setEnabled(!swingButton.isEnabled());
            });
```

```
        });
        SwingNode swingNode = new SwingNode();
        SwingUtilities.invokeLater(() -> {
            swingButton = new JButton("Swing Button");
            swingButton.addActionListener((e) -> {
                Platform.runLater(() -> {
                    jfxButton.setDisable(!jfxButton.isDisabled());
                });
            });
            swingNode.setContent(swingButton);
        });
        VBox myPane = new VBox();
        myPane.setPadding(new Insets(12));
        myPane.setAlignment(Pos.CENTER);
        myPane.setSpacing(12);
        myPane.getChildren().addAll(jfxButton, swingNode);
        Scene myScene = new Scene(myPane);
        primaryStage.setScene(myScene);
        primaryStage.show();
    }
    public static void main(String[] args) {
        launch(args);
    }
}
```

In the example, a JavaFX application is created like in most other examples in this book, but this sample uses the `SwingNode` and integrates a Swing button. Therefore, a `JButton` instance is created and defined as the content of the `SwingNode`. The `JButton` instance must be created on the EDT, and because of that, the creation is wrapped in a `SwingUtilities` `.invokeLater(…)` method. Like in the demo of the `JFXPanel`, both buttons can be used to modify the other one. Therefore, `SwingUtilities.invokeLater(…)` and `Platform` `.runLater(…)` calls are needed. Using these methods is equal to the functionalities covered with the `JFXPanel`, so I won't discuss that again here. As in the `JFXPanel` example, the complete event handling of Swing and JavaFX is supported by the use of the `SwingNode`.

It is important to use only lightweight Swing components in a `SwingNode`. Swing extends the old AWT UI toolkit, and therefore, heavyweight AWT components can be added to a Swing component hierarchy. If the hierarchy of Swing components that is defined as the content of a `SwingNode` contains heavyweight components, the `SwingNode` may fail to paint them.

NOTE
As mentioned earlier in the book, only components that extend the Node *class can be part of a JavaFX scene graph, but a Swing component doesn't extend this class. So, how can a Swing component be added to an application with the help of the* SwingNode*? The* SwingNode *uses a* BufferedImage *internally to paint the Swing component into it. This* BufferedImage *will be shown in the JavaFX scene graph. As a result, the Swing* JButton *instance isn't a real part of the scene graph.*

Using the Experimental Single-Thread Mode

JavaFX provides an experimental mode to sync the EDT and JavaFX application thread. In this mode, both UI toolkits will share a single thread, and all events of both toolkits that normally will be handled on the specific UI thread will be on a single thread. To activate the experimental mode, you must set an environment property when starting the application:

```
-Djavafx.embed.singleThread=true
```

Once an application is started with this property, Swing and JavaFX will use just one thread, making the EDT the same thread as the JavaFX application thread. Doing this decreases the complexity of the examples shown so far. Let's take a look at the JFXPanel demo and refactor it to a version that can be used once the singleThread flag is set:

```java
package com.guigarage.masteringcontrols;
import javafx.embed.swing.JFXPanel;
import javafx.scene.Scene;
import javafx.scene.control.Button;
import javafx.scene.layout.StackPane;
import javax.swing.*;
import java.awt.*;

public class JFXPanelDemo1 {

    private static JButton swingButton;
    private static Button jfxButton;

    public static void main(String[] args) {
        final JFXPanel jfxPanel = new JFXPanel();
        SwingUtilities.invokeLater(() -> {
            JFrame swingFrame = new JFrame("Integrate JavaFX in Swing");
            swingFrame.getContentPane().setLayout(new BorderLayout());
            swingButton = new JButton("I'm a Swing button");
            swingFrame.getContentPane().add(BorderLayout.NORTH, swingButton);
            swingButton.addActionListener((e) -> {
                jfxButton.setDisable(!jfxButton.isDisable());
            });
            swingFrame.getContentPane().add(BorderLayout.CENTER, jfxPanel);
            jfxButton = new Button("I'm a JavaFX button");
            StackPane jfxPane = new StackPane(jfxButton);
            Scene jfxScene = new Scene(jfxPane);
            jfxPanel.setScene(jfxScene);
            jfxButton.setOnAction((e) -> {
                swingButton.setEnabled(!swingButton.isEnabled());
            });
            swingFrame.setVisible(true);
        });
    }
}
```

As you can see in the code, all the `Platform.runLater(...)` calls are removed. Because Swing and JavaFX share a single thread, only one `SwingUtilities.invokeLater(...)` call is needed here. In the sample, the creation of the `JFXPanel` instance is extracted to the main method and isn't part of the lambda expression that is passed to the `invokeLater(...)` method. By calling the constructor of the `JFXPanel`, JavaFX will set up the single-threaded event-dispatching mechanism.

Pros and Cons of the Integration

Mixing JavaFX and Swing brings both benefits and also potential issues. Let's start with the positive effects. By using the `SwingNode` or the `JFXPanel`, you can mix Swing components and JavaFX controls. This is useful if a company needs to migrate a Swing application to JavaFX. For applications where custom Swing components were specifically developed for that application, a developer wouldn't need to reimplement these custom components once migrated to JavaFX. The components could be still used in a JavaFX porting by using `SwingNode`, or you could migrate and refactor the application so only a few views and dialogs will be re-created in JavaFX. Here, the `JFXPanel` would be helpful because the new JavaFX views can be integrated in the given Swing application.

You should also be aware of potential problems that must be managed when doing such a migration. As mentioned, the complexity of the code will rise when two different UI toolkits are used. The main concepts of these toolkits are different, and therefore a developer must be an expert in both of them to manage the migration and its issues. In addition, the visual representation of JavaFX and Swing is completely different. JavaFX uses the so-called Modena theme to render its controls onscreen. Modena is a cross-platform theme that is used on every OS. Swing contains cross-platform themes like Metal or Nimbus, but these themes define a completely different look than Modena does. A user will always notice this break in the UI because the application will look inconsistent. In addition to Modena, JavaFX can use the Caspian theme that was already defined in JavaFX 2. Swing provides a platform-specific look and feel that can define the visualization of all Swing-based components as they would be rendered by the underlying OS. Often, this look and feel includes native code to render the skin of the Swing components directly by the operating system, but there is no match in any of them. Figure 8-2 shows how a button is rendered by the different JavaFX themes and Swing look and feel.

Additionally, mixing both UI toolkits can result in lags in performance. As mentioned, `BufferedImages` are used here to store the rendering of one toolkit and render it in the other one.

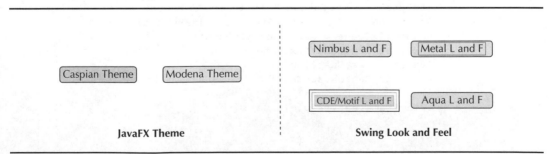

FIGURE 8-2. *Different representations of JavaFX and Swing*

NOTE
Some other third-party JavaFX themes have been released. AquaFX is one of them, and it can be used to imitate the look of native Mac OS controls. The platform-specific look and feel on Mac OS does the same in Swing, so on a Mac, these two themes can be used to create a more consistent look. Ideally, other JavaFX themes that do the same for other operating systems will follow.

Combining JavaFX and SWT

SWT is the default UI toolkit of the Eclipse IDE. It uses the native OS controls, so it cannot easily be configured to use custom UI features like you can do with JavaFX controls. Therefore, JavaFX provides a set of helpful classes that can be used to integrate JavaFX in SWT-based applications.

Because SWT is not part of the JDK or JRE, the integration is not as easy as it is with Swing. First, the SWT JAR must be added to the Java classpath. Since developers typically want to integrate JavaFX into an existing SWT application, this would already be arranged. If you still need the SWT JAR file, you can download it from the SWT release page (www.eclipse.org/swt/), or you can find it as part of an Eclipse installation at `eclipse/plugins/org.eclipse.swt**.jar`. Because SWT depends on the OS, you will need different JARs depending on the operating system where the application will be running. For Mac OS, you can use the `org.eclipse.swt.cocoa .macosx.x86_64_3.100.1.v4236b.jar` file that is defined in Eclipse Juno, for example.

In addition to the SWT JAR, specific JavaFX classes are needed. Because SWT is not part of the JDK, the complete SWT support of JavaFX is defined in a special JAR that is not part of the default Java class path. In a JDK 8 installation, the JAR can be found under `JAVA_HOME/jre/lib/ jfxswt.jar`. This JAR must be added to the classpath too. Once this is done, you will find the following class: `javafx.embed.swt.FXCanvas`.

Using the FXCanvas

All you need to integrate JavaFX with SWT is the `FXCanvas` class. This class extends the SWT `Canvas` class and can be used anywhere that an SWT canvas can appear. I won't take a deep dive into how SWT is internally working or what an SWT Canvas does. Instead, let's focus on the basic features of the `FXCanvas` class that are useful for SWT developers.

The `FXCanvas` class can be used to integrate a scene graph into your SWT application; the class provides two methods: `getScene()` and `setScene(Scene scene)`. The class can be used like the JFXPanel that was shown earlier. The following example defines an SWT application that contains an SWT button and a JavaFX button that can interact with each other:

```
package com.guigarage.masteringcontrols;
import javafx.embed.swt.FXCanvas;
import javafx.event.ActionEvent;
import javafx.event.EventHandler;
import javafx.scene.Scene;
import javafx.scene.control.Button;
import javafx.scene.layout.StackPane;
import org.eclipse.swt.SWT;
import org.eclipse.swt.graphics.Point;
import org.eclipse.swt.layout.RowLayout;
```

```java
import org.eclipse.swt.widgets.Display;
import org.eclipse.swt.widgets.Event;
import org.eclipse.swt.widgets.Listener;
import org.eclipse.swt.widgets.Shell;
public class SwtDemo {
    public static void main(String[] args) {
        final Display display = new Display();
        final Shell shell = new Shell(display);
        shell.setText("SWT meets JavaFX");
        final RowLayout layout = new RowLayout();
        shell.setLayout(layout);
        final org.eclipse.swt.widgets.Button swtButton =
                new org.eclipse.swt.widgets.Button(shell, SWT.PUSH);
        swtButton.setText("SWT Button");
        final FXCanvas fxCanvas = new FXCanvas(shell, SWT.NONE) {
            public Point computeSize(int wHint, int hHint, boolean changed) {
                getScene().getWindow().sizeToScene();
                int width = (int) getScene().getWidth();
                int height = (int) getScene().getHeight();
                return new Point(width, height);
            }
        };
        final Button jfxButton = new Button("JavaFX Button");
        Scene scene = new Scene(new StackPane(jfxButton));
        fxCanvas.setScene(scene);
        swtButton.addListener(SWT.Selection, new Listener() {
            public void handleEvent(Event event) {
                jfxButton.setDisable(!jfxButton.isDisable());
                shell.layout();
            }
        });
        jfxButton.setOnAction(new EventHandler<ActionEvent>() {
            public void handle(ActionEvent event) {
                swtButton.setEnabled(!swtButton.isEnabled());
                shell.layout();
            }
        });
        shell.open();
        while (!shell.isDisposed()) {
            if (!display.readAndDispatch()) {
                display.sleep();
            }
        }
        display.dispose();
    }
}
```

This code uses some SWT-specific classes such as the `Shell` and `Display` classes. These classes are used to create an SWT application that contains one frame. The frame contains an SWT button and an `FXCanvas` instance that is used as a wrapper around the JavaFX scene graph that holds the JavaFX button. Both buttons have an action listener defined that will handle their action events. Whenever the SWT button is clicked, the JavaFX button will change its `disabled` property. When the user clicks the JavaFX button, the enabled bean property of the SWT button will change. Figure 8-3 shows how the application will look at run time.

NOTE
To start the sample on a Mac, the special VM option
-XstartOnFirstThread must be specified.

When looking at the example, you will see a great benefit compared to the interoperability with Swing. When mixing SWT and JavaFX, the SWT event dispatch thread and the JavaFX application thread are automatically the same, so you will not need to handle two different threads like with Swing and JavaFX.

NOTE
The jfxswt.jar file that contains the FXCanvas class provides some additional classes. One of them, the SWTFXUtils class, can be used to convert between org.eclipse.swt.graphics.ImageData instances and JavaFX Image instances.

Because SWT uses the native OS to render the GUI components, these components will almost always look like native controls. Therefore, you will have the same problems with this approach as when mixing Swing and JavaFX: The controls will look different. As you can see in Figure 8-3, an SWT button doesn't look like a JavaFX button. So, it is a best practice to use this mix only for custom controls or controls that can't be created using SWT.

FIGURE 8-3. *AN SWT application with an internal JavaFX button*

Summary

JavaFX provides some helpful classes to create interoperability with Swing or SWT. These classes can be used to migrate big applications, but it's important to remain aware of the potential issues raised when mixing two different toolkits. If a mix is needed, choose wisely, and always consider how users will be impacted by visual inconsistencies in the UI.

I recommend using these techniques sparingly. The complexity of an application will always increase when you add a second UI toolkit. While it's fine to create some intermediate results in a migration that contains Swing and JavaFX controls, for example, the final goal of an application is to target only one UI toolkit. Issues aside, having JavaFX offer these classes is a great option when you need to mix JavaFX with other UI toolkits.

CHAPTER
9

Styling a Control

s shown in Chapter 5, you can style a control in Java code, setting different properties such as the text color of a button. If you need to style a complete application with several different controls, however, this workflow creates a lot of code. JavaFX supports CSS, though, allowing you to style a complete application or control. In this chapter, you'll learn how to apply CSS styling in JavaFX.

Using Themes to Style an Application

The fastest way to style a complete application in JavaFX is to use a custom theme. By default, all JavaFX applications use the Modena theme to style content (which is the theme applied to all the samples shown in this book). Prior to JavaFX 8, the default theme was Caspian, which is still available as an alternative theme in JavaFX 8. Both themes are considered cross-platform, ensuring a consistent look across all operating systems.

> **NOTE**
> *A theme in JavaFX is defined by a CSS style sheet. Even Modena is defined by a CSS file; the Modena CSS file is part of JavaFX and can be found in the* `jfxrt.jar` *file at* `com/sun/javafx/scene/control/skin/modena/modena.css`.

You can change the theme of an application with just one line of code, shown here:

```
setUserAgentStylesheet(Application.STYLESHEET_CASPIAN);
```

This code snippet sets the application's theme to Caspian. JavaFX contains static fields for Modena and Caspian, so you can easily change an application back to Modena, like so:

```
setUserAgentStylesheet(Application.STYLESHEET_MODENA);
```

The method `setUserAgentStylesheet(…)` is part of the `Application` class.

Figure 9-1 shows the sample application created in Chapter 5. This time, the application is styled with Caspian.

As you can see in Figure 9-1, Caspian isn't as modern as Modena. In addition to the visual appeal, Modena offers a number of benefits that I will cover later in the chapter. It is definitely a best practice to use Modena instead of Caspian, but an application that was developed with JavaFX 2.*x* and migrated to JavaFX 8 could use Caspian to retain its look, for example.

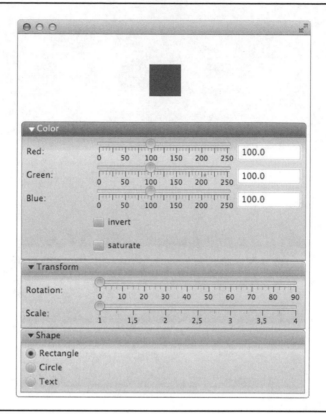

FIGURE 9-1. *The Caspian theme*

In addition to Caspian and Modena, the JavaFX community has developed a number of third-party themes. The most popular one is AquaFX (http://aquafx-project.com/). Unlike Modena or Caspian, AquaFX was designed as a native theme, so the theme aims to mimic the look of a specific operating system. In this case, AquaFX styles all default JavaFX controls in the Mac OS Aqua style, so you would use AquaFX for applications that run on a Mac. Figure 9-2 shows the sample application styled by AquaFX.

As mentioned, each JavaFX theme is defined by a CSS style sheet that contains the styling information for JavaFX controls. To understand how this works, you will now take a deeper look at using CSS in JavaFX.

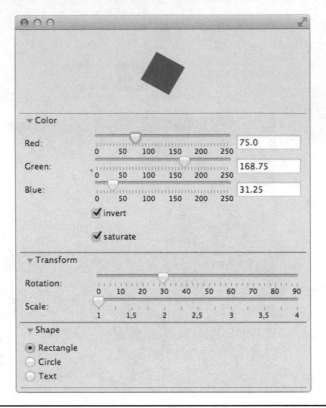

FIGURE 9-2. *The AquaFX theme*

CSS Basics

Some developers may not have experience using CSS, so I'll quickly review the basics. Cascading Style Sheets (CSS) is a style sheet language that can be used to define the look and format of documents. It is the default language for styling web pages, and the CSS specification is maintained by the World Wide Web Consortium (W3C). The main goal of CSS is to separate the content from the presentation of documents. Think about a simple static web page; all the content such as tables, text, and hyperlinks can be defined by HTML. To style and format all the containing components, though, you should use CSS. While this is the main use case, CSS can be used in other ways, such as styling text documents or print layouts. In general, CSS describes different style and layout attributes of components, and in JavaFX, it is used to style controls.

Here is a simple CSS definition:

```
#headline {
    background-color: blue;
}
```

The CSS snippet defines the font color for an element called headline, and the `background-color` property is set to the value blue. To bind this definition to the defined element, you use a selector. The selector in the example is `#headline`, which defines the component that is affected by the given rule. Here are some definitions of CSS terms:

- CSS has *rules* that define how a component should be styled.
- A *style sheet* contains a set of CSS rules. Usually, this is a CSS file.
- Each rule has a *selector* that defines what components should be styled by the rule.
- Each rule contains a set of *properties*.
- For each property, a *value* is defined.

The given example is a CSS rule that can be used for web development. In JavaFX, the CSS properties have other names than in the CSS definitions for HTML. Each JavaFX property starts with the `-fx-` prefix. To style a JavaFX control like the previous HTML example, you would use the following rule:

```
#headline {
       -fx-background-color: blue;
}
```

Note that JavaFX supports the CSS 2.1 specification. That means most of the functionalities in CSS 2.1 can be used in JavaFX. The biggest difference between how the specification is used for web design versus in JavaFX is the `-fx-` prefix, but there are other minor changes in JavaFX, including the following:

- There is no @ keyword.
- Some CSS pseudoclasses and elements such as `:first-line`, `:first-letter`, `:before`, and `:after` aren't supported.
- `:active` and `:focus` are replaced by `:pressed` and `:focused`.
- `:link` and `:visited` are not supported in general (the `Hyperlink` control supports `:visited`).
- No comma-separated series of font family names in the `-fx-font-family` property are allowed.
- The HSB color model is used instead of the HSL model.

An important feature of CSS is its cascading functionality. CSS defines a priority hierarchy for the properties that affect the style of a component. This functionality is useful when you are styling a complete application or view instead of a single control. The CSS rule shown previously defines the background color of an element with the given ID headline. Let's assume that this element is a JavaFX label in a custom application, and in this application all labels should have gray text. In addition, the headline of the application should have a blue background. Without the cascading functionality, developers must define CSS rules for all `Label` instances that are used in the application. Here is a short abstract of a CSS style sheet that would do it this way:

```
#headline {
        -fx-background-color: blue;
        -fx-text-fill: gray;
```

```
}
#label1 {
      -fx-text-fill: gray;
}
#label2 {
      -fx-text-fill: gray;
}
```

Styling an application this way would be hard because you would need to write a lot of CSS rules, and every time a change request appears, it would be a big problem to change several aspects of the design. If the customer decides to change all labels to a light gray color, for example, you would need to change this in all the CSS rules for all the labels.

To avoid these problems, you can use the cascading functionality of CSS where property declarations are inherited. The following code defines a solution that solves the given problems with only two CSS rules:

```
.label {
      -fx-text-fill: gray;
}
#headline {
      -fx-background-color: blue;
}
```

In this code, you define a global rule for all `Label` instances by using a different selector syntax. The # prefix defines that a selector specifies an ID of a component and affects only those components with the given ID. A dot defines an element type that is a control type in JavaFX. This rule sets the text color of all labels to gray, which includes the headline label. The second rule adds a property to the definition of the headline label. In this rule, the `-fx-text-fill` property could be overridden to change the text color of this specific label. Later in the chapter, I'll show different selector types and properties that are supported for JavaFX controls, as well as some best practices in terms of inheritance and cascading.

CSS in JavaFX

JavaFX provides a couple of ways to apply CSS to the nodes of a scene graph. In Chapter 5, you created a simple login dialog. As an example, let's style this dialog. To do this, let's change the source code of the application and define some unique IDs for all the components that should be styled, as shown here:

```
...
gridPane.setId("login-pane");
userLabel.setId("login-user-label");
passwordLabel.setId("login-password-label");
button.setId("login-button");
userNameField.setId("login-user-textfield");
passwordField.setId("login-password-textfield");

Scene myScene = new Scene(gridPane);
```

As a next step, you need a CSS style sheet that defines rules for all the nodes. I won't describe all the possible properties that can be used in the CSS rules for JavaFX because this is a really huge list, as you might know from web development. You can find a complete overview of all possibilities and the syntax of how CSS can be used in JavaFX in the JavaFX CSS Reference Guide (http://download.java.net/jdk8/jfxdocs/javafx/scene/doc-files/cssref.html). The following code defines a sample style sheet for the login dialog:

```
#login-pane {
    -fx-background-color: #000000;
}
#login-button {
    -fx-background-color: #008000;
    -fx-text-fill: #f5f5f5;
}
#login-user-label {
    -fx-text-fill: #f5f5f5;
}
#login-password-label {
    -fx-text-fill: #f5f5f5;
}
#login-user-textfield {
    -fx-background-color: #191970;
    -fx-background-radius: 10.0;
    -fx-text-fill: #f5f5f5;
    -fx-prompt-text-fill: #5ecbea;
}
#login-user-textfield {
    -fx-background-color: #191970;
    -fx-background-radius: 10.0;
    -fx-text-fill: #f5f5f5;
    -fx-prompt-text-fill: #5ecbea;
}
```

In the style sheet, all the rules are defined by a selector. Each selector starts with the # prefix that defines an ID. Each node that has been defined with the given ID will be styled by the rule, and all the different JavaFX node types can be styled by specified CSS properties.

NOTE
All color information in the CSS file is defined by hex values. As you will see later, that is one of many ways that a color can be defined in CSS.

Before looking more closely at the properties and values used, let's look at the result of the example. Just add the defined style sheet to the JavaFX application using the following code snippet:

```
String stylesheet = getClass().getResource("custom.css").toExternalForm();
myScene.getStylesheets().add(stylesheet);
```

In this line of Java code, the CSS style sheet that is saved in the `custom.css` file is applied to the scene graph of the application. Figure 9-3 shows the styled login dialog.

FIGURE 9-3. *The styled login dialog*

As already mentioned, I don't have room for a complete overview of all these properties, but here are the ones that can be used to style a node:

- `-fx-blend-mode`
- `-fx-cursor`
- `-fx-effect`
- `-fx-focus-traversable`
- `-fx-opacity`
- `-fx-rotate`
- `-fx-scale-x`
- `-fx-scale-y`
- `-fx-scale-z`
- `-fx-translate-x`
- `-fx-translate-y`
- `-fx-translate-z`
- `visibility`

Because all node and control types in JavaFX extend the `Node` class, all possible controls will support the shown CSS properties by default. As you can see, the `Node` class defines a lot of CSS properties. These properties can be used in all nodes in JavaFX, and the CSS properties will be inherited. All the properties can hold a value of a given type, and each has a default value. Sometimes, an enumeration is defined for a CSS property, and its value must be a value of the enumeration. An example of this property type is the `-fx-alignment` property, which is defined by the `TextField` class. This property can hold one of the following values:

- `top-left`
- `top-center`
- `top-right`
- `center-left`
- `center`
- `center-right`
- `bottom-left`
- `bottom-center`
- `bottom-right`
- `baseline-left`
- `baseline-center`
- `baseline-right`

Other property types that can be used are boolean or number, for example. In addition to the raw values, CSS supports units. Some value types, such as length, define a set of units that can be used as additional information. To define a unit, you must add the keyword of the unit to the value of a property; in these cases, no whitespace is allowed between the number and its unit. The following example defines the font size of a control by using the points unit:

```
#my-action-button {
    -fx-font-size: 16pt;
}
```

Unit	Description
px	Pixels; relative to the viewing device
em	The font size of the relevant font
ex	The x-height of the relevant font
in	Inches; 1 inch is equal to 2.54 centimeters
cm	Centimeters
mm	Millimeters
pt	Points; the points used by CSS 2.1 are equal to 1/72 of an inch
pc	Picas; 1 pica is equal to 12 points

TABLE 9-1. *Units of the Length Type*

Table 9-1 defines the units that can be used by the length type. Other value types define units too. You can find all the allowed units in the CSS documentation of JavaFX.

Let's also look at the paint type, which will mostly be used when defining the fill or the border color of a control. This type can define a color, a linear gradient, or a radial gradient. You can find an example for a linear gradient in the following rule:

```
#my-control {
    -fx-fill: linear-gradient(from 0% 0% to 100% 100%, red 0%, black 100%);
}
```

The value for the `-fx-fill` property defines a linear gradient that goes from red to black. The colors of the gradient are specified by red and black values, and CSS contains a huge set of predefined colors that can be used directly in the CSS rules. Figure 9-4 contains an abstract of the list. You can find the complete list in the JavaFX documentation.

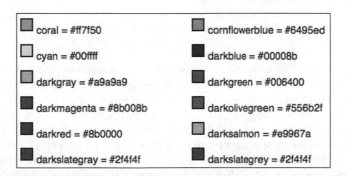

coral = #ff7f50   cornflowerblue = #6495ed

cyan = #00ffff   darkblue = #00008b

darkgray = #a9a9a9   darkgreen = #006400

darkmagenta = #8b008b   darkolivegreen = #556b2f

darkred = #8b0000   darksalmon = #e9967a

darkslategray = #2f4f4f darkslategrey = #2f4f4f

FIGURE 9-4. *Abstract of CSS colors*

NOTE
You can also define color information by its RGB values. In this case,
the alpha of the color can be specified too. An example for this case is
rgba(255,0,0,1).

As mentioned, a property of the paint type can hold a color. Therefore, the following rules would also be correct:

```
#my-control {
    -fx-fill: linear-gradient(from 0% 0% to 100% 100%, #ff0000 0%, #000000
100%);
}

#my-control2 {
    -fx-fill: cyan;
}

#my-control3 {
    -fx-fill: #56c8f2;
}
```

After looking at the basics of styling with CSS in JavaFX, let's refactor the CSS style sheet of the first example in this chapter. Here, only ID-based selectors were used, and all colors were specified by hex values. You can refactor the CSS by using class-based selectors and more readable color information, as shown here:

```
#login-button {
    -fx-background-color: green;
    -fx-text-fill: whitesmoke;
}
.label {
    -fx-text-fill: whitesmoke;
}
.text-field {
    -fx-background-color: rgb(25.0, 25.0, 112.0);
    -fx-background-radius: 10.0;
    -fx-text-fill: whitesmoke;
    -fx-prompt-text-fill: rgb(94.0, 203.0, 234.0);
}
```

As you can see in the example, the selector that is defined to style the button is referenced using the ID of the button. Because this rule is needed for only one specific button in this example, it is a best practice to use this kind of selector. Because the sample has more than one `Label` and `TextField` that needs styling, you use the class-based selector to define a rule. By doing this, only one rule is needed to style all `Label` instances instead of one rule for each `Label`. In addition, keywords are used for most color information. If no keyword is needed, I change the color definition to an RGB value because this format is normally more readable than a hex value.

Another feature of JavaFX is that you can define CSS properties directly in Java code. Because this feature isn't a best practice, though, developers should usually not use it; I'm only showing it as a reference. You can use the following code snippet in the demo instead of a CSS file. In this case, no CSS file is needed, and the complete styling is done in the Java class.

```
gridPane.setStyle("-fx-background-color: black");
userLabel.setStyle("-fx-text-fill: whitesmoke");
passwordLabel.setStyle("-fx-text-fill: whitesmoke");
button.setStyle("-fx-background-color: green;" +
        "    -fx-text-fill: whitesmoke;");
userNameField.setStyle("-fx-background-color: #191970;" +
        "    -fx-background-radius: 10.0;" +
        "    -fx-text-fill: whitesmoke;" +
        "-fx-prompt-text-fill: rgb(94.0, 203.0, 234.0);");
passwordField.setStyle("-fx-background-color: #191970;" +
        "    -fx-background-radius: 10.0;" +
        "    -fx-text-fill: whitesmoke;" +
        "-fx-prompt-text-fill: rgb(94.0, 203.0, 234.0);");
```

Note that because of the cascading functionality of CSS, you can mix all of the approaches shown so far. If you do that, though, you should know the different priorities in the cascade and what rules will overwrite other ones. If you need a lot of custom CSS styling in an application, make sure to plan the CSS structure accurately. If you mix CSS styling in Java code and in CSS files, it can be hard to change a special property later.

NOTE
All Node classes in JavaFX can be styled by CSS. The CSS styling functionality is defined in the Styleable interface that is implemented by the Node class.

Using Selectors

In the previous examples, you saw two different CSS selector types. CSS provides a complex syntax to create complex selectors that can be used to define style rules for sets of controls in a JavaFX application. The following examples define different selectors that can be used in JavaFX:

```
#id {
    ...
}
```

This defines a rule for a node with the given ID. The Node class provides the id property that must be defined to use the ID-based selector.

The next selector type is the class selector. Here, the dot prefix will be used:

```
.label {
    ...
}
```

Most node types in JavaFX already have one defined class. You can find the style classes that are defined by default for different Node classes in the JavaDoc. In addition, you can add a style class to each control. A style class is defined by its name and can be accessed in CSS like the default style classes, as shown here:

```
.my-class {
     ...
}
```

To use the given CSS rule for a node, you must set the style class to the Node instance. Therefore, the Node class contains the getStyleClass() method that returns an ObservableList<String> of all style classes that are defined for the node. An additional style class can be easily added to the list:

```
myButton.getStyleClass().add("my-class");
```

By using style classes, different controls can share a rule. In the following snippet, a CSS rule is defined for a custom class:

```
.orange-bordered {
     -fx-stroke: orange;
     -fx-stroke-width: 8;
}

.blue-filled {
     -fx-fill: blue;
}

.green-filled {
     -fx-fill: blue;
}
```

The first rule says that all nodes that have defined the orange-bordered style class and support the -fx-stroke and -fx-stroke-width properties will have an orange border with a line width of 8. The other rule defines a fill color. In Java, you can create some Shape instances that will get styled by the CSS, as shown here:

```
Rectangle r = new Rectangle(100, 100);
r.getStyleClass().add("orange-bordered");
r.getStyleClass().add("blue-filled");

Circle c = Circle(50);
c.getStyleClass().add("orange-bordered");
c.getStyleClass().add("green-filled");
```

Rendering these shapes will result in a blue circle with an orange border and a green circle with an orange border. In this sample, the style classes of both Node instances contain the orange-bordered style class. Therefore, both of them will be rendered with an orange border.

NOTE
By convention, style class names that consist of more than one word use a hyphen (-) between words. If a developer creates new style classes for a custom control, the style classes should correspond to class names. For example, the default style class for the ToolBar *control is named* tool-bar.

If you use a lot of style classes, it is useful to define some rules for a set of style classes. This can be done using the CSS selector syntax too. The following example defines a rule for all nodes that have the `dark-control` and the `big-button` class defined:

```
.dark-control.big-button {
    -fx-font-size: 24;
    -fx-background-color: black;
    -fx-text-fill: gray;
}
```

NOTE
As you will see, it is important not to add a space between the two pseudoclass names in the selector.

In addition to style classes, CSS supports pseudoclasses, which can be used to define a special state of a component. A pseudoclass selector is defined by a colon prefix, as shown in the following sample:

```
.button :hover {
    -fx-scale-x: 2;
    -fx-scale-y: 2;
    -fx-scale-z: 2;
}
```

The defined rule will be used for all `Button` instances once the hover variable is true. This will happen whenever the mouse cursor enters the node. The node types that are part of JavaFX define a huge set of pseudoclasses. Table 9-2 gives an overview of all pseudoclasses that are defined for the `Node` class. These pseudoclasses can be used for each node.

In addition to these pseudoclasses, each control type defines its specific ones. Table 9-3 describes the pseudoclasses of the `IndexedCell` class. All cells that are part of a `TableView` or `ListView` can be styled by using these pseudoclasses.

CSS Pseudoclass	Comments
disabled	Applies when the `disabled` variable is true
focused	Applies when the `focused` variable is true
hover	Applies when the `hover` variable is true
pressed	Applies when the `pressed` variable is true
show-mnemonic	Applies when the mnemonic affordance should be shown

TABLE 9-2. *Pseudoclasses for the Node Class*

CSS Pseudoclass	Comments
even	Applies if this cell's index is even
odd	Applies if this cell's index is odd

TABLE 9-3. *Pseudoclasses for the IndexedCell Class*

By using the shown pseudoclasses, it is simple to define a striped "zebra" effect for all rows of a ListView:

```
.list-cell:even {
    -fx-background-color: yellow;
}
.list-cell:odd {
    -fx-background-color: lightyellow;
}
```

Once the style sheet that contains the given rules is applied to a JavaFX application that contains `TreeView` or `TableView` instances, the rows of these controls will be styled. Figure 9-5 shows an example at run time.

In addition to the shown selector definitions, you can use the CSS selector syntax to define more complex selectors. For example, maybe you want to change the border of all buttons that are on a toolbar. By using the previously described selectors, you can add a style class to all the `Button` instances inside the `Toolbar` instance. With CSS, you can define selectors that look up

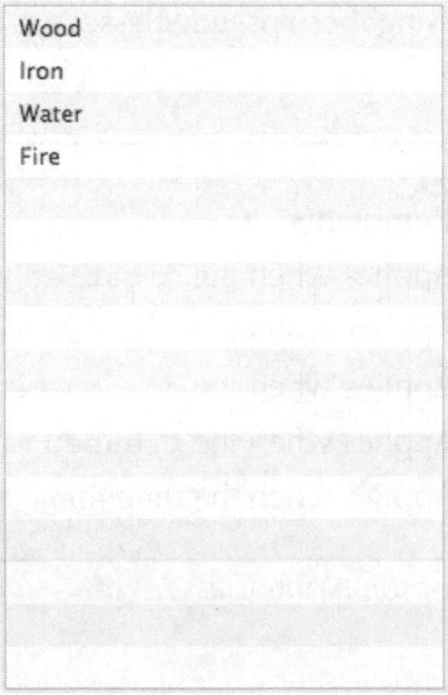

FIGURE 9-5. *Styled cells*

all `Button` instances in a `Toolbar` instance. Here is an example of a CSS rule with the described selector:

```
#my-toolbar .button {
    ...
}
```

By using the selector, all `Node` instances that contain the `button` style class and that are part of the `Node` hierarchy in the `Toolbar` with the given ID of `my-toolbar` will be styled by the rule. Here, a `Button` instance doesn't have to be a direct child node of the `Toolbar` instance. If you want to look up only direct children of the `Toolbar`, you can use the > sign. By adding this between the two parts of the selector, only direct children will be affected:

```
#my-toolbar > .button {
    ...
}
```

NOTE
*Using the > sign in a CSS selector will improve performance somewhat.
By using it, the complete child hierarchy under the `Toolbar` control
will not need to be scanned. Matching nodes will be searched only in
the first hierarchy of children.*

You can mix all the shown selector types. Here's an example:

```
.list-view .text:disabled {
    -fx-fill: yellow;
}
```

By using this rule, all `Text` nodes that are children of all `ListView` instances of the application will be rendered with yellow text.

NOTE
*Most control types in JavaFX include `Node` instances that can have their
own style definition. An example of this is the text of a `Button` control.
The text is internally defined as a `Text` shape. These inner nodes can
be styled by using descendant classes too, as shown in the previous
examples. Some examples of these descendant classes are `.check-
box .label`, `.check-box .box`, or `.radio-button .dot`.*

If you have a basic CSS rule that defines some general styling, you can combine several of the selector types by using a comma. Here is an example that defines the color for the top and bottom arrows in a scroll bar:

```
.scroll-bar > .increment-button > .increment-arrow,
.scroll-bar > .decrement-button > .decrement-arrow {
    -fx-background-color: white;
}
```

As you can see, the selector of the rule is more complex than the selectors that were shown here. The first line defines all nodes that have defined the `increment-arrow` class and are direct children of a node that has defined the `increment-button` CSS class. This node must be a direct child of a node that has defined the `scroll-bar` CSS class. The second line is similar to the first one and defines the selector for nodes that have defined the `decrement-arrow` class. The shown CSS classes in this example are defined by JavaFX. The up and down icons of a default JavaFX `ScrollBar` can be styled like the shown selectors of the code snippet. As stated earlier, a control in JavaFX contains several subnodes that can be styled too. In this example, the `ScrollBar` of JavaFX contains a node that has the defined CSS class `increment-button`. When getting started with CSS styling in JavaFX, it's not easy to find all these internal CSS classes and inner nodes of controls. A good tool to analyze the controls and its inner nodes is the CSS Analyzer, shown in Figure 9-6, that is part of Scene Builder. You can select parts of JavaFX controls with the mouse, and the tool will analyze each one's pseudoclasses and CSS values.

To see how all these different selector types can be used and how the cascading feature of CSS is working, let's look at an example application. This application contains several buttons that will be styled by CSS. Here is the Java source code of the application:

```
package com.guigarage.masteringcontrols;
import javafx.application.Application;
import javafx.geometry.Insets;
```

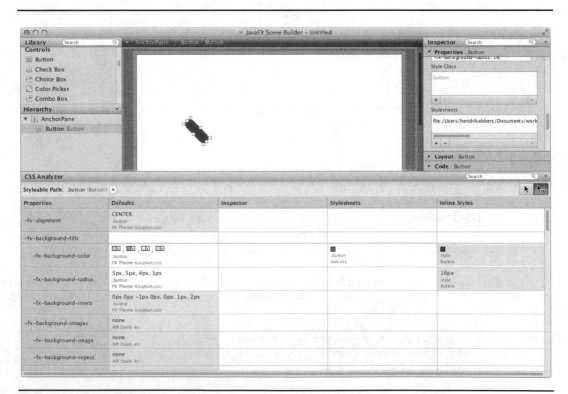

FIGURE 9-6. *CSS Analyzer of Scene Builder*

```
import javafx.geometry.Pos;
import javafx.scene.Scene;
import javafx.scene.control.Button;
import javafx.scene.control.ToolBar;
import javafx.scene.layout.Priority;
import javafx.scene.layout.StackPane;
import javafx.scene.layout.VBox;
import javafx.stage.Stage;
public class CssStylingDemo extends Application {
    public static void main(String[] args) {
        launch(args);
    }
    @Override
    public void start(Stage primaryStage) throws Exception {
        Button bottomButton = new Button("Click");
        bottomButton.setId("bottomButton");

        Button toolbarButton1 = new Button("Click");
        toolbarButton1.setId("button-custom");

        Button toolbarButton2 = new Button("Click");
        toolbarButton2.setId("my-action-button");

        Button centerButton = new Button("Click");
        centerButton.setId("centerButton");

        ToolBar toolbar = new ToolBar(toolbarButton1, toolbarButton2);
        StackPane centerPane = new StackPane(centerButton);
        VBox myPane = new VBox(toolbar, centerPane, bottomButton);
        VBox.setVgrow(centerPane, Priority.ALWAYS);
        myPane.setAlignment(Pos.CENTER);
        myPane.setSpacing(12);
        myPane.setPadding(new Insets(0, 0, 6, 0));

        Scene myScene = new Scene(myPane);
        primaryStage.setScene(myScene);
        primaryStage.setTitle("App");
        primaryStage.setWidth(300);
        primaryStage.setHeight(200);
        primaryStage.show();
    }
}
```

The example contains four `Button` instances that are placed in different parts of the scene graph hierarchy. In addition, all instances have custom IDs defined. In this first step, no CSS and styling are defined. Therefore, the application will be rendered by using the default styling defined by Modena. Figure 9-7 contains all the steps of styling this application that will be discussed in the following text. Without any additional CSS information, the application will appear as in the first dialog of Figure 9-7.

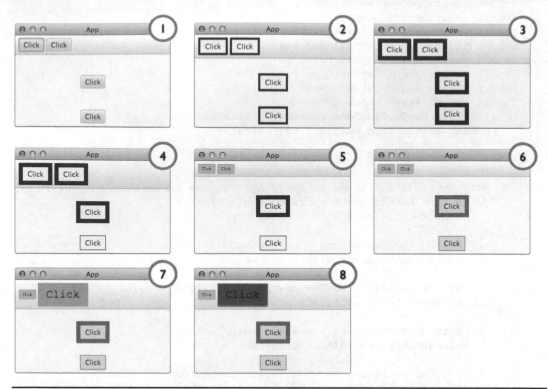

FIGURE 9-7. *Styling a JavaFX application, step by step*

As a first step, you need a CSS file. Name it `customstyle.css` and place it in the same package as the application. You can then apply the CSS file as the style sheet for the application using the following code:

```
String stylesheet = getClass().getResource("customstyle.css").toExternalForm();
myScene.getStylesheets().addAll(stylesheet);
```

Let's define the first rule in the CSS file. This rule should affect all buttons that are part of the application, so you can use a class selector, as mentioned earlier. The following code snippet defines the rule:

```
.button {
    -fx-border-width: 4;
    -fx-border-color: blue;
    -fx-background-color: yellow;
}
```

When running the application, all buttons will look the same. As defined in the CSS rule, they have a yellow background and a thick blue border. You can see the result in the second dialog of Figure 9-7.

As a next step, all Button instances that are part of the VBox should be in a different style. Therefore, you need to define an additional rule:

```
.vbox .button {
    -fx-border-width: 8;
}
```

Because the VBox class in JavaFX doesn't define a default style class, you need to add a class in JavaFX, as shown by the following code snippet:

```
myPane.getStyleClass().add("vbox");
```

You can see the result in the third dialog of Figure 9-7. As shown, all Button instances in the application are part of the children of the VBox, so they have changed slightly. The defined rule doesn't handle buttons that are direct children of the VBox only; recursively, all children will be found. The defined rule has a higher priority than the first one, and therefore the defined -fx-border-width of the last rule will be used when styling is applied to the control instances.

With the next rule, you want to change only the Button instances that are direct children of the VBox. As shown earlier, you can do this by defining a rule with the > sign:

```
.vbox > .button {
    -fx-border-width: 1;
}
```

By using this rule, you create the first difference in the style of the buttons. Because only the bottomButton is a direct child of the VBox, its border width will be changed. As you can see, this rule has again a higher priority than all the other ones. You can see the result in the fourth dialog in Figure 9-7.

As a next step, you want to change the style of all the Button instances in the toolbar. The ToolBar class in JavaFX already defines a CSS class called tool-bar. You can use this class for the next rule:

```
.tool-bar .button {
    -fx-background-color: lightskyblue;
    -fx-border-width: 1;
    -fx-border-color: darkgrey;
    -fx-font-size: 6pt;
}
```

As expected, the style of all buttons in the toolbar has changed after the rule is added. Dialog 5 in Figure 9-7 represents the current state.

Next, all Button instances that are not part of the toolbar should be changed. Therefore, create a new style class called dialog-button. By using this class, you can define a CSS selector. Because you want to change the style of all buttons that are not part of the toolbar, the centerButton and bottomButton instances need this new CSS class. You can apply the class in Java as shown:

```
centerButton.getStyleClass().add("dialog-button");
bottomButton.getStyleClass().add("dialog-button");
```

Here is the additional CSS rule:

```
.dialog-button {
    -fx-background-color: khaki;
    -fx-border-width: 20;
    -fx-border-color: red;
}
```

You can see the result in the sixth dialog of Figure 9-7. At first, you might think an error has occurred. In the new rule, the -fx-border-width property is defined with a value of 20 that defines very thick borders, but when looking at Figure 9-7, you will notice that the border width hasn't changed. This isn't an error. As already mentioned, the cascading feature of CSS is defined by priorities of the CSS rules. The new rule has a lower priority than the two with the .tool-bar .button and .vbox > .button selectors. Because of that, the values of the -fx-border-width property that are defined by these two rules will be used when styling the buttons. These rules don't define an additional background color or border color, so these values will be extracted from the last rule that is defined by the .dialog-button selector.

> **NOTE**
> *The priority level of CSS rules is defined by the weight of the selector. The weight defines how specific a style is. The more specific style will be used over the less specific one, meaning it has a higher priority. To calculate the weight of a selector, you can use the following formula:*
>
> *(number of IDs in the selector) × 100 + (number of classes in the selector) × 10 + (pseudoclasses in the selector)*
>
> *When comparing two rules, the one with the bigger weight of its selector has the higher priority.*

As a next step, you want to define a rule that affects only one button. So, you need a selector that defines the Button instance by its ID:

```
#my-action-button {
    -fx-background-color: darkorange;
    -fx-font-size: 16pt;
    -fx-font-family: "Courier New";
}
```

Because an ID is used in the selector, this CSS rule will have a higher priority than all the other ones, and all properties of the rule will be used for styling. Dialog 7 in Figure 9-7 shows the current state of the dialog.

As a last step, you want to add a CSS property inline in Java code. As already mentioned, this is bad practice, and it is done here only to show how the cascade feature is working and how the priority of inline styling is defined. Therefore, you add the following code snippet to the application:

```
toolbarButton2.setStyle("-fx-background-color: green;");
```

As you can see in dialog 8 of Figure 9-7, the button has changed its color. So, this rule that is defined directly in Java has a higher priority than the rules that are defined by CSS. A CSS rule that is defined in Java code always has a higher priority than a rule that is part of a CSS style sheet file. In addition, CSS supports two types of style sheets. The user agent style sheet is the global basic style sheet. In JavaFX, Modena is defined as the default user agent style sheet. All other style sheets, like the one being used in this application, are normal style sheets. These have a higher priority than the user agent style sheet, so the rules in the custom CSS file can override the definitions that are part of Modena. The inline CSS that is part of the Java code always has the highest priority.

NOTE
The example shown here was created solely to show the different selector possibilities and priority of rules. This code should not be used for a real application. The cascade of the CSS rules is complex, and many properties are defined several times.

Summary of the Cascading Feature

In the previous section, I discussed a lot of information about the priority of styles and the cascading functionality of CSS. Now, let's turn to a complete overview.

As you saw in this chapter, you can define styles in style sheets or as inline styles in the `Java` class. With style sheets, you can set one user agent style sheet for the application by using the `setUserAgentStylesheet(...)` method of the `Application` class and add several style sheets to the scene graph by using the `getStylesheets()` method of the `Scene` class. In addition, the `Parent` class provides the `getStylesheets()` method, so a style sheet can be defined for a subtree of nodes in a scene graph. In addition to the style defined in CSS, you can set a JavaFX property for a node, for instance, setting the text color by using the `textFill` property of a `Button` instance. For these types of style definitions, the following rules are valid:

- A style from a user agent style sheet has a lower priority than setting a JavaFX property.
- The value of a JavaFX property has a lower priority than a style sheet that is defined for the scene graph.
- A scene graph style sheet has a lower priority than a style sheet of a parent node.
- An inline style sheet has the highest priority.

Additionally, several CSS rules defined in one style sheet can affect the same JavaFX node. Here, the following rules are valid:

- The priority of a rule can be calculated by its selector's weight.
- The following formula should be used: (number of IDs in the selector) × 100 + (number of classes in the selector) × 10 + (pseudoclasses in the selector).
- The rule with the bigger weight has the higher priority.

There is one additional flag that can be used to modify the priority of a CSS property. By adding the !important flag to a value of a CSS property, this value will get the highest priority, as shown here:

```
.my-button-class {
    -fx-background-color: blue !important;
}
```

Styling a Chart

In the previous sample, mostly JavaFX control types were styled by CSS. But as mentioned, each node type could be styled with CSS. Therefore, the following example will show how a chart can be styled with CSS. In the demo application, a pie chart is created and shown onscreen.

```
package com.guigarage.masteringcontrols;

import javafx.application.Application;
import javafx.collections.FXCollections;
import javafx.collections.ObservableList;
import javafx.scene.Scene;
import javafx.scene.chart.PieChart;
import javafx.scene.layout.StackPane;
import javafx.stage.Stage;

public class PieChartExample extends Application {

    @Override
    public void start(Stage primaryStage) throws Exception {
        ObservableList<PieChart.Data> pieChartData =
                FXCollections.observableArrayList();
        pieChartData.addAll(
                new PieChart.Data("Christopher Eccleston", 1),
                new PieChart.Data("David Tennant", 5),
                new PieChart.Data("Matt Smith", 3));
        PieChart chart = new PieChart(pieChartData);
        chart.setTitle("Tenure of Doctor Who");

        StackPane myPane = new StackPane();
        myPane.getChildren().add(chart);
        Scene myScene = new Scene(myPane);
        primaryStage.setScene(myScene);
        primaryStage.setTitle("Pie Chart");
        primaryStage.setWidth(800);
        primaryStage.setHeight(600);
        primaryStage.show();
    }

    public static void main(String[] args) {
        launch(args);
    }
}
```

Figure 9-8 shows this chart on the top.

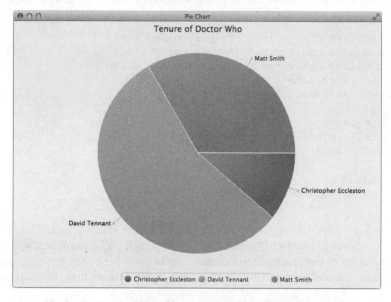

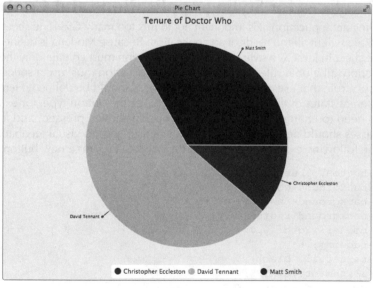

FIGURE 9-8. *A styled PieChart*

As a next step, say you want to style the `PieChart` with CSS. You create a new style sheet and apply it to the scene graph, as shown here:

```
.default-color0.chart-pie { -fx-pie-color: blue; }
.default-color1.chart-pie { -fx-pie-color: lightblue; }
.default-color2.chart-pie { -fx-pie-color: darkblue; }
.chart-pie-label-line {
    -fx-stroke: black;
}
.chart-pie-label {
    -fx-fill: black;
    -fx-font-size: 0.7em;
}
.chart-legend {
    -fx-background-color:  lightyellow;
}
```

Figure 9-8 shows the result on the bottom. In the style sheet, you will find an additional feature of the CSS support in JavaFX. When styling charts, JavaFX will automatically create CSS classes for all the data parts of the chart. In the example, the classes `default-color0`, `default-color1`, and `default-color3` can be used to style each of the data sections of the pie chart.

Best Practices for Styling Applications and Controls

When styling an application, it is important not to mix too many CSS style sheets. In most cases, a single CSS file will fit all the needs of an application. Because Modena is defined as the default user agent style sheet in JavaFX, a style sheet for an application must contain only the changes to Modena.

First, apply all global rules. Let's assume the application must use a special skin for buttons. In this case, a rule that uses the `.button` pseudoclass should be defined. Here, it is important that all the different states of the control will be tested. For the button type, for example, developers will often need to change the style for states, such as hover, pressed, and focused, so CSS pseudoclasses should be used. If this isn't done, a user gets no visual feedback when clicking a button. The following example defines how the needed rules for a new button style may look:

```
.toggle-button, .button{
    -fx-background-color: red;
    -fx-background-insets:  0.0;
    -fx-background-radius: 2.0;
    -fx-border-width: 0.0;
    -fx-padding: 6;
    -fx-text-fill: black;
    -fx-alignment: CENTER;
    -fx-content-display: LEFT;
}


.toggle-button:focused,
.button:focused,
.button:default:focused {
    -fx-background-color: lightcoral;
}
```

```
.toggle-button:focused:selected {
    -fx-background-color: lightcoral, lightcyan;
    -fx-background-insets: 0.0, 0.2em;
}

.toggle-button:armed,
.toggle-button:selected,
.button:armed,
.button:default:armed {
    -fx-background-color: darkred;
}
```

As you can see, the selectors of the rules contain comma-separated lists. By doing this, only a few rules are needed to specify all the needed styling information for a `Button` and a `ToggleButton` in the different states.

As a next step, define special types of the controls. In this case, it is best to define custom CSS classes. Let's say all buttons in menus should have a smaller font. Here, an `app-menu-button` CSS class is defined that contains a value for the `-fx-font-size` property:

```
.app-menu-button {
    -fx-font-size: 8pt;
}
```

If the application contains some special buttons that are used in only one view, you can define these controls with a unique ID. In this case, the ID selector of CSS should be used:

```
#shut-down-button {
    -fx-font-size: 16pt;
}
```

Doing this for all the needed control types defines a clear hierarchy of styling.

To create an even better overview of the CSS styling and create a more refactorable style sheet, you should use the `root` style class. The `root` class is applied to the `root` node of the scene graph, and properties that are defined in the `root` style can be used in any other CSS rule. If, for example, you define a style for an application that has blue as its main color, you can define the `root` style class as shown in the following snippet:

```
.root {
    -fx-color-base: blue;
}
```

Here, the property `-fx-color-base` is defined in the `root`. The big benefit of this is that the property can be reused in each CSS rule of the style sheet. The following code shows another abstract of the application CSS:

```
.button{
    -fx-background-color: -fx-color-base;
}

.context-menu .label {
    -fx-text-fill: -fx-color-base;
}
```

The `-fx-color-base` property is reused in two rules here. Once you have extracted all the basic values as global properties to the `root` rule of a style sheet, it is easy to refactor the styling by changing only one value. Another benefit is that you automatically provide more consistency in the UI because the same values will be used in a lot of control types.

When looking at the Modena CSS file, you will see that a lot of properties are defined in the `root` section of the style sheet. You can reuse these properties in custom application style sheets or define new values for them. By doing this, you can change the complete style of an application with only a few lines of CSS, as shown here:

```
.root{
    -fx-font-size: 14pt;
    -fx-font-family: "Verdana";
    -fx-base: orange;
    -fx-background: yellow;
}
```

A custom style sheet that contains only these lines will change the complete look of an application. Figure 9-9 shows the sample application that is styled by this style sheet.

NOTE
In theory, an application can be styled by multiple style sheets. A style sheet will be added to a scene graph by calling `myScene .getStylesheets().add(…)`. The `getStylesheets()` method returns a List, and therefore it can hold and manage several style sheets. Suppose you have a default style for all your applications that is wrapped in one default style sheet. If one application needs some additional styles for specific components or the customer needs a special color for all button backgrounds, these features could be implemented in a separate style sheet. In this case, the order of the CSS style sheets in the list defines its priority. When possible, though, it is a best practice to define the styling of an application in a single style sheet.

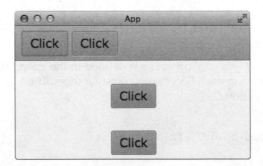

FIGURE 9-9.   *A styled application*

A final best practice for developers creating huge CSS style sheets is the proper use of the `derive(...)` and `ladder(...)` functions. These two functions can be used to define color values in CSS. When thinking about a style for a complete application, you will mostly use some basic colors that specify the color theme of the application. In general, these colors will be used in several modifications in the UI of the application. For instance, maybe the basic color for an application is a light blue. In this case, the background of all buttons will be defined as `lightblue`, and the border of all buttons should appear in a darker blue. In this case, the `derive(...)` function can be used to derive the border color from the base color. To do this, the `derive(...)` function takes a color and computes a brighter or darker version of that color. The second parameter of the `derive(...)` function is the brightness offset that can be defined in a range from –100% to 100%. You can use the `derive(...)` function as a value for a CSS property, as shown in the following snippet:

```
.root{
    -fx-base: lightblue;
    -fx-border-base: derive(-fx-base, -50%);
    -fx-focus-base: derive(-fx-base, 50%);
}
```

In this case, only the value of the `-fx-base` property needs to be changed to affect all defined colors. In addition to the `derive(...)` function, the `ladder(...)` function can be used to interpolate between colors. Here, a gradient must be specified, and the brightness of the provided color parameter is used to look up a color value within that gradient. The calculated color depends on the brightness of the passed color. At 0 percent brightness, the returned color will be the start color of the gradient. At 100 percent brightness, the color at the 1.0 end of the gradient is used. Here's an example:

```
#dark-button{
 -fx-background-color: darkred;
 -fx-text-fill: ladder(darkred, white 0%, black 100%);
}
#light-button{
 -fx-background-color: lightyellow;
 -fx-text-fill: ladder(lightyellow, white 0%, black 100%);
}
```

In the CSS style sheet, the `ladder(...)` function is used to define the text color for two buttons. You create these buttons in a JavaFX application without defining any additional parameters next to their IDs:

```
..
Button darkButton = new Button("Dark");
darkButton.textFId("dark-button");
Button lightButton = new Button("Light");
lightButton.setId("light-button");
...
```

When running the application, the two buttons will have different text colors. The color of the text fits perfectly to the light and dark backgrounds of the buttons, as shown in Figure 9-10.

FIGURE 9-10. *Result of the ladder() function*

By using the brightness of the background color, the `ladder(...)` function calculates the perfect color for the text.

With the two methods shown here, it is easy to define global base colors in CSS and use derived colors in specific rules.

An Interview with Claudine Zillmann, software developer at maredit GmbH

Hi, Claudine. Many JavaFX developers know you as a CSS expert for JavaFX styling and the maintainer of AquaFX. Therefore, I think you can add some useful information and tips about styling to the more general information about CSS mentioned in this book. But before we start, can you please introduce yourself and how you came to JavaFX and CSS?

Hello, Hendrik, it's a pleasure to contribute to your work with an interview and share tips and knowledge on this topic.

Right now, I work at maredit GmbH as one of three lead developers for e-commerce projects and specialize in developing controls with our recently created web framework.

But to introduce myself, I take a step further back in time.

I will start with my first steps in styling and HTML. At the beginning, I tried some things just for fun, using 1x1-pixel images or marquee tags. Soon, school projects made me concentrate on using CSS and what it stands for. You find out a lot of benefits and concepts, such as the box model and separation of markup and styling in general. But I realized that those components were not comfortable. Especially proper usage of positioning made me mad at times.

During my studies at university, I concentrated on Java development and started to work in a company with a client-server application, specializing on development of the Swing client for seven years. In that time, JavaFX came up and became a successor of Swing. Soon, the idea of AquaFX was born at the completion of my degree. It was like, "Hey, I think JavaFX really rocks, and I want a deep dive in that technology. JavaFX is young and could need contributions. Let's create a skin!" Since that time, JavaFX has been my hobby and my favorite UI framework.

It sounds to me as you played with most of the different layout solutions that appeared over the last few years, beginning with a 1-pixel blank.gif to the CSS styling that we have today with Bootstrap and JavaFX CSS styling. Can you tell me what are the biggest differences between CSS styling for web content and JavaFX content?

The differences are not really that big, on the one hand. On the other hand, they are immense (but control-based web design comes up more and more). In an exaggerated way, I think I was lucky by not getting too serious in web design, so I do not miss a lot of stuff that might be possible with web CSS. JavaFX adapted the CSS standard and adjusted it for its UI controls. So, you have nodes (a box model), which can be styled with colors, borders, padding, effects, and so on, and which also can inherit styles by parent nodes, as known from conventional web design. If you know those concepts and the possibilities that CSS offers, it is not hard to style JavaFX applications. You just have to be aware of some tiny things:

- The naming is different: not `background-color` but `-fx-background-color`.
- You are within a control, especially when it's about positioning. This is the part where you should not forget about the concept of layout managers in UI frameworks.
- Not everything is possible with JavaFX CSS, but almost. Just stick to the reference guide before you start. That will help.
- Things that might seem impossible are not really impossible because you also might realize them in a programmatic way.

All in all, it is pretty similar. Like in web-based design, all those possibilities can be used in a good and a "less good" way. This could cause ugly code, unwanted visual results, or performance issues.

In conclusion, JavaFX combines the strength of UI frameworks with web design, so cool results can be achieved straightforwardly, even if you do not know CSS very well or at all.

Let me ask a last general CSS question before we talk about CSS for JavaFX and your AquaFX project. There are different ways you can apply CSS: by using several style sheets, defining all CSS rules in one big style sheet, or adding all styles inline, for example. Do you have any tips or a best-practice workflow for how developers should organize their CSS styles?

There is no general best-practice workflow that fits every need. I think the answer is, "It depends." You have to ask yourself a couple of questions to find the proper organization of styles for your project. For example:

- Do I want to reuse styles?
- Can some characteristics be generalized?
- Should colors/sizes vary? Or are there other variations?

So, define the individual requirements of your own project, and then you can decide how to realize it.

Generally, if you just want to try something or modify some tiny things, inline styles might be enough. I'm not a friend of that technique at all, though.

If you create a set of your own controls, try to put all general definitions in one style sheet and add individual styles for each control. For a complete skin, I used one style sheet because you touch every single control.

(Continued)

Thanks for this hint. Let's change the focus and talk about JavaFX in combination with CSS. Why do you think each JavaFX developer should know CSS and use it when developing JavaFX applications?

This answer is pretty simple: because it makes development so much easier. The times of programmatic styling and drawing each component are over. Formatting, colors, and style information shouldn't live within your code. Why not use proven concepts of web development and apply them? Your application gets much more flexible as well. On top of that, CSS is no mystery and not that hard to learn. Does it need more reasons?

The CSS support in JavaFX is based on CSS 2.1 and adds some useful functions like `derive(...)` and `ladder(...)`. These functions are normally not part of CSS and help a developer to create flexible and more readable CSS definitions. Do you have some other hints how a developer can create readable and flexible CSS rules?

There are several hints to achieve readable and flexible CSS definitions. I think the five most important tips are

- Get to know all possibilities JavaFX already ships with by default. Take more than one look at the JavaFX CSS Reference Guide. It tells you about all those cool functions JavaFX offers for CSS.

- The other important thing to address is the source of the Modena skin. When you look at the CSS shipped with JavaFX, there are no more mysteries about the usage of CSS.

- Make your CSS flexible by learning how to use selectors properly. The smarter your selection is, the more efficient the parsing of the scene graph is.

- When it comes to colors, use looked-up colors. Looked-up colors enable a global definition of colors in some sort of variable. This then can be used in the whole CSS and, for example, altered by the functions `derive(...)` and `ladder(...)` you mentioned. With that approach, you can use a few color definitions that are held centrally and avoid a complete revision of all CSS definitions when changing the whole color scheme. This concept could even be widened by implementing your own functions. As I mentioned, almost everything is possible with JavaFX.

Many web developers started to use a dynamic style sheet language like LESS to optimize their CSS style sheets. Do you know whether workflows like this can be used in JavaFX, too?

Oh, well, actually Tom Schindl has already experimented with LESS and JavaFX. He published a little blog post about his thoughts and experiments in this promising area. If you want to know more, read it at http://tomsondev.bestsolution.at/2013/08/07/using-less-in-javafx/. This trend is really noteworthy.

Let's talk about AquaFX. With this project, you created a complete skin for all the basic JavaFX controls. Can you share some of the pitfalls with that you were confronted with and experiences that you earned while developing the theme?

Sure, I can. But where to start? I think, with the concept. One of the first questions I asked myself was, do I base the skin on an existing JavaFX skin, or shall I create it independently? Since AquaFX will explicitly be the look and feel of OS X for JavaFX, it couldn't be dependent on future changes in the base skin. So, adjusting the base skin was no option, which means that every control had to be styled from scratch.

When it comes to styling controls, this is pure work and good eyes. One pitfall can be the vertical alignment of text. If you work a lot with padding, check your new controls next to each other. Some other tips for all kinds of questions can be found on my slides, loaded up on SlideShare: http://de.slideshare.net/ClaudineZillmann/lets-get-wetbestpracticesforskinningjavafxcontrols.

Thank you very much for this interview. Let me ask one last question: Are you planning to create some other JavaFX themes in the future?

Thank you very much for conducting this interview. It is always a pleasure. To your last question: Well, yes, the next skin, FlatterFX, is still in progress and will be published when it is finished. I guess the next steps are maybe some experiments with LESS and some optimization of AquaFX. After that, we will see what the community might ask for.

Summary

As you saw in this chapter, the CSS support in JavaFX is detailed and could therefore warrant a book of its own. This chapter covered the basics, so you should be able to create style sheets based on these practices and features. It is also important to take a deeper look at the CSS documentation of JavaFX as you begin working with CSS; all the classes, pseudoclasses, and properties are described in the documentation.

By using CSS to style a JavaFX application, you can create a perfect separation between the styling and the logic of an application. By using CSS and FXML in combination, only the business and controller logic of an application must be implemented in Java. All the layout and styling topics can be defined in languages that fit your needs. If you've already used CSS for web development, you should have no trouble becoming familiar with the functions covered in this chapter. However, the benefits of using CSS are so important that everyone should use it. Your application will be more structured, and changes in the style of an application can be defined quickly if the CSS style sheet of the application is well structured.

CHAPTER
10

Custom Controls

I n this chapter, I show how the internal layout and rendering mechanisms of a control work and how you can create custom JavaFX controls or extend the basic controls with new cool features. To do either of these things, you will need to create a skin, because in JavaFX, the layout and behavior of a control are defined in its skin. In this chapter, you will learn how to define the skin and how its interaction with the `Control` class works. In addition, you'll create your first custom control, which will use some exciting JavaFX features.

The Structure of a Control

It is important to know how a JavaFX control works internally. In the previous chapters, I showed most of the internals of the `Control` class and classes that inherit from it, like `Button` and `CheckBox`. All these classes define the model of a control in JavaFX, which means all properties of a control are encapsulated in the `Control` class (Chapters 5 and 6 described the architecture and properties of `Control`). To render a `Control` instance on the screen, you're missing some important information, though. Specifically, how are all the different components of the control laid out in its bounds?

This functionality is one of the main features of a JavaFX skin. In JavaFX, a skin is defined for each `Control` instance, and the skin defines the look and feel of the control. As mentioned in Chapter 3 (see Figure 3-6 for an example for the `CheckBox`), all controls are defined as a composition of basic JavaFX `Node` instances. Each basic control is created by using JavaFX `Shape` objects such as `Text`, `Rectangle`, or `Line`. All these basic nodes are managed in the skin of a control. This part defines the look and layout of a control. In addition, the skin manages the "feel," or behavior, of a control; in other words, the skin defines the events and actions that will be called and handled when the user does some input action. If a user presses CTRL-A in a `TextField` instance, the complete text in the `TextField` will be selected, for example. Figure 10-1 shows the structure of a JavaFX control.

As you can see in the figure, the internal architecture of JavaFX controls is based on the Model-View-Controller (MVC) pattern. Since the other parts of a control were already described in earlier chapters, let's take a look at the skin definition in JavaFX so you understand the complete architecture of JavaFX controls.

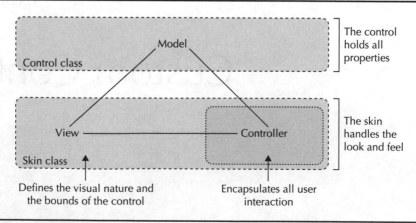

FIGURE 10-1. *Internal structure of a control*

The Skin

The skin of a control is defined by the Skin<C extends Skinnable> interface. The interface defines the visual representation of user interface controls and defines three methods, as described in Table 10-1.

As defined in the interface, a skin needs an object of type Skinnable. The Skinnable instance will be returned by the getSkinnable() method. Skinnable is an interface that defines the basic methods for an object that can hold a Skin instance. The Control class in JavaFX implements the Skinnable interface, and therefore each control can hold a skin. Almost all skins in JavaFX extend the SkinBase<C extends Control> class that implements the Skin interface. Figure 10-2 shows the inheritance of all the named classes and interfaces in an UML diagram.

As you can see, a custom control implementation will extend the Control class, and its skin implementation will normally extend the SkinBase class. The two classes will look like the following code snippet:

```
//Control
public class CustomControl extends Control {

    @Override
    protected Skin<?> createDefaultSkin() {
        return new CustomControlSkin(this);
    }

}

//Skin
public class CustomControlSkin extends SkinBase<CustomControl> {
    public CustomControlSkin(CustomControl control) {
        super(control);
    }
}
```

All basic controls that are part of JavaFX and mentioned in this book are structured like this example. The skin and control are defined as a one-to-one relationship. The skin is defined by the skin property of the Control class, and the control can be referenced in a skin by calling the getSkinnable() method. The skin is designed as a black box from the perspective of the control. Normally, it will listen only to changes in the state of the control and handle them.

Method	Description
C getSkinnable()	Returns the Skinnable instance to which this skin is assigned. In most cases, this will be the Control class.
Node getNode()	Returns the node that represents this skin. In most cases, this will be the Control class.
void dispose()	Called by the Skinnable when the skin is replaced. The method can be overridden to clean up the skin.

TABLE 10-1. *Methods of the Skin Interface*

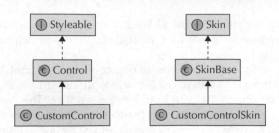

FIGURE 10-2. *UML diagram of Control and Skin*

NOTE
The Skin classes of the basic JavaFX controls don't extend SkinBase
directly. All these skins are part of the private API and extend the
com.sun.javafx.scene.control.skin.BehaviorSkinBase
*class. As you can see in the package, this class is part of the private
API, too. So, you shouldn't extend this class for custom controls.
Instead, the* SkinBase *class should be extended directly. The*
BehaviorSkinBase *class is used internally to separate the behavior
and the look of a control. If you want this architecture for custom
controls, an additional custom basic* Skin *class is needed. Maybe the*
BehaviorSkinBase *class will become part of the public API in a
future version of JavaFX. Until then, it shouldn't be used.*

As mentioned, all skins that are defined for custom controls should extend the SkinBase
class, so you will now take a deeper look at this class.

The SkinBase Class

The abstract SkinBase class defines a basic implementation of a skin for a JavaFX control. As
described earlier, the Skin interface can be used for each Skinnable instance. The SkinBase
class directly works with the Control class that implements the Skinnable interface, and
therefore SkinBase contains some useful basic implementations and methods when skinning a
Control instance. Therefore, each skin that is used to skin a control should extend this class.

The SkinBase class defines a set of methods containing some basic implementation; it can
be simply overridden in concrete implementations to define a custom look and behavior of a
control. Table 10-2 contains the methods of the SkinBase class.

To get a better understanding of these methods and how they can be used or must be
overridden when creating custom skins, let's first create a custom control that uses a skin that
extends the SkinBase class and defines a set of special features for the control. In the following
section, you will create a custom button-like control and extend its skin with new features.

Method	Description
`public final ObservableList<Node> getChildren()`	This returns the children of the control.
`public static List<CssMetaData<? extends Styleable, ?>> getClassCssMetaData()`	This is a static helper method that returns the `CssMetaData` instances that are associated with the skin.
`public List<CssMetaData<? extends Styleable, ?>> getCssMetaData()`	This returns the `CssMetaData` instances that are associated with the skin. In most cases, this will call the static helper class mentioned in the previous row.
`public final void pseudoClassStateChanged(PseudoClass pseudoClass, boolean active)`	This is used to specify that a pseudoclass has changed.
`protected double compute...(...)`	The `SkinBase` class defines a set of methods that compute the minimum, maximum, and preferred sizes of the control. Examples are `protected double computeMaxWidth(...)` and `protected double computePrefHeight(...)`.
`protected final void consumeMouseEvents(boolean value)`	This determines if all mouse events of the control should be automatically consumed.
`protected void layoutChildren(final double contentX, final double contentY, final double contentWidth, final double contentHeight)`	This method is called during the layout process of the JavaFX scene graph and will lay out all children of the control.
`protected void layoutInArea(Node child, ...)`	This is a utility method that lays out the given child within an area of the control. These methods will change the size and position of the child.
`protected positionInArea(Node child, ....)`	This is a utility method that positions the given child within an area of the control. This method won't change the size of the child.

(continued)

TABLE 10-2. *Methods of the SkinBase Class*

Method	Description
`protected double snapped...Inset()`	This is a utility method that returns an inset that includes padding and the border inset of the control. If `getSkinnable().isSnapToPixel()` is true, the value will be rounded up. Here are two examples: `protected double snappedBottomInset()` and `protected double snappedRightInset()`.
`protected double snapPosition(double value)`	If `getSkinnable().isSnapToPixel()` is true, the utility method will return a value rounded to the nearest pixel.
`protected double snapSize(double value)`	If `getSkinnable().isSnapToPixel()` is true, the utility method will return a value rounded to the nearest pixel.
`protected double snapSpace(double value)`	If `getSkinnable().isSnapToPixel()` is true, the utility method will return a value rounded to the nearest pixel.

TABLE 10-2.   *Methods of the SkinBase Class* (continued)

Creating a Custom Control

To create your first control in JavaFX, you need a specification of the control and its features. For this example, you will create a button-like control that is a triangle. Figure 10-3 shows how the control will look in its basic version.

Later you will add action handling and different visual states for when the control is clicked, but first you will focus on the basic layout and rendering of the control. In its initial version, the control should have a property that defines its background color, so you need the model of the control. As mentioned, the model will be defined in the class that extends the `Control` class. Here's the source code of the class:

```
package com.guigarage.masteringcontrols;

import javafx.beans.property.ObjectProperty;
import javafx.beans.property.SimpleObjectProperty;
import javafx.scene.control.Control;
import javafx.scene.control.Skin;
import javafx.scene.paint.Color;

public class TriangleButton extends Control {
```

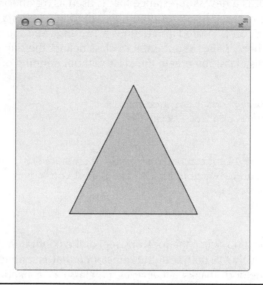

FIGURE 10-3. *The TriangleButton control onscreen*

```java
    private ObjectProperty<Color> backgroundFill;
    public TriangleButton() {
        backgroundFill = new SimpleObjectProperty<>(Color.DARKORCHID);
    }


    public Color getBackgroundFill() {
        return backgroundFill.get();
    }

    public ObjectProperty<Color> backgroundFillProperty() {
        return backgroundFill;
    }

    public void setBackgroundFill(Color backgroundFill) {
        this.backgroundFill.set(backgroundFill);
    }
}
```

This class contains only a property that will be used to define the background color of the control. As mentioned, a skin is needed for this custom control. A `Control` instance must hold its skin, and to define the default skin of a `Control` instance, the `Control` class defines the `Skin<?> createDefaultSkin()` method. To define a default skin for the `TriangleButton` control, you override only this method, as shown here:

```java
@Override
protected Skin<?> createDefaultSkin() {
    return new TriangleButtonSkin(this);
}
```

The method returns a new skin instance that is used as a skin for an instance of the `TriangleButton` control. The method will be called whenever a new instance of the `TriangleButton` is created and defines a `TriangleButtonSkin` instance as the skin of the control. The `TriangleButtonSkin` class defines the skin of the custom control. So, let's take a look at this class. You create the class without defining or overriding any methods, as shown here:

```
package com.guigarage.masteringcontrols;
import javafx.scene.control.SkinBase;


public class TriangleButtonSkin extends SkinBase<TriangleButton> {
    protected TriangleButtonSkin(TriangleButton control) {
        super(control);
    }
}
```

Once this is done, you define the look and feel of the control. In the `TriangleButtonSkin` class, you can access the `TriangleButton` instance that is managed by the skin by calling the `getSkinnable()` method. Thanks to Generics, no class cast is needed here. Let's start with the size of the control. The `SkinBase` class defines some methods that will be used to calculate the control's size. To define a specific size for the custom control, you override all these methods, as shown in the following code snippet:

```
    @Override
    protected double computePrefHeight(double width, double topInset,
        double rightInset, double bottomInset, double leftInset) {
        return  topInset + bottomInset + 200;
    }

    @Override
    protected double computePrefWidth(double height, double topInset,
        double rightInset, double bottomInset, double leftInset) {
        return  rightInset + leftInset + 200;
    }

    @Override
    protected double computeMinHeight(double width, double topInset,
        double rightInset, double bottomInset, double leftInset) {
        return 20 + topInset + bottomInset;
    }

    @Override
    protected double computeMinWidth(double height, double topInset,
        double rightInset, double bottomInset, double leftInset) {
        return 20 + rightInset + leftInset;
    }

    @Override
    protected double computeMaxWidth(double height, double topInset,
        double rightInset, double bottomInset, double leftInset) {
        return computePrefWidth(height, topInset, rightInset, bottomInset, leftInset);
    }
```

```
@Override
protected double computeMaxHeight(double width, double topInset,
    double rightInset, double bottomInset, double leftInset) {
    return computePrefHeight(width, topInset, rightInset, bottomInset, leftInset);
}
```

By adding these methods, the skin defines preferred, maximum, and minimum sizes for the `TriangleButton` control:

- The control has a minimum size (width and height) that is equal to its insets + 20.
- The control has a preferred size (width and height) that is equal to its insets + 200.
- The control has a maximum size (width and height) that is equal to its preferred size.

So, if you add a `TriangleButton` control to a huge `StackPane` instance and don't define any insets (padding or border) for it, the control will have a size of 200 × 200 pixels.

NOTE
*There are some other ways to define the size of the control.
Because the maximum width is always equal to the preferred one,
getSkinnable().setMaxWidth(Region.USE_PREF_SIZE) could
be called in the constructor of the skin. For more information about
the size calculation, refer to Chapter 4.*

The shown methods are not abstract methods in the `SkinBase` class, and therefore they don't need to be overridden. Its default implementation calculates the needed sizes by using the managed children of the control when they are positioned at their current positions at their preferred size. You should look at the source of these methods as they are defined in the `SkinBase` class to decide when they should be overridden or not.

After you define the size of the control, it needs a visualization. So, define a shape that is used as the visual representation of the control. To create a triangle, you will use the `Path` class, which extends the `Shape` class and defines a simple shape with its geometric path. (You can find a complete feature overview of the `Path` class in the JavaDoc.) The path that is needed to visualize the `TriangleButton` is defined as shown in the following code snippet:

```
Path triangle = new Path();
triangle.getElements().add(new MoveTo(width / 2, 0));
triangle.getElements().add(new LineTo(width, height));
triangle.getElements().add(new LineTo(0, height));
triangle.getElements().addAll(new ClosePath());
```

The path is created by three lines that span a triangle. In the last line of the snippet, the path is closed. A closed path can be filled by a color, and that is exactly what you need for the `TriangleButton`. The following code defines the first version of a skin that defines a triangle as the visual representation of the `TriangleButton`:

```
package com.guigarage.masteringcontrols;
import javafx.geometry.HPos;
import javafx.geometry.VPos;
import javafx.scene.control.SkinBase;
import javafx.scene.paint.Color;
```

```java
import javafx.scene.shape.ClosePath;
import javafx.scene.shape.LineTo;
import javafx.scene.shape.MoveTo;
import javafx.scene.shape.Path;

public class TriangleButtonSkin extends SkinBase<TriangleButton> {
    private Path triangle;

    private boolean invalidTriangle = true;

    protected TriangleButtonSkin(TriangleButton control) {
        super(control);
        control.widthProperty().addListener(observable ->
            invalidTriangle = true);
        control.heightProperty().addListener(observable ->
            invalidTriangle = true);
        control.backgroundFillProperty().addListener(observable ->
            updateTriangleColor());
    }

    public void updateTriangleColor() {
        if(triangle != null) {
            triangle.setFill(getSkinnable().getBackgroundFill());
            getSkinnable().requestLayout();
        }
    }

    public void updateTriangle(double width, double height) {
        if(triangle != null) {
            getChildren().remove(triangle);
        }
        triangle = new Path();
        triangle.getElements().add(new MoveTo(width / 2, 0));
        triangle.getElements().add(new LineTo(width, height));
        triangle.getElements().add(new LineTo(0, height));
        triangle.getElements().addAll(new ClosePath());
        triangle.setStroke(Color.BLACK);
        triangle.setFill(getSkinnable().getBackgroundFill());
        getChildren().add(triangle);
    }

    @Override
    protected void layoutChildren(double contentX, double contentY,
        double contentWidth, double contentHeight) {
        if(invalidTriangle) {
            updateTriangle(contentWidth, contentHeight);
            invalidTriangle = false;
        }
        layoutInArea(triangle, contentX, contentY, contentWidth,
            contentHeight, -1, HPos.CENTER, VPos.CENTER);
    }
```

```
//ComputeSizeMethods
//...

}
```

NOTE
In the code, I've omitted all the methods to compute the size of the control to give you a better overview of the code. Because the demo classes in this chapter are huge, I will do this in most of the code snippets in this chapter.

Let's take a look at the new methods and how they work. The `updateTriangle(...)` method creates a new triangle and adds it as a child to the control. So, the triangle shape will be rendered onscreen whenever the `TriangleButton` control is rendered. The method changes the internal node hierarchy of the control, and therefore it should be called on every rendering loop. This would result in poor performance; therefore, the `invalidTriangle` flag is introduced. Whenever the size of the control changes, you set the flag to true. You do this in the constructor of the skin by adding listeners to the `width` and `height` property of the control. Whenever the flag is true, the control changes its size. Because the triangle is defined by a static size, it must be re-created in this case. The re-creation is triggered in the `layoutChildren(...)` method of the skin. This method is called whenever the layout of the control needs to be recalculated by the JavaFX rendering loop. If `invalidTriangle` is true, the layout method will trigger the `updateTriangle(...)` method to create a new version of the triangle that matches the current size of the control. In addition to this, the `updateTriangleColor()` method is introduced. This method changes the fill color of the triangle shape to the color that is defined by the `backgroundFill` property of the `TriangleButton` class. Whenever the value of this property changes, the method is called.

NOTE
You might wonder why the triangle isn't created directly when the size of the control changes. This is done because of a performance issue. Maybe the size changes but the control isn't visible onscreen. In this case, the triangle mustn't be re-created until the control appears onscreen. As you will see later in this chapter, there are a lot of performance tricks that can be used to create a reusable control. Most of these tricks are reproduced by analyzing the basic `Control` and `Skin` classes that are part of JavaFX.

Once all this is done, you can use the `TriangleButton` in JavaFX and add it to a scene graph. The following code shows an example that adds an instance of the custom control to a scene. The result was shown in Figure 10-3.

```
package com.guigarage.masteringcontrols;
import javafx.application.Application;
import javafx.geometry.Insets;
import javafx.scene.Scene;
import javafx.scene.layout.StackPane;
import javafx.scene.paint.Color;
import javafx.stage.Stage;
import java.util.Random;
```

```
public class TriangleButtonDemo extends Application {
    @Override
    public void start(Stage primaryStage) throws Exception {
        TriangleButton button = new TriangleButton();
        button.setId("my_triangle_button");
        button.setPadding(new Insets(20));
        button.setOnMouseClicked((e) -> {
            Random random = new Random(System.currentTimeMillis());
            button.setBackgroundFill(Color.color(random.nextDouble(),
                random.nextDouble(),random.nextDouble()));
        });
        StackPane myPane = new StackPane();
        myPane.getChildren().add(button);
        Scene myScene = new Scene(myPane);
        primaryStage.setScene(myScene);
        primaryStage.setWidth(300);
        primaryStage.setHeight(200);
        primaryStage.show();
    }
    public static void main(String[] args) {
        launch(args);
    }
}
```

Adding Event Handling

As a next step, you should add event handling to the control. Like the event handling that is defined in the basic controls of JavaFX, the EventHandler class should be used here. The TriangleButton should fire action events whenever the button is clicked, so you can reuse the ActionEvent class that is a specific event implementation and used by the JavaFX Button control. To do this, you introduce a new property in the TriangleButton class called onAction:

```
public class TriangleButton extends Control {

    //…

    public final ObjectProperty<EventHandler<ActionEvent>> onActionProperty() { return
        onAction; }

    public final void setOnAction(EventHandler<ActionEvent> value) {
        onActionProperty().set(value); }


    public final EventHandler<ActionEvent> getOnAction() { return onActionProperty().
        get(); }

    private ObjectProperty<EventHandler<ActionEvent>> onAction =
        new ObjectPropertyBase<EventHandler<ActionEvent>>() {
        @Override protected void invalidated() {
            setEventHandler(ActionEvent.ACTION, get());
        }
        @Override
        public Object getBean() {
```

```
            return TriangleButton.this;
        }
        @Override
        public String getName() {
            return "onAction";
        }
    };
}
```

As you can see in the code, the onAction property is defined as ObjectProperty<Event
Handler<ActionEvent>>, and it can be used like all the other properties that are mentioned in
earlier examples in this book. In the following code snippet, a custom event handler is defined to
handle the action events of the TriangleButton instance. Once this is done, the background
color of the TriangleButton will change whenever the action event is fired:

```
TriangleButton button = new TriangleButton();
button.setOnAction((e) -> {
    Random random = new Random(System.currentTimeMillis());
    button.setBackgroundFill(Color.color(random.nextDouble(),
        random.nextDouble(),random.nextDouble()));
});
```

Once this is done, a developer can programmatically react to action events. But until now,
these events will never be fired. Because the skin of a class should handle its behavior, the event
should be fired in the TriangleButtonSkin. As mentioned, new ActionEvent instances should
be fired whenever the user clicks the triangle button. To do this, a mouse handler will be defined
for the triangle shape. Therefore, the updateTriangle(...) method in the skin will be extended:

```
public class TriangleButtonSkin extends SkinBase<TriangleButton> {

    //...

    public void updateTriangle(double width, double height) {
        if(triangle != null) {
            getChildren().remove(triangle);
        }
        triangle = new Path();
        ...
        triangle.setOnMouseClicked((e) -> getSkinnable().fireEvent(new ActionEvent()));
        getChildren().add(triangle);
    }

    //...
}
```

The fireEvent(...) method that is defined in the Node class is used here. You should
always use this method instead of dealing directly with the event handlers when firing events.
Whenever this method is called, the created event will travel through the hierarchy from the stage
to the TriangleButton node. Any event filter encountered will be notified and can consume
the event. If the event is not consumed by the filters, the event handlers on the TriangleButton
are notified. This workflow can be guaranteed only when using the fireEvent(...) method.
Once this is done, an ActionEvent will be fired whenever the user clicks the triangle. In the
sample, the RectangleButton will change its background color once the user clicks it.

NOTE
*In the example, an ActionEvent will be fired only when the
visible triangle is clicked. As with each node, the bounds of the
TriangleButtons are defined as a rectangle. This is specified in the basic
functionality of the scene graph. But whenever a user clicks an empty
area of the control, nothing will happen. If the mouse-click event
handler were registered on the control, the events would be fired
whenever a user clicks any area inside the bounds of the control. By
using the demonstrated approach, a developer can specify the event
handling behavior in a much better way.*

Styling the Control

Next, you should style the `TriangleButton` with CSS, so you'll need some additional classes
and interfaces. Before the `TriangleButton` classes are refactored, I will introduce the needed
classes. Until now, the `TriangleButton` class contained an `ObjectProperty` that defined
the background color. To make this property stylable by CSS, you need a property of type
`StyleableProperty<T>`. This interface defines a JavaFX property that can be styled by CSS.
The interface defines three methods, as described in Table 10-3.

Normally, you don't need to implement these methods and implement the
`StyleableProperty<T>` by yourself. JavaFX provides a set of default implementations
that can be used in almost all use cases. When refactoring the `TriangleButton` later, you'll
use a default implementation. When taking a look at the methods of the interface, you'll see two
new types are mentioned: `StyleOrigin` and `CssMetaData`. `StyleOrigin` is an enumeration
that defines the origin of a CSS style such as a user-agent style sheet or inline style. (You can find
more information about different CSS origins in Chapter 9.)

The abstract `CssMetaData<? extends Styleable, T>` class defines information about
the CSS property that can be used to style the JavaFX property. In addition, the class defines the
hooks that allow CSS to set a property value. So, for an additional CSS property definition that
should be used to style the JavaFX property of a control, you need a `CssMetaData` instance.

You can find examples that show how the `CssMetaData` class and stylable properties should
be used in the source of the default JavaFX `Control` classes. As a first step, you will define this
structure in the `TriangleButton` class. Because the `CssMetaData` instance and the stylable

Method	Description
`void applyStyle(StyleOrigin origin, T value)`	This method is called from JavaFX's CSS mechanism to set the value of the property.
`StyleOrigin getStyleOrigin()`	This defines the origin of the current value.
`CssMetaData<? extends Styleable, T> getCssMetaData()`	This returns the `CssMetaData` that corresponds to the property.

TABLE 10-3. *Methods of the StyleableProperty Interface*

property depend on each other, the code is complex at first sight. So, let's take a deeper look at the source code:

```java
public class TriangleButton extends Control {

private StyleableObjectProperty<Paint> backgroundFill;

public Paint getBackgroundFill() {
      return backgroundFill == null ? Color.DARKGRAY : backgroundFill.get();
    }
    public void setBackgroundFill(Paint backgroundFill) {
        this.backgroundFill.set(backgroundFill);
    }
    public StyleableObjectProperty<Paint> backgroundFillProperty() {
        if (backgroundFill == null) {
            backgroundFill = new SimpleStyleableObjectProperty<Paint>(
                StyleableProperties.BACKGROUND_FILL, TriangleButton.this,
                "backgroundFill", Color.DARKGRAY);
        }
        return backgroundFill;
    }

    //…

    private static class StyleableProperties {
      private static final CssMetaData<TriangleButton, Paint> BACKGROUND_FILL =
            new CssMetaData<TriangleButton, Paint>("-fx-triangle-fill",
                    PaintConverter.getInstance(), Color.BLACK) {
                @Override
                public boolean isSettable(TriangleButton control) {
                    return control.backgroundFill == null || !control.
                        backgroundFill.isBound();
                }
                @Override
                public StyleableProperty<Paint> getStyleableProperty
                    (TriangleButton control) {
                    return control.backgroundFillProperty();
                }
            };
        private static final List<CssMetaData<? extends Styleable, ?>> STYLEABLES;
        static {
            final List<CssMetaData<? extends Styleable, ?>> styleables =
                    new ArrayList<CssMetaData<? extends Styleable, ?>>(Control.
                        getClassCssMetaData());
            Collections.addAll(styleables,
                    BACKGROUND_FILL
            );
            STYLEABLES = Collections.unmodifiableList(styleables);
        }
    }
    @Override
    public List<CssMetaData<? extends Styleable, ?>> getControlCssMetaData() {
        return getClassCssMetaData();
    }
```

```
public static List<CssMetaData<? extends Styleable, ?>> getClassCssMetaData() {
    return StyleableProperties.STYLEABLES;
}

}
```

As mentioned, there is a lot of new code in the `TriangleButton` class, but I've removed all unchanged methods in the code example to give you a better overview. The complete source of the class will follow after this example.

The class type of the `backgroundFill` property has changed. It is now defined as a `Simple StyleableObjectProperty<Paint>`. This class is one of the default implementations of the `StyleableProperty` interface. But the biggest change is the new internal class `StyleableProperties`. This class contains all the static information needed for CSS styling. In this class, the `CssMetaData` instances that define the link between the JavaFX properties and the CSS properties are defined. This is done in a static inner class because of some performance issues. All the information defined here is the same for all instances of the custom `Skin` class. Therefore, the defined instances mustn't be created for each new `Skin` instance. The private class contains the `CssMetaData` instance that defines the CSS property that is linked to the `backgroundFill` property of the control. The CSS property name `-fx-triangle-fill` and its default value are passed to the constructor of the `CssMetaData` class. In addition, the two methods `isSettable(…)` and `getStyleableProperty(…)` of the `CssMetaData` class are overridden. As a result, the static `CssMetaData` instance can work with the `backgroundFill` property of a given `Control` instance. This is achieved by passing the static `CssMetaData` instance as a parameter to the constructor of the `StyleableProperty`. So, the property of a specific `Control` instance will use the static `CssMetaData` instance that describes the link to the CSS styling internally.

In addition to the `CssMetaData` instance, the static class `StyleableProperties` defines a list of all `CssMetaData` instances that can be used to style the control. This list contains the `CssMetaData` instances that are defined by the control and all instances that are added by the skin. In addition, the method `getControlCssMetaData()` has been overridden. This method returns a list of all `CssMetaData` instances. Because you defined this list in the inner static private class, it can be returned here. Instead of returning the static list directly, a static utility method called `getClassCssMetaData()` is defined and called. In this first example, the static method theoretically isn't needed, but as you will see later, this structure is useful.

NOTE
The shown structure looks complex at first, but it is a best practice when defining custom controls. JavaFX uses the same approaches internally, which results in great performance: All global objects are defined in a static class and therefore need to be created only one time. In addition, no listener instances are needed. When working with controls, especially on mobile or embedded devices, memory usage and performance are important topics. Therefore, custom controls should be designed as shown here and done in the default JavaFX controls. Even if internal classes and anonymous inner classes are not a best practice when talking about design, they should be used in this case.

After all these changes, the `TriangleButton` class will look like this:

```java
package com.guigarage.masteringcontrols;
import com.sun.javafx.css.converters.PaintConverter;
import javafx.beans.property.ObjectProperty;
import javafx.beans.property.ObjectPropertyBase;
import javafx.css.*;
import javafx.event.ActionEvent;
import javafx.event.EventHandler;
import javafx.scene.control.Control;
import javafx.scene.control.Skin;
import javafx.scene.paint.Color;
import javafx.scene.paint.Paint;
import java.util.ArrayList;
import java.util.Collections;
import java.util.List;
public class TriangleButton extends Control {

    private StyleableObjectProperty<Paint> backgroundFill;
    private ObjectProperty<EventHandler<ActionEvent>> onAction =
        new ObjectPropertyBase<EventHandler<ActionEvent>>() {
         @Override
         protected void invalidated() {
             setEventHandler(ActionEvent.ACTION, get());
         }
         @Override
         public Object getBean() {
             return TriangleButton.this;
         }
         @Override
         public String getName() {
             return "onAction";
         }
    };
    @Override
    protected Skin<?> createDefaultSkin() {
        return new TriangleButtonSkin(this);
    }
    public Paint getBackgroundFill() {
        return backgroundFill == null ? Color.DARKGRAY : backgroundFill.get();
    }

    public void setBackgroundFill(Paint backgroundFill) {
        this.backgroundFill.set(backgroundFill);
    }

    public StyleableObjectProperty<Paint> backgroundFillProperty() {
        if (backgroundFill == null) {
           backgroundFill = new SimpleStyleableObjectProperty<Paint>(
               StyleableProperties.BACKGROUND_FILL, TriangleButton.this,
               "backgroundFill", Color.DARKGRAY);
        }
        return backgroundFill;
    }
```

```java
    public final ObjectProperty<EventHandler<ActionEvent>> onActionProperty() {
        return onAction;
    }

    public final EventHandler<ActionEvent> getOnAction() {
        return onActionProperty().get();
    }

    public final void setOnAction(EventHandler<ActionEvent> value) {
        onActionProperty().set(value);
    }

    private static class StyleableProperties {
        private static final CssMetaData<TriangleButton, Paint> BACKGROUND_FILL =
                new CssMetaData<TriangleButton, Paint>("-fx-triangle-fill",
                        PaintConverter.getInstance(), Color.BLACK) {
                    @Override
                    public boolean isSettable(TriangleButton control) {
                        return control.backgroundFill == null || !control.
                        backgroundFill.isBound();
                    }
                    @Override
                    public StyleableProperty<Paint> getStyleableProperty(
                    TriangleButton control) {
                        return control.backgroundFillProperty();
                    }
                };
        private static final List<CssMetaData<? extends Styleable, ?>> STYLEABLES;
        static {
            final List<CssMetaData<? extends Styleable, ?>> styleables =
                    new ArrayList<CssMetaData<? extends Styleable, ?>>(
                    Control.getClassCssMetaData());
            Collections.addAll(styleables,
                BACKGROUND_FILL
            );
            STYLEABLES = Collections.unmodifiableList(styleables);
        }
    }

    @Override
    public List<CssMetaData<? extends Styleable, ?>> getControlCssMetaData() {
        return getClassCssMetaData();
    }

    public static List<CssMetaData<? extends Styleable, ?>> getClassCssMetaData() {
        return StyleableProperties.STYLEABLES;
    }
}
```

Once this is done, you can style instances of the `TriangleButton` with CSS. Here is an example of a CSS rule that can be used to style a `TriangleButton`:

```css
#my_triangle_button {
    -fx-triangle-fill: yellow;
}
```

Using a CssHelper for Styling

As you saw in the previous sample, a lot of code is needed to make a JavaFX control stylable. Most of the code must be defined again for each stylable property of a control. By doing this, you'll create a lot of boilerplate code. Therefore, you can use helper classes to simplify the definition of stylable controls. One API that can be used is the `CssHelper` class that is provided at www.guigarage.com. You can find a description of the API here: http://www.guigarage.com/2014/03/javafx-css-utilities/. By using the `CssHelper` class, you can define the stylable properties and the needed `CssMetaData` instances in only a few lines of code; the following code block is an example. Here, a second stylable property is added to the `TriangleButton`.

```
package com.guigarage.masteringcontrols;
import com.sun.javafx.css.converters.PaintConverter;
import javafx.beans.property.ObjectProperty;
import javafx.beans.property.ObjectPropertyBase;
import javafx.css.CssMetaData;
import javafx.css.Styleable;
import javafx.css.StyleableObjectProperty;
import javafx.event.ActionEvent;
import javafx.event.EventHandler;
import javafx.scene.control.Control;
import javafx.scene.control.Skin;
import javafx.scene.paint.Color;
import javafx.scene.paint.Paint;
import java.util.List;

public class TriangleButton extends Control {
    private StyleableObjectProperty<Paint> backgroundFill;

    private StyleableObjectProperty<Paint> strokeFill;

    public Paint getBackgroundFill() {
        return backgroundFill == null ? Color.DARKGRAY : backgroundFill.get();
    }

    public void setBackgroundFill(Paint backgroundFill) {
        this.backgroundFill.set(backgroundFill);
    }

    public StyleableObjectProperty<Paint> backgroundFillProperty() {
        if (backgroundFill == null) {
            backgroundFill = CssHelper.createProperty(StyleableProperties.
            BACKGROUND_FILL, TriangleButton.this);
        }
        return backgroundFill;
    }

    public Paint getStrokeFill() {
        return strokeFill == null ? Color.DARKGRAY : strokeFill.get();
    }

    public void setStrokeFill(Paint strokeFill) {
        this.strokeFill.set(strokeFill);
    }
```

```
    public StyleableObjectProperty<Paint> strokeFillProperty() {
        if (strokeFill == null) {
            strokeFill = CssHelper.createProperty(StyleableProperties.STROKE_FILL,
            TriangleButton.this);
        }
        return strokeFill;
    }

    ...

    private static class StyleableProperties {
        private static final CssHelper.PropertyBasedCssMetaData<TriangleButton,
            Paint> BACKGROUND_FILL = CssHelper.createMetaData("-fx-triangle-fill",
            PaintConverter.getInstance(), "backgroundFill", Color.LIGHTGREEN);
        private static final CssHelper.PropertyBasedCssMetaData<TriangleButton,
            Paint> STROKE_FILL = CssHelper.createMetaData("-fx-triangle-stroke",
            PaintConverter.getInstance(), "strokeFill", Color.BLUE);
        private static final List<CssMetaData<? extends Styleable, ?>> STYLEABLES
            = CssHelper.createCssMetaDataList(Control.getClassCssMetaData(),
            BACKGROUND_FILL, STROKE_FILL);
    }

    @Override
    public List<CssMetaData<? extends Styleable, ?>> getControlCssMetaData() {
        return getClassCssMetaData();
    }

    public static List<CssMetaData<? extends Styleable, ?>> getClassCssMetaData() {
        return StyleableProperties.STYLEABLES;
    }
}
```

As you can see in the example, the `CssHelper` class provides static methods to generate stylable properties and `CssMetaData` instances.

For the second `StyleableProperty`, some changes in the `TriangleButtonSkin` are needed, as shown here:

```
public class TriangleButtonSkin extends SkinBase<TriangleButton> {

    public TriangleButtonSkin(TriangleButton control) {
        super(control);
        control.widthProperty().addListener(observable ->
            invalidTriangle = true);
        control.heightProperty().addListener(observable ->
            invalidTriangle = true);
        control.backgroundFillProperty().addListener(observable ->
            updateTriangleColor());
        control.strokeFillProperty().addListener(observable ->
            updateTriangleColor());
    }

    public void updateTriangleColor() {
        if(triangle != null) {
```

```
            triangle.setFill(getSkinnable().getBackgroundFill());
            triangle.setStroke(getSkinnable().getStrokeFill());
            getSkinnable().requestLayout();
        }
    }

    public void updateTriangle(double width, double height) {
        if(triangle != null) {
            getChildren().remove(triangle);
        }
        triangle = new Path();
        triangle.getElements().add(new MoveTo(width / 2, 0));
        triangle.getElements().add(new LineTo(width, height));
        triangle.getElements().add(new LineTo(0, height));
        triangle.getElements().addAll(new ClosePath());
        triangle.setStroke(getSkinnable().getStrokeFill());
        triangle.setStrokeWidth(4);
        triangle.setFill(getSkinnable().getBackgroundFill());
        triangle.setOnMouseClicked((e) -> getSkinnable().fireEvent(
            new ActionEvent()));
        getChildren().add(triangle);
    }

    //…
}
```

The `TriangleButton` control can now be styled in CSS by using all the properties that are defined for the basic `Control` class and the new CSS properties that are added to the `TriangleButton` class. Normally, a control inherits the stylable property of its parent class for CSS styling. If you want to eliminate a stylable property from a parent class, don't add the `CSSMetaData` from the parent class to the `CSSMetaData` list of the control. You can use the `CssHelper` class like in the following code snippet:

```
private static final List<CssMetaData<? extends Styleable, ?>> STYLEABLES =
    CssHelper.createCssMetaDataList(null, BACKGROUND_FILL, STROKE_FILL);
```

Here, null is used for the first parameter of the `createCssMetaDataList(…)` method. This parameter defines the basic list of `CssMetaData` instances. The complete list of all `CssMetaData` instances that are used for the class are defined by this list and all additional instances that are committed as parameters to the method. Normally, the static `getClassCssMetaData()` method of the parent class will be used here.

Defining Custom CSS Value Types
As mentioned in this and the previous chapter, CSS supports a lot of different types, such as String, color, and number, in JavaFX. In addition to this, you can define custom value types in JavaFX. As a next step, let's add some animation to the `TriangleButton`; aspects of the animation will be changeable by CSS.

Because the JavaFX animation API wasn't mentioned until now in this book, it's time to take a short look at it.

JavaFX contains an API that can be used to easily create animations. The basic class is the `Animation` class, and all animations should extend this class. JavaFX already contains a set of specific animations. One of them will be shown in the next example. An animation can run either only one time or in a loop, and in addition, it can run forward and backward while looping. The `Animation` class provides methods such as `play()` and `pause()` to handle the state of an animation. In most use cases, the animation API will be used to animate JavaFX properties such as the `rotation` property of a control. For some property types, JavaFX contains default classes that can be used to define an animation for a property instance. An example is the `ScaleTransition` class. This class can be easily used to define an animation for the scale properties (`scaleX`, `scaleY`, `scaleZ`) of a control.

NOTE
If you need an animation for a property type that isn't supported directly by a concrete `Animation` class in JavaFX, you can use a more general `Animation` class. This class can be found at www.guigarage.com/2012/12/bindabletransition/.

To provide better feedback for the user, the `TriangleButton` should zoom in and out once the user enters the mouse over the control. Because this feature is part of the behavior and look of the control, it should be defined in the `Skin` class. Therefore, the `TriangleButtonSkin` class will be extended, as shown here:

```
package com.guigarage.masteringcontrols;
import javafx.animation.ScaleTransition;
import javafx.event.ActionEvent;
import javafx.geometry.HPos;
import javafx.geometry.VPos;
import javafx.scene.control.SkinBase;
import javafx.scene.shape.ClosePath;
import javafx.scene.shape.LineTo;
import javafx.scene.shape.MoveTo;
import javafx.scene.shape.Path;
import javafx.util.Duration;
public class TriangleButtonSkin extends SkinBase<TriangleButton> {

    private ScaleTransition scaleTransition;

    protected TriangleButtonSkin(TriangleButton control) {
        super(control);
        control.widthProperty().addListener(observable -> invalidTriangle =
            true);
        control.heightProperty().addListener(observable -> invalidTriangle =
            true);
        control.backgroundFillProperty().addListener(observable ->
            updateTriangleColor());
        control.strokeFillProperty().addListener(observable ->
            updateTriangleColor());
    }
```

```java
    public void updateTriangle(double width, double height) {
        if(triangle != null) {
            getChildren().remove(triangle);
        }
        triangle = new Path();
        //...
        triangle.setOnMouseEntered((e) -> zoomIn());
        triangle.setOnMouseExited((e) -> zoomOut());
        getChildren().add(triangle);
    }

    private void zoomIn() {
        if(scaleTransition != null) {
            scaleTransition.pause();
        }
        scaleTransition = new ScaleTransition(Duration.millis(250), triangle);
        scaleTransition.setFromX(triangle.getScaleX());
        scaleTransition.setFromY(triangle.getScaleY());
        scaleTransition.setToX(1.5);
        scaleTransition.setToY(1.5);
        scaleTransition.play();
    }
    private void zoomOut() {
        if(scaleTransition != null) {
            scaleTransition.pause();
        }
        scaleTransition = new ScaleTransition(Duration.millis(250), triangle);
        scaleTransition.setFromX(triangle.getScaleX());
        scaleTransition.setFromY(triangle.getScaleY());
        scaleTransition.setToX(1.0);
        scaleTransition.setToY(1.0);
        scaleTransition.play();
    }

    @Override
    public void dispose() {
        if(scaleTransition != null) {
            scaleTransition.stop();
            scaleTransition = null;
        }
        super.dispose();
    }
    //...
}
```

Two new methods were added to the class: `zoomIn()` and `zoomOut()`. These methods will be called whenever the mouse cursor enters or exits the triangle and starts an animation. The animation automatically changes the values of the `scaleX` and `scaleY` properties of the control. As a result, the triangle will zoom in or out as a reaction to a mouse hover. In addition, the `dispose()` method of the `SkinBase` class has been overridden. In JavaFX, the skin of a control can change at run time. Therefore, the animation must stop whenever the skin is disposed. Figure 10-4 shows an example of the current state.

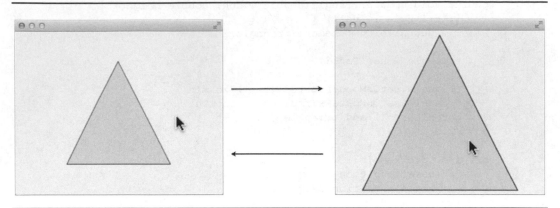

FIGURE 10-4. *Animation of the control*

At the moment, a hard-coded duration of 250 ms is defined for the animation. As a next step, this duration should be changeable by CSS. It would be easy to define a CSS property that could handle any number value and use this as the duration in milliseconds. But sometimes you need an animation that will take 20 seconds, for example. In this case, it would be better to write 20s instead of 20000 for the CSS value. Therefore, you will define a new CSS converter that can be used to define duration values in CSS.

To create a special converter, JavaFX provides the StyleConverter<F, T> class, which can be extended to define new converters for special data types. Therefore, you must override the convert(…) method that is defined by the StyleConverter class. The following code defines a StyleConverter that will create Duration instances from CSS values:

```java
package com.guigarage.masteringcontrols;
import javafx.css.ParsedValue;
import javafx.css.StyleConverter;
import javafx.scene.text.Font;
import javafx.util.Duration;

public class DurationStyleConverter extends StyleConverter<String, Duration> {

    @Override
    public Duration convert(ParsedValue<String, Duration> value, Font font) {
        String cssProperty = value.getValue();
        if(cssProperty.endsWith("ms")) {
            return Duration.millis(Long.parseLong(cssProperty.substring(0,
            cssProperty.length() - 2)));
        } else if(cssProperty.endsWith("s")) {
            return Duration.seconds(Long.parseLong(cssProperty.substring(0,
            cssProperty.length() - 1)));
        }
        return Duration.millis(Long.parseLong(cssProperty));
    }
}
```

The converter currently supports seconds and milliseconds, and values can be specified like 3s or 250ms. This converter can be used in `CssMetaData` instances to convert the value that is defined in a CSS rule and set it to a stylable property.

NOTE
The Font parameter of the `convert (...)` method normally isn't needed. But sometimes you will specify CSS types that are defined as relative values. These values specify a length relative to another length. Normally, the font size will be taken as a reference in this case. You can find more information about relative values at www.w3.org/TR/ css3-values/#relative-lengths.

Once the converter class is defined, it can be used by any `CssMetaData` instance. Let's make the duration of the example animation in the `TriangleButtonSkin` stylable. You define the `CssMetaData` instance as shown in the following code snippet:

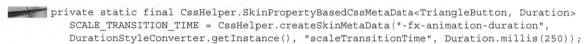

```
private static final CssHelper.SkinPropertyBasedCssMetaData<TriangleButton, Duration>
    SCALE_TRANSITION_TIME = CssHelper.createSkinMetaData("-fx-animation-duration",
    DurationStyleConverter.getInstance(), "scaleTransitionTime", Duration.millis(250));
```

After all these changes, the `TriangleButtonSkin` should look like this:

```
package com.guigarage.masteringcontrols;
import javafx.animation.ScaleTransition;
import javafx.css.CssMetaData;
import javafx.css.Styleable;
import javafx.css.StyleableObjectProperty;
import javafx.event.ActionEvent;
import javafx.geometry.HPos;
import javafx.geometry.VPos;
import javafx.scene.control.SkinBase;
import javafx.scene.shape.ClosePath;
import javafx.scene.shape.LineTo;
import javafx.scene.shape.MoveTo;
import javafx.scene.shape.Path;
import javafx.util.Duration;
import java.util.List;
public class TriangleButtonSkin extends SkinBase<TriangleButton> {

    private Path triangle;
    private boolean invalidTriangle = true;
    private ScaleTransition scaleTransition;
    private StyleableObjectProperty<Duration> scaleTransitionTime;

    protected TriangleButtonSkin(TriangleButton control) {
        super(control);
        control.widthProperty().addListener(observable -> invalidTriangle = true);
        control.heightProperty().addListener(observable -> invalidTriangle = true);
        control.backgroundFillProperty().addListener(observable ->
            updateTriangleColor());
        control.strokeFillProperty().addListener(observable -> updateTriangleColor());
    }
    public Duration getScaleTransitionTime() {
```

```java
            return scaleTransitionTime.get();
        }

    public StyleableObjectProperty<Duration> scaleTransitionTimeProperty() {
        if (scaleTransitionTime == null) {
            scaleTransitionTime = CssHelper.createSkinProperty(StyleableProperties.
            SCALE_TRANSITION_TIME, TriangleButtonSkin.this);
        }
        return scaleTransitionTime;
    }

    public void setScaleTransitionTime(Duration scaleTransitionTime) {
        this.scaleTransitionTime.set(scaleTransitionTime);
    }

    private static class StyleableProperties {
        private static final CssHelper.SkinPropertyBasedCssMetaData<TriangleButt
            on, Duration> SCALE_TRANSITION_TIME = CssHelper.createSkinMetaData("-fx-
            animation-duration", DurationStyleConverter.getInstance(),
            "scaleTransitionTime", Duration.millis(250));
        private static final List<CssMetaData<? extends Styleable, ?>> STYLEABLES =
            CssHelper.createCssMetaDataList(SCALE_TRANSITION_TIME);
    }

public List<CssMetaData<? extends Styleable, ?>> getCssMetaData() {
        return StyleableProperties.STYLEABLES;
    }

    public void updateTriangleColor() {
        if(triangle != null) {
            triangle.setFill(getSkinnable().getBackgroundFill());
            triangle.setStroke(getSkinnable().getStrokeFill());
            getSkinnable().requestLayout();
        }
    }
    public void updateTriangle(double width, double height) {
        if(triangle != null) {
            getChildren().remove(triangle);
        }
        triangle = new Path();
        triangle.getElements().add(new MoveTo(width / 2, 0));
        triangle.getElements().add(new LineTo(width, height));
        triangle.getElements().add(new LineTo(0, height));
        triangle.getElements().addAll(new ClosePath());
        updateTriangleColor();
        triangle.setOnMouseEntered((e) -> zoomIn());
        triangle.setOnMouseExited((e) -> zoomOut());
        triangle.setOnMouseClicked((e) -> getSkinnable().fireEvent(new
            ActionEvent()));
        getChildren().add(triangle);
    }
    private void zoomIn() {
        if(scaleTransition != null) {
            scaleTransition.pause();
        }
```

```
            scaleTransition = new ScaleTransition(scaleTransitionTime.get(), triangle);
            scaleTransition.setFromX(triangle.getScaleX());
            scaleTransition.setFromY(triangle.getScaleY());
            scaleTransition.setToX(1.5);
            scaleTransition.setToY(1.5);
            scaleTransition.play();
        }
        private void zoomOut() {
            if(scaleTransition != null) {
                scaleTransition.pause();
            }
            scaleTransition = new ScaleTransition(scaleTransitionTime.get(), triangle);
            scaleTransition.setFromX(triangle.getScaleX());
            scaleTransition.setFromY(triangle.getScaleY());
            scaleTransition.setToX(1.0);
            scaleTransition.setToY(1.0);
            scaleTransition.play();
        }
        @Override
        protected double computePrefHeight(double width, double topInset, double
            rightInset, double bottomInset, double leftInset) {
            return  topInset + bottomInset + 200;
        }

        @Override
        protected double computePrefWidth(double height, double topInset, double
            rightInset, double bottomInset, double leftInset) {
            return  rightInset + leftInset + 200;
        }

        @Override
        protected double computeMinHeight(double width, double topInset, double
            rightInset, double bottomInset, double leftInset) {
            return 20 + topInset + bottomInset;
        }

        @Override
        protected double computeMinWidth(double height, double topInset, double
            rightInset, double bottomInset, double leftInset) {
            return 20 + rightInset + leftInset;
        }

        @Override
        protected double computeMaxWidth(double height, double topInset, double
            rightInset, double bottomInset, double leftInset) {
            return computePrefWidth(height, topInset, rightInset, bottomInset, leftInset);
        }

        @Override
        protected double computeMaxHeight(double width, double topInset, double
            rightInset, double bottomInset, double leftInset) {
            return computePrefHeight(width, topInset, rightInset, bottomInset, leftInset);
        }
```

```
@Override
protected void layoutChildren(double contentX, double contentY, double
    contentWidth, double contentHeight) {
    if(invalidTriangle) {
        updateTriangle(contentWidth, contentHeight);
        invalidTriangle = false;
    }
    layoutInArea(triangle, contentX, contentY, contentWidth, contentHeight, -1,
        HPos.CENTER, VPos.CENTER);
}

@Override
public void dispose() {
    if(scaleTransition != null) {
        scaleTransition.stop();
        scaleTransition = null;
    }
    super.dispose();
}
}
```

As you can see in the code, the getCssMetaData() method has been overridden. In addition, a static section was added to define the CssMetaData of the class. Why this has been done and how the CssMetaData objects that are defined in the skin are bound to a CSS style sheet will be discussed in a moment. But before this, it's time to change the style sheet of the control and test all the changes.

```
.triangle {
    -fx-animation-duration: '2s';
    -fx-triangle-fill: orange;
    -fx-triangle-stroke: black;
}
```

Once you change the style sheet, the triangle will be shown in orange with a black border. Whenever the mouse enters or leaves the triangle, the animation will start. This will now look very slow because the complete animation will take 2s instead of 250ms.

NOTE
Whenever a control is styled with CSS, JavaFX will fetch the list of CssMetaData objects by the skin of the control. By default, the List<CssMetaData<? extends Styleable, ?>> getCssMetaData() method that is defined in the Region class will be called to fetch all CssMetaData instances. Therefore, each class that extends the Region class can define its own CSS properties. This method is overridden by the Control class that merges the metadata of the Control instance and its skin. So, you can specify stylable properties in custom Control and Skin classes.

Adding a CSS Pseudoclass

As a next step, a CSS pseudoclass will be added for the TriangleButton; you can define a CSS pseudoclass in JavaFX by using the PseudoClass class. Each CSS pseudoclass is defined with a unique name and can be used to style different states of a control. Chapter 9 shows how this can be done with CSS.

You create a new `PseudoClass` instance as shown in this code snippet:

```
private static final PseudoClass ARMED_PSEUDO_CLASS = PseudoClass.
    getPseudoClass("armed");
```

This creates the new pseudoclass `armed`. The `Node` class in JavaFX provides the `pseudoClassStateChanged(...)` method that should be used to activate a pseudoclass. The method `getPseudoClassStates()` returns a set with all currently active pseudoclasses. The following sample shows how pseudoclasses can be used and combined:

```
PseudoClass ARMED_PSEUDO_CLASS = PseudoClass.getPseudoClass("armed");
PseudoClass HIGHLIGHTED_PSEUDO_CLASS = PseudoClass.
    getPseudoClass("highlighted");

getPseudoClassStates(); // returns an empty set

pseudoClassStateChanged(ARMED_PSEUDO_CLASS, true);
getPseudoClassStates(); // set contains "armed"

pseudoClassStateChanged(HIGHLIGHTED_PSEUDO_CLASS, true);
getPseudoClassStates(); // set contains "armed" and "highlighted"

pseudoClassStateChanged(HIGHLIGHTED_PSEUDO_CLASS, false);
getPseudoClassStates(); // set contains "armed"
```

For the `TriangleButton` control, you need to define an `armed` pseudoclass, and the CSS pseudoclass should be active whenever the button is armed by a mouse click. This means that whenever the mouse is pressed on the triangle, the custom control should have an active `armed` pseudoclass. The same behavior is defined for the default JavaFX button.

To implement this feature, you add a new `BooleanProperty` instance called `armed` to the `TriangleButton`. Whenever the value of this property is true, the pseudoclass should be active. The following code shows the new version of the `TriangleButton` class:

```
package com.guigarage.masteringcontrols;

import com.sun.javafx.css.converters.PaintConverter;
import javafx.beans.property.BooleanProperty;
import javafx.beans.property.BooleanPropertyBase;
import javafx.beans.property.ObjectProperty;
import javafx.beans.property.ObjectPropertyBase;
import javafx.css.CssMetaData;
import javafx.css.PseudoClass;
import javafx.css.Styleable;
import javafx.css.StyleableObjectProperty;
import javafx.event.ActionEvent;
import javafx.event.EventHandler;
import javafx.scene.control.Control;
import javafx.scene.control.Skin;
import javafx.scene.paint.Color;
import javafx.scene.paint.Paint;
import java.util.List;
```

```java
public class TriangleButton extends Control {

    //...

    private static final PseudoClass ARMED_PSEUDO_CLASS = PseudoClass.
        getPseudoClass("armed");

    private BooleanProperty armed;

    public final void setArmed(boolean armed) {
        armedProperty().set(armed);
    }

    public final boolean isArmed() {
        return armed == null ? false : armed.get();
    }

    public final BooleanProperty armedProperty() {
        if (armed == null) {
            armed = new BooleanPropertyBase(false) {
                @Override protected void invalidated() {
                    pseudoClassStateChanged(ARMED_PSEUDO_CLASS, get());
                }
                @Override
                public Object getBean() {
                    return TriangleButton.this;
                }
                @Override
                public String getName() {
                    return "armed";
                }
            };
        }
        return armed;
    }

    //...
}
```

You set the definition and implementation of the armed property like how pseudoclasses are defined in the JavaFX basic controls. Whenever you create custom controls that should be used heavily in applications or released as open source controls, this is the most performant way to do this. The invalidated() method of the property class is overridden to directly change the pseudoclass. The same behavior can be defined by the following code:

```java
package com.guigarage.masteringcontrols;

//imports

public class TriangleButton extends Control {

    private static final PseudoClass ARMED_PSEUDO_CLASS = PseudoClass.
        getPseudoClass("armed");

    private BooleanProperty armed;
```

```
    public TriangleButton() {
      armedProperty().addListener((observable, oldValue, newValue) ->
        pseudoClassStateChanged(ARMED_PSEUDO_CLASS, newValue));
    }

    public final BooleanProperty armedProperty() {
      if (armed == null) {
          armed = new SimpleBooleanProperty(false);
      }
      return armed;
    }

    //...

}
```

This code looks much cleaner than the first version: The `armed` property is defined as a `SimpleBooleanProperty` like in some of the earlier examples. In the constructor of the `TriangleButton`, you add a `ChangeListener<Boolean>` instance to the property, and whenever its value changes, the `armed` pseudoclass is activated or deactivated. In addition, no anonymous classes are used in the code. But the code has some performance drawbacks in comparison to the first approach: In the second code snippet, the `armed` property will be instantiated directly in the constructor of the class. So, memory will be used for the property object even if it's never used. In addition, a `ChangeListener` instance is created. When taking a look at the internal JavaFX classes, you will learn that a lot more objects will be generated when the `ChangeListener` is registered. So, the second approach uses a lot more objects and therefore more memory. Thus, you should always use the first approach when developing reusable controls.

Once the `armed` property and the pseudoclass are defined in the `Control` class, the behavior of the control will be adapted in the `Skin` class. Therefore, you add two mouse handlers to the `updateTriangle(...)` method, as shown here:

```
public void updateTriangle(double width, double height) {
        if (triangle != null) {
            getChildren().remove(triangle);
        }
        triangle = new Path();
        //...
        triangle.setOnMousePressed((e) -> getSkinnable().setArmed(true));
        triangle.setOnMouseReleased((e) -> getSkinnable().setArmed(false));
        getChildren().add(triangle);
    }
```

Once this is done, the control will handle its armed state and automatically activate and deactivate the `armed` pseudoclass. You can now use the pseudoclass in a CSS style sheet, as shown here:

```
.triangle {
    -fx-border-color: black;
    -fx-triangle-fill: yellow;
    -fx-triangle-stroke: black;
    -fx-animation-duration: '250ms';
}
```

```
.triangle:armed {
    -fx-triangle-fill: orange;
}
```

By defining these CSS rules, the background color of the TriangleButton will change whenever the mouse is pressed on it.

Adding an Effect

To create even better visual feedback whenever the TriangleButton is armed, let's add an effect to it. JavaFX provides an effect API with several effect types. You can find the API in the javafx .scene.effect package. The following sample shows how to assign effects to any JavaFX node:

```java
package com.guigarage.masteringcontrols;

import javafx.application.Application;
import javafx.geometry.Insets;
import javafx.geometry.Pos;
import javafx.scene.Scene;
import javafx.scene.control.Button;
import javafx.scene.effect.*;
import javafx.scene.layout.VBox;
import javafx.stage.Stage;


public class EffectsDemo extends Application {

    public static void main(String[] args) {
        launch(args);
    }


    @Override
    public void start(Stage primaryStage) throws Exception {
        Button reflectionButton = new Button("Reflection");
        reflectionButton.setEffect(new Reflection());
        Button dropShadowButton = new Button("DropShadow");
        dropShadowButton.setEffect(new DropShadow());
        Button boxBlurButton = new Button("BoxBlur");
        boxBlurButton.setEffect(new BoxBlur());
        Button sepiaToneButton = new Button("SepiaTone");
        sepiaToneButton.setEffect(new SepiaTone());
        Button multipleEffectsButton = new Button("Mixed");
        SepiaTone effect = new SepiaTone();
        effect.setInput(new Reflection());
        multipleEffectsButton.setEffect(effect);

        VBox myPane = new VBox();
        myPane.setPadding(new Insets(24));
        myPane.setAlignment(Pos.CENTER);
        myPane.setSpacing(42);
        myPane.getChildren().addAll(reflectionButton, dropShadowButton,
            boxBlurButton, sepiaToneButton, multipleEffectsButton);
```

```
        Scene myScene = new Scene(myPane);
        primaryStage.setScene(myScene);
        primaryStage.setWidth(300);
        primaryStage.setHeight(200);
        primaryStage.show();
    }
}
```

The demo defines some JavaFX buttons and applies different effects on the `Button` instances. Figure 10-5 shows the result. As you can see in the code, an effect can simply be applied to a node by using its `effect` property. Effects will transform the visualization of the node by adding shadows and reflections, or will render the node by using a blur filter, for example. As shown with the last button of Figure 10-5, most JavaFX effects can be stacked on top of one another by using its `input` property. All effect types that are defined by JavaFX can be configured. To see all the different effect types and how they can be configured and used, refer to the JavaDoc of the `javafx.scene.effect` package.

NOTE
The `Node` class defines the `-fx-effect` CSS property, and therefore you can define an effect for each JavaFX node using CSS. At the moment, JavaFX CSS supports only the DropShadow and InnerShadow effects. You can learn how these effects can be applied in CSS in the JavaFX CSS documentation: http://download.java.net/jdk8/jfxdocs/ javafx/scene/doc-files/cssref.html#typeeffect.

FIGURE 10-5. *Effect example that can be created with JavaFX*

As mentioned, the `TriangleButton` should be rendered with an effect whenever it is armed. To do this, you add the method `updateEffect()` to the `Skin` class. The method will be triggered whenever the armed state of the `TriangleButton` changes. Whenever the control is armed, an inner shadow will be applied as an effect on the triangle. Figure 10-6 shows how the control will now look in the armed state.

Because the `TriangleButtonSkin` won't be changed anymore, here is the final code of the class:

```java
package com.guigarage.masteringcontrols;

import javafx.animation.ScaleTransition;
import javafx.css.CssMetaData;
import javafx.css.Styleable;
import javafx.css.StyleableObjectProperty;
import javafx.event.ActionEvent;
import javafx.geometry.HPos;
import javafx.geometry.VPos;
import javafx.scene.control.SkinBase;
import javafx.scene.effect.InnerShadow;
import javafx.scene.shape.ClosePath;
import javafx.scene.shape.LineTo;
import javafx.scene.shape.MoveTo;
import javafx.scene.shape.Path;
import javafx.util.Duration;
import java.util.List;

public class TriangleButtonSkin extends SkinBase<TriangleButton> {

    private Path triangle;
    private boolean invalidTriangle = true;
    private ScaleTransition scaleTransition;
    private StyleableObjectProperty<Duration> scaleTransitionTime;
```

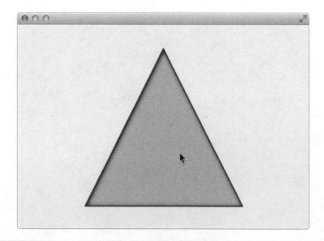

FIGURE 10-6. *An inner shadow effect*

```
protected TriangleButtonSkin(TriangleButton control) {
    super(control);
    control.widthProperty().addListener(observable -> invalidTriangle = true);
    control.heightProperty().addListener(observable -> invalidTriangle = true);
    control.backgroundFillProperty().addListener(observable ->
        updateTriangleColor());
    control.strokeFillProperty().addListener(observable -> updateTriangleColor());
    control.armedProperty().addListener(observable -> updateEffect());
}

protected void updateEffect() {
    if (getSkinnable().isArmed()) {
        if (triangle != null) {
            InnerShadow innerShadow = new InnerShadow();
            innerShadow.setOffsetX(1.0f);
            innerShadow.setOffsetY(1.0f);
            triangle.setEffect(innerShadow);
        }
    } else {
        if (triangle != null) {
            triangle.setEffect(null);
        }
    }
}

public Duration getScaleTransitionTime() {
    return scaleTransitionTime.get();
}

public void setScaleTransitionTime(Duration scaleTransitionTime) {
    this.scaleTransitionTime.set(scaleTransitionTime);
}

public StyleableObjectProperty<Duration> scaleTransitionTimeProperty() {
    if (scaleTransitionTime == null) {
        scaleTransitionTime = CssHelper.createSkinProperty(StyleableProperties.
            SCALE_TRANSITION_TIME, TriangleButtonSkin.this);
    }
    return scaleTransitionTime;
}

public List<CssMetaData<? extends Styleable, ?>> getCssMetaData() {
    return StyleableProperties.STYLEABLES;
}

public void updateTriangleColor() {
    if (triangle != null) {
        triangle.setFill(getSkinnable().getBackgroundFill());
        triangle.setStroke(getSkinnable().getStrokeFill());
        getSkinnable().requestLayout();
    }
}

public void updateTriangle(double width, double height) {
    if (triangle != null) {
        getChildren().remove(triangle);
```

```
        }
        triangle = new Path();
        triangle.getElements().add(new MoveTo(width / 2, 0));
        triangle.getElements().add(new LineTo(width, height));
        triangle.getElements().add(new LineTo(0, height));
        triangle.getElements().addAll(new ClosePath());
        updateTriangleColor();
        updateEffect();
        triangle.setOnMouseEntered((e) -> zoomIn());
        triangle.setOnMouseExited((e) -> zoomOut());
        triangle.setOnMouseClicked((e) -> getSkinnable().fireEvent(new
            ActionEvent()));
        triangle.setOnMousePressed((e) -> getSkinnable().setArmed(true));
        triangle.setOnMouseReleased((e) -> getSkinnable().setArmed(false));
        getChildren().add(triangle);
    }

    private void zoomIn() {
        if (scaleTransition != null) {
            scaleTransition.pause();
        }
        scaleTransition = new ScaleTransition(scaleTransitionTime.get(), triangle);
        scaleTransition.setFromX(triangle.getScaleX());
        scaleTransition.setFromY(triangle.getScaleY());
        scaleTransition.setToX(1.5);
        scaleTransition.setToY(1.5);
        scaleTransition.play();
    }

    private void zoomOut() {
        if (scaleTransition != null) {
            scaleTransition.pause();
        }
        scaleTransition = new ScaleTransition(scaleTransitionTime.get(), triangle);
        scaleTransition.setFromX(triangle.getScaleX());
        scaleTransition.setFromY(triangle.getScaleY());
        scaleTransition.setToX(1.0);
        scaleTransition.setToY(1.0);
        scaleTransition.play();
    }

    @Override
    protected double computePrefHeight(double width, double topInset, double
        rightInset, double bottomInset, double leftInset) {
        return topInset + bottomInset + 200;
    }

    @Override
    protected double computePrefWidth(double height, double topInset, double
        rightInset, double bottomInset, double leftInset) {
        return rightInset + leftInset + 200;
    }
```

```java
    @Override
    protected double computeMinHeight(double width, double topInset, double
        rightInset, double bottomInset, double leftInset) {
        return 20 + topInset + bottomInset;
    }

    @Override
    protected double computeMinWidth(double height, double topInset, double
        rightInset, double bottomInset, double leftInset) {
        return 20 + rightInset + leftInset;
    }

    @Override
    protected double computeMaxWidth(double height, double topInset, double
        rightInset, double bottomInset, double leftInset) {
        return computePrefWidth(height, topInset, rightInset, bottomInset, leftInset);
    }

    @Override
    protected double computeMaxHeight(double width, double topInset, double
        rightInset, double bottomInset, double leftInset) {
        return computePrefHeight(width, topInset, rightInset, bottomInset, leftInset);
    }

    @Override
    protected void layoutChildren(double contentX, double contentY, double
        contentWidth, double contentHeight) {
        if (invalidTriangle) {
            updateTriangle(contentWidth, contentHeight);
            invalidTriangle = false;
        }
        layoutInArea(triangle, contentX, contentY, contentWidth, contentHeight, -1,
            HPos.CENTER, VPos.CENTER);
    }
    private static class StyleableProperties {
        private static final CssHelper.SkinPropertyBasedCssMetaData<TriangleButton,
            Duration> SCALE_TRANSITION_TIME = CssHelper.createSkinMetaData
            ("-fx-animation-duration", DurationStyleConverter.getInstance(),
            "scaleTransitionTime", Duration.millis(250));
        private static final List<CssMetaData<? extends Styleable, ?>> STYLEABLES
            = CssHelper.createCssMetaDataList(TriangleButton.getClassCssMetaData(),
            SCALE_TRANSITION_TIME);
    }

@Override
    public void dispose() {
        if(scaleTransition != null) {
            scaleTransition.stop();
            scaleTransition = null;
        }
        super.dispose();
    }
}
```

Adding a Second Skin

You have seen how to develop a custom control and its skin, but the most important benefit of this structure wasn't mentioned until now. By splitting a JavaFX control into a `Control` class and a `Skin` class, you can easily change the skin. This can be done even at run time or with CSS. To see this feature, you need another skin; it should render a triangle button with a triangle that has one of its apexes on the bottom instead of on the top. Figure 10-7 shows an example of how this will look.

To do this, you need an additional `Skin` class. For this example, the `Skin` class will look mostly like the current one. Only the definition of the triangle in the `updateTriangle(...)` method has changed. Here is the code of the second skin:

```
package com.guigarage.masteringcontrols;

import javafx.event.ActionEvent;
import javafx.geometry.HPos;
import javafx.geometry.VPos;
import javafx.scene.control.SkinBase;
import javafx.scene.layout.Region;
import javafx.scene.shape.ClosePath;
import javafx.scene.shape.LineTo;
import javafx.scene.shape.MoveTo;
import javafx.scene.shape.Path;


public class AlternativeTriangleButtonSkin extends SkinBase<TriangleButton> {

    private Path triangle;
    private boolean invalidTriangle = true;

    public AlternativeTriangleButtonSkin(TriangleButton control) {
        super(control);
        control.widthProperty().addListener(observable -> invalidTriangle =
            true);
```

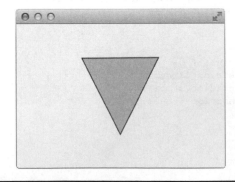

FIGURE 10-7. *The TriangleButton with an alternative skin*

```
        control.heightProperty().addListener(observable -> invalidTriangle =
            true);
        control.backgroundFillProperty().addListener(observable ->
            updateTriangleColor());
        control.strokeFillProperty().addListener(observable ->
            updateTriangleColor());
        getSkinnable().setMaxWidth(Region.USE_PREF_SIZE);
        getSkinnable().setMaxHeight(Region.USE_PREF_SIZE);
        getSkinnable().setMinWidth(Region.USE_PREF_SIZE);
        getSkinnable().setMinHeight(Region.USE_PREF_SIZE);
    }

    public void updateTriangleColor() {
        if (triangle != null) {
            triangle.setFill(getSkinnable().getBackgroundFill());
            triangle.setStroke(getSkinnable().getStrokeFill());
            getSkinnable().requestLayout();
        }
    }

    public void updateTriangle(double width, double height) {
        if (triangle != null) {
            getChildren().remove(triangle);
        }
        triangle = new Path();
        triangle.getElements().add(new MoveTo(width / 2, height));
        triangle.getElements().add(new LineTo(width, 0));
        triangle.getElements().add(new LineTo(0, 0));
        triangle.getElements().addAll(new ClosePath());
        updateTriangleColor();
        triangle.setOnMouseClicked((e) -> getSkinnable().fireEvent(new
            ActionEvent()));
        triangle.setOnMousePressed((e) -> getSkinnable().setArmed(true));
        triangle.setOnMouseReleased((e) -> getSkinnable().setArmed(false));
        getChildren().add(triangle);
    }


    @Override
    protected double computePrefHeight(double width, double topInset,
        double rightInset, double bottomInset, double leftInset) {
        return topInset + bottomInset + 120;
    }


    @Override
    protected double computePrefWidth(double height, double topInset,
        double rightInset, double bottomInset, double leftInset) {
        return rightInset + leftInset + 120;
    }
```

```
    @Override
    protected void layoutChildren(double contentX, double contentY,
        double contentWidth, double contentHeight) {
      if (invalidTriangle) {
          updateTriangle(contentWidth, contentHeight);
          invalidTriangle = false;
      }
      layoutInArea(triangle, contentX, contentY, contentWidth,
          contentHeight, -1, HPos.CENTER, VPos.CENTER);
    }
}
```

Once you define the second skin, you can use it for the example. There are several different ways to apply the skin to the control. As mentioned earlier, the `Control` class defines the `createDefaultSkin(...)` method that can be overridden. If the new skin should be the default skin of the `TriangleButton`, you do it like this:

```
@Override
protected Skin<?> createDefaultSkin() {
        return new AlternativeTriangleButtonSkin(this);
}
```

But, as mentioned, there are other ways to change the skin of a control. One way is to set a new skin to the `skin` property of the control. The following code snippet shows how to do this:

```
TriangleButton button = new TriangleButton();
button.setSkin(new AlternativeTriangleButtonSkin(button));
```

This code snippet can easily be wrapped in an action handler. As a result, the skin of a control can theoretically be changed by clicking a button.

In addition to this, the `Control` class provides the CSS property `-fx-skin`. By using this property, the `Skin` class of a control can be defined in CSS. Therefore, the class of the skin must be defined as its CSS value in a style sheet, as shown here:

```
.triangle {
    -fx-skin: 'com.guigarage.masteringcontrols.AlternativeTriangleButtonSkin';
    -fx-triangle-fill: orange;
    -fx-triangle-stroke: black;
}
```

NOTE
CSS properties can be defined in the `Control` class and the `Skin` class. In the `TriangleButtonSkin`, you defined the CSS property `-fx-animation-duration`, for example. Once the skin changed, this property isn't used anymore because it is not defined in the current skin. Frameworks such as AquaFX use this approach to add custom CSS properties to the default JavaFX control types by providing custom `Skin` classes for these controls and adding new CSS metadata to these skins.

Dispose a Skin

Whenever the skin of a control changes, the old instance should be removed by Java's garbage collection. To do this, all references of the old skin should be removed. Additionally, it is important that for all listeners the old skin registered to properties of the control are removed too. If this doesn't happen, the old skin will still be alive and could change the behavior of the control. To avoid this, the SkinBase class defines the dispose() method. As already mentioned, this method will be called each time the skin of a control changes. The method will be called on the old skin instance of the control.

In our example, the skin implementations register some listeners to properties of the control. These listeners should be removed whenever the skin instance is changed. To do so, and to provide a fully useable skin implementation, we need to change one last thing in our Skin class. In the following code, the listeners that are registered to the properties of the control are extracted as fields of the Skin class. As a result, they can easily be registered in the constructor of the skin and deregistered in the dispose() method:

```
public class TriangleButtonSkin extends SkinBase<TriangleButton> {

private InvalidationListener invalidTriangleListener =
    observable -> invalidTriangle = true;

private InvalidationListener updateTriangleColorListener =
    observable -> updateTriangleColor();

private InvalidationListener updateEffectListener =
    observable -> updateEffect();

protected TriangleButtonSkin(TriangleButton control) {
        super(control);
        control.widthProperty().addListener(
                            invalidTriangleListener);
        control.heightProperty().addListener(
                            invalidTriangleListener);
        control.backgroundFillProperty().addListener(
                            updateTriangleColorListener);
        control.strokeFillProperty().addListener(
                            updateTriangleColorListener);
        control.armedProperty().addListener(
                            updateEffectListener);
    }

    @Override
    public void dispose() {
        if(scaleTransition != null) {
            scaleTransition.stop();
            scaleTransition = null;
        }
        getSkinnable().widthProperty().
            removeListener(invalidTriangleListener);
        getSkinnable().heightProperty().
            removeListener(invalidTriangleListener);
```

```
    getSkinnable().backgroundFillProperty().
        removeListener(updateTriangleColorListener);
    getSkinnable().strokeFillProperty().
        removeListener(updateTriangleColorListener);
    getSkinnable().armedProperty().
        removeListener(updateEffectListener);
    getChildren().clear();
    super.dispose();
    }
}
```

NOTE
For default control implementations that are part of JavaFX, there is a special mechanism that registers and deregisters all these listeners automatically. But, sadly, this is defined in the `BehaviorSkinBase` class that is part of the private API of JavaFX and, therefore, shouldn't be used. If you want to develop a lot of custom controls, you should have a look at this class and define your own basic class for skin implementations, that provides comparable functionality.

An Interview with Gerrit Grunwald, Canoo Engineering

Hi, Gerrit. Most JavaFX developers know you as @hansolo_ and have seen your awesome custom controls that you have created for JavaFX in the last two years. But before we talk about this cool stuff, can you please introduce yourself?

Hi, Hendrik. My name is Gerrit Grunwald, and I'm working for Canoo Engineering in Switzerland. I started coding Java around 10 years ago when I was working as an engineer in the nanotechnology and semiconductor industry. I'm mainly doing front-end-related stuff, and I'm also very interested in IoT and embedded technologies that run Java and JavaFX. But the thing I like most are still custom controls, preferably in JavaFX.

So, as I understand it, the development of custom controls is one of your hobbies. I know that you already did this with the help of different UI toolkits before you started to create controls with JavaFX. Maybe you can give a short overview of the different languages and frameworks you have already used to create and design controls.

Yes, creating custom controls is something that drives me. For me, trying to transfer a real object into a custom control is a challenge that I simply can't withstand. So, I started to create my own components around eight years ago in Java Swing and was fascinated by the possibilities of that technology. It was always nice to figure out how to create certain visual effects in Swing manually (which was needed due to the lack of built-in visual effects). Then I tried Microsoft .NET with C#. I created a couple of C#-based controls, but the way that worked in .NET was not that nice, so when HTML5 came along, I saw the canvas element and was thrilled. Now I had a technology that made it possible to create components that ran also on my iOS and Android devices. The only thing with HTML5 that I did not like was JavaScript; it somehow didn't work for me. So when JavaFX 2 was born in 2011, I gave it a try, and now I'm addicted. It's powerful, it has lots of nice features, and it's Java…I love it.

So you tried a lot of different technologies to create custom control, and in the end, you decided to use JavaFX. What are the biggest benefits of JavaFX in this case?

First, and most important for me, is the fact that JavaFX is just Java, so you don't have to learn a new language, but only a new API. The second important thing is the availability of JavaFX on all major platforms with the same feature set plus the ARM port, which makes it also available to embedded devices. So with this technology, I can create controls that I can reuse wherever I need them. In addition, the JavaFX API is really nice to code with, and the features you get with JavaFX are powerful. Because I've tried the other platforms, I know how much time one can save if you don't have to create everything by yourself.

Let's talk about custom controls in JavaFX. What is your best-practice workflow when developing a new control?

Usually, I start with drawing a prototype of the control in a vector drawing program. With this approach, I can easily modify the shapes and colors of the control with direct visual feedback. When this is done, I transfer the shapes and colors into code by using SVG for the shapes. In my IDE I've created some templates for different kinds of controls, for example, those that are based on extending a `Region` node, and so on. If possible, I stick with the `Region`-based control because it's stylable by CSS and only one file. But when I create controls for a library, I usually use the approach where you create a `Control` class and a `Skin` class in combination with a CSS file.

In your workflow description, you mention two steps that are different from the basic practices that are described in this book: SVG as a base for the UI and the usage of the `Region` class as the base class for custom controls instead of using the `Control` class. Let's discuss these two topics in more detail. How do you convert an SVG file to a Java-based UI?

One of the many great things in JavaFX is the SVG support in CSS, which means that one can define an SVG path in CSS by defining something like this:

```
-fx-shape: "M 0 0, H 50 0, V 50 50, L 0 50, Z";
```

Now you simply could apply the CSS class that contains the definition to a `Region` node and the node will be filled with the shape that is defined in `-fx-shape`. If you would like to scale that shape automatically, you simply have to set `-fx-scale-shape: true;`, and the SVG path will always be scaled to the size of the `Region` node. So what you need to create an SVG shape is a vector-drawing program like Inkscape, Illustrator, or others that are capable of handling SVG. With such a program, you can draw the shapes in the program, export them as an SVG file, and use the paths in the CSS file of your JavaFX application.

That's a cool tip that wasn't mentioned in the book until now. So, thank you for that. The next topic I want to talk about is your basic control structure. You said that some of your custom controls extend the `Region` class instead of the `Control` class. Can you explain this decision?

The `Region` node is a lightweight container that is stylable via CSS. That makes it a perfect component to extend and use as a custom control. If you would like to create a not-too-complex control, the `Region` is a perfect choice because it's only one class and a CSS file. That means you combine the logic with visualization code within one class. Like I said, that's fine for simple controls, but if it gets more complex, it's a good idea to split the logic from the visualization by extending the `Control` class for the logic and creating a skin for the visualization.

(Continued)

So, you have two different ways how you create controls. Some people have tried to use FXML or the `Canvas` class to create custom controls. Have you tested these approaches too? If so, can you explain in a few words the problems in these approaches and why a developer should use the architecture that is described here?

Yes, I've also created controls based on the `Canvas` node. This approach is useful if you have to draw very complex things in your control. Because the `Canvas` node is more like an image you can draw on, you can reduce the number of nodes on the scene graph. The disadvantage of using the `Canvas` node for a control is the fact that you can't easily attach event listeners to subareas of your control but only to the `Canvas` node alone. This means controls based on the `Canvas` node are great for controls that only visualize something and don't offer any user interaction. I've never really tried the FXML-based approach because in my eyes, FXML is not meant to be for creating controls but more to be read/written by a computer and not for manual editing.

Have you seen any differences in the performance of the discussed approaches?

My experience (especially on embedded devices) is that it really depends on the control itself. Because with JavaFX we get hardware-accelerated graphics (also on embedded), the drawing performance most times is not the problem. One of the reasons for bad performance might be the fact that paths will be calculated by the CPU before they will be rendered by the GPU. That means if you use a lot if complex paths in your control, it might slow down the performance of your control. One thing that also is true is that nothing is faster than code, which means if you overuse CSS, it might also be slower than a pure-code approach. But keep in mind that you might lose flexibility in styling when using code only.

Your answer leads perfectly to the last topic of this interview. You already mentioned embedded devices, and I know that you developed a lot of custom controls for different devices like desktop, mobile, and embedded. Can you share some pitfalls or best practices when developing controls for different devices?

Well, on the desktop, you simply can do everything you like.

With embedded, it's a bit different; first of all, it depends on the hardware you use. When using a Pi, you have to keep in mind that it has a really good GPU but a really slow CPU. This means every path you use in your controls will be calculated by the relatively slow CPU before it will be rendered by the fast GPU. So, the CPU is the main bottleneck on the Pi. Using an i.MX6-based device with a Vivante GPU might be completely different. Here, you have a fast CPU in combination with a good GPU. So, there is no general rule, but everything depends on the target platform and its capabilities.

As a last tip, let me tell you that on iOS and Android devices you might want to use `Regions` for your controls. Somehow, the control approach doesn't work on these platforms at the moment. This might change in the future, but at the moment you are bound to JDK 7 and JavaFX 2 on these platforms, and only `Region`-based custom controls work.

Do you have any experience with controls that are made for all the different devices? I think a big problem might be the significant difference in the screen resolution of these devices. How can that be handled?

If you want your controls to run on all devices, you should extend `Region` and make sure that the controls resize correctly. With this approach, the controls will run on JavaFX 2 and JavaFX 8 and also on all devices. The screen resolution really could be a problem, especially if you use fonts. You have to make sure that the control also renders nicely when it is very small or very big. So, getting that right is the hardest part, and unfortunately, there is only one way to figure it out...you have to try it on the device.

Most developers don't have all these devices. Can emulators be used to test the behavior and performance of custom controls?

Unfortunately not. I've tested the same control on the Raspberry Pi, an i.MX6 quadcore, an iPad, and Android, and performance-wise it behaves completely differently on all of these platforms. If you use the iPad emulator on the Mac to test your JavaFX application, you will figure out that it is really slow, and if you put it on an iPad mini retina, it will show good performance. But if you put the same code on an iPhone 5 (which is not that old), it will be slow again. Again, it all depends on the target platform.

Thank you for all these important tips. Do you want to mention any other helpful notes about developing custom controls to all the JavaFX developers out there?

I know developers are not designers, but believe me that everyone can learn at least some things related to design, so my advice is...learn how to use a vector-drawing program! Thanks for the interview.

Thanks for your time. I hope to see a lot of cool custom controls designed by you in the future!

Summary

The chapter described how to develop custom controls in JavaFX and showed a lot of best practices used in the default JavaFX control classes. Theoretically, all the functionality shown here could be developed more easily: If you need a special control that is used one time and will never change, you could extend the `Region` class instead of the `Control` class and develop all the features in only one class. However, in that case, you won't get all the benefits of the `Skin` class and the performance tricks shown in this chapter. Therefore, usually you should invest the time to design a custom control as shown in this chapter. The workflows that are shown here were used to develop the default controls of JavaFX and were used in some other important open source libraries such as ControlsFX.

APPENDIX

JavaFX Resources and Where to Go from Here

I n this book I have described all the JavaFX APIs that you need to know to work with JavaFX controls. After reading the book, you should be prepared to create the front end of an application with JavaFX. But when developing complete JavaFX applications, you'll need to know more than this book can contain. Thankfully, the JavaFX community is growing every day, and more information about JavaFX is available than ever before. In this appendix, I introduce additional topics that will be important for developers who are learning JavaFX and provide additional resources where you can learn more. I have also included some statements, knowledge, and approaches from the JavaFX community.

Make Your UI Shine

User experience (UX) is about so much more than a user interface (UI). Whatever you develop should be clean, as intuitive as possible to use, and work in expected ways.
—Mark Heckler (@MkHeck)

Make use of effects and animation. They are cool and can make a big difference. Keep them small and targeted to a specific purpose.

—Dierk König (@mittie)

Most of the samples in this book aren't very spectacular when you start thinking about all the fancy UI stuff you could add like animations and effects. For a regular business application, these additions aren't the most important part, and besides, thanks to the Modena theme, all the basic JavaFX controls look good and their skins match each other. But it is still important to choose a good layout, place and use all the controls in the right way, and design an understandable flow through your application. For example, when developing an application such as a music player, all these effects and animations will become more important. Figure A-1 shows a JavaFX demo created by Gerrit Grunwald. As you can see, the UI is completely different from a regular, data-driven JavaFX business application.

JavaFX-Related Middleware and Application Frameworks

JavaFX offers new possibilities to implement UI Architectures. That's why we created a framework which supports the developer to follow the MVVM approach by using the JavaFX Properties API.
—Alexander Casall (@sialcasa)

As soon as you start writing real-life enterprise applications with JavaFX, you have to consider questions that go beyond widgets and their APIs. You need to set up structures for organizing your code and rules for how to expose functionality to your user. In other words, you need an application *architecture*. Here I introduce two projects that allow you to implement architecture: DataFX and OpenDolphin.

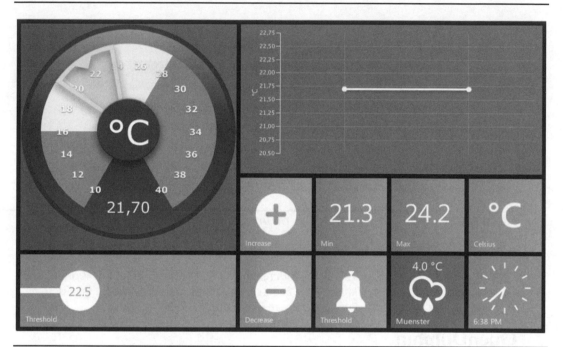

FIGURE A-1. *An embedded JavaFX application*

DataFX

DataFX is an application framework for JavaFX. Its main goal is to provide useful architecture and utilities when developing business and enterprise applications. DataFX contains many modules that cover a lot of use cases and technologies that are needed when developing a JavaFX enterprise application.

The DataSource API of DataFX lets you read and write different data sources. This data can be stored in a database or accessed by a REST service on a server. By using the DataSource API, you don't have to handle all the multithreading issues that are important when working with background tasks or long-running requests. This API is based on the Core module of DataFX and provides a lot of useful functionality to handle concurrent tasks in JavaFX.

Another important part of the DataFX framework is the Flow module. With the help of this module, you can define view-based flows for an application and, therefore, structure the views by using the Model-View-Controller (MVC) pattern. With the Flow API, you can then combine these MVC-based views to create a large flow and links or internal actions. Figure A-2 shows the schematic flow of a master-detail application that can be easily created with DataFX.

All DataFX modules can be combined by using dependency injection. With the Flow API, DataFX even supports context dependency injection (CDI) by providing different scopes.

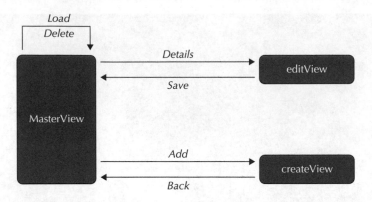

FIGURE A-2.   *A design flow that can be implemented with the help of DataFX*

Currently, DataFX is the best choice for creating a JavaFX enterprise application that will communicate with a server that provides access by middleware standards such as REST or WebSocket. See www.javafxdata.org for more information about DataFX.

OpenDolphin

OpenDolphin makes prolific use of the Presentation Model pattern. You bind your JavaFX views to a presentation model, while your application code and your tests operate solely by working on this model.

Models are automatically kept in sync between the client and the server such that your controllers can reside on the enterprise server (where enterprise applications are supposed to live and where they can share information).

With the clean separation of concerns that OpenDolphin enforces (controllers managing "what" to display and views knowing "how" to display) comes a long list of benefits: The system becomes easier to modify and extend. It can be easily tested. The UI specifics are kept separate and are thus easier to adapt to new versions and even entirely new UI toolkits. When the UI changes, the server-side logic remains untouched, so all your investment in application logic is protected.

There is even the option to create a totally new class of applications that run on many devices, follow you wherever you go, and foster teamwork by allowing all team members to work on a shared presentation state.

But since seeing is believing, you can head over to http://open-dolphin.org and take a look at the demos.

Best of Open Source Projects

Know your tools: Scene Builder, ScenicView, Gerrit's converter, your favorite painting program, color picker, gradient editor, and 3D modeling tool in case you do 3D.

—Dierk König (@mittie)

When developing a JavaFX application, you don't have to do everything on your own. A lot of APIs and frameworks based on JavaFX have been developed in the past few months. Here is a quick overview of some of the most important open source projects:

- **ControlsFX**, http://fxexperience.com/controlsfx/ An open source project that provides high-quality UI controls
- **JFXtras**, http://jfxtras.org A general library that provides those pieces developers often need in their day-to-day work but that are currently missing from JavaFX
- **AquaFX**, http://aquafx-project.com A Mac OS theme for JavaFX
- **DataFX**, www.javafxdata.org An application framework for JavaFX
- **TestFX**, https://github.com/SmartBear/TestFX An easy-to-use library for testing JavaFX
- **ReactFX**, https://github.com/TomasMikula/ReactFX An exploration of reactive programming techniques for JavaFX

Projects are constantly popping up, and I will add an up-to-date list on my web site at www.guigarage.com/javafx-book/.

Important JavaFX Links

Maintain a list of resources for cool designs, tutorials, code snippets, and so on. Prefer "stealing" good work over being original.

—Dierk König (@mittie)

In the past few years, a lot of great JavaFX web sites and blogs have sprung up. The following are the most important ones and will give you a great entry point to the JavaFX community:

- **http://fxexperience.com** This JavaFX blog was created by some of the JavaFX experts and architects at Oracle: Jasper Potts, Jonathan Giles, and Richard Bair. The blog releases a weekly update of JavaFX news.
- **http://harmoniccode.blogspot.de** This is Gerrit Grunwalds' JavaFX blog. Here you can find a lot of interesting articles about JavaFX on embedded devices. (See the end of Chapter 10 for an interview with Gerrit.)
- **www.guigarage.com** Okay, this is more of an ad because this is my blog! Here you can find general articles about JavaFX architecture.
- **http://docs.oracle.com/javase/8/javase-clienttechnologies.htm** This is the official JavaFX tutorial site by Oracle.
- **https://www.java.net/community/javafx** This is the JavaFX community web site. Here you can find some interesting news about JavaFX.

JavaFX Books

Learn the many JavaFX 8 ways to be productive when building UIs.

—Carl Dea (@carldea)

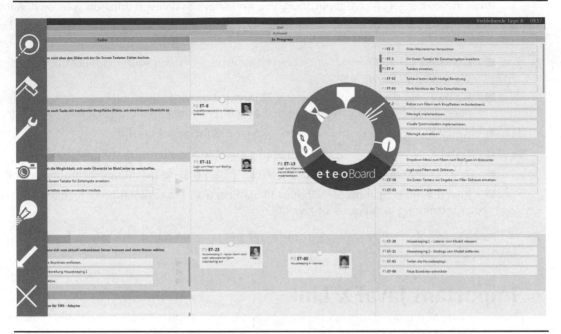

FIGURE A-3.   *The eteoBoard in action*

In addition to this book, a few other JavaFX books have been released. Most of these books are general JavaFX books that try to describe the complete JavaFX framework without going too deep into the specific elements. Here are the other books that I recommend:

- DiMarzio, J.F. *Quick Start Guide to JavaFX*. McGraw-Hill Professional, 2014.
- Dea, C, et al. *JavaFX 8: Introduction by Example*, Second Edition. Apress, 2014.
- Johan Vos, et al. *Pro JavaFX* 8. Apress, 2014.

JavaFX Application

One last thing I want to mention is that if you ask yourself whether there are any productive JavaFX applications out there, you'll find that the answer is yes. For example, at www.eteoboard.de/de/, you can find a scrum board application that was written completely in JavaFX and is used by a lot of companies. The application looks really great, has a cool UI, and is completely touch-based (see Figure A-3). This is a perfect example of what can be done with JavaFX.

Summary

As you can see, the JavaFX community is really big and growing every day. I think JavaFX has a lot of potential and will be used in a lot of cool applications in the next few years. I can't wait to see all this, and I hope you feel the same after reading this book.

Index

Join the Largest Tech Community in the World

 Download the latest software, tools, and developer templates

 Get exclusive access to hands-on trainings and workshops

 Grow your professional network through the Oracle ACE Program

 Publish your technical articles – and get paid to share your expertise

Join the Oracle Technology Network
Membership is free. Visit oracle.com/technetwork

@OracleOTN facebook.com/OracleTechnologyNetwork

Reach More than 700,000 Oracle Customers with Oracle Publishing Group

Connect with the Audience that Matters Most to Your Business

Oracle Magazine
The Largest IT Publication in the World
Circulation: 550,000
Audience: IT Managers, DBAs, Programmers, and Developers

Profit
Business Insight for Enterprise-Class Business Leaders to
Help Them Build a Better Business Using Oracle Technology
Circulation: 100,000
Audience: Top Executives and Line of Business Managers

Java Magazine
The Essential Source on Java Technology, the Java
Programming Language, and Java-Based Applications
Circulation: 125,000 and Growing Steady
Audience: Corporate and Independent Java Developers,
Programmers, and Architects

For more information
or to sign up for a FREE
subscription:
Scan the QR code to visit
Oracle Publishing online.